The penny politics of Victorian popular fiction

Manchester University Press

Series editors: Anna Barton, Andrew Smith

Editorial board: David Amigoni, Isobel Armstrong, Philip Holden, Jerome McGann, Joanne Wilkes, Julia M. Wright

Interventions: Rethinking the Nineteenth Century seeks to make a significant intervention into the critical narratives that dominate conventional and established understandings of nineteenth-century literature. Informed by the latest developments in criticism and theory the series provides a focus for how texts from the long nineteenth century, and more recent adaptations of them, revitalise our knowledge of and engagement with the period. It explores the radical possibilities offered by new methods, unexplored contexts and neglected authors and texts to re-map the literary-cultural landscape of the period and rigorously re-imagine its geographical and historical parameters. The series includes monographs, edited collections, and scholarly sourcebooks.

Already published

Engine of modernity: The omnibus and urban culture in nineteenth-century Paris   Masha Belenky

Spectral Dickens: The uncanny forms of novelistic characterization   Alexander Bove

Worlding the South: Nineteenth-century literary culture and the southern settler colonies   Sarah Comyn and Porscha Fermanis (eds)

Pasts at play: Childhood encounters with history in British culture, 1750–1914   Rachel Bryant Davies and Barbara Gribling (eds)

The Case of the Initial Letter: Charles Dickens and the politics of the dual alphabet   Gavin Edwards

Spain in the nineteenth century: New essays on experiences of culture and society   Andrew Ginger and Geraldine Lawless

Instead of modernity: The Western canon and the incorporation of the Hispanic (c. 1850–75)   Andrew Ginger

The Victorian aquarium: Literary discussions on nature, culture, and science   Silvia Granata

Marie Duval: Maverick Victorian cartoonist   Simon Grennan, Roger Sabin and Julian Waite

Creating character: Theories of nature and nurture in Victorian sensation fiction   Helena Ifill

Margaret Harkness: Writing social engagement 1880–1921   Flore Janssen and Lisa C. Robertson (eds)

Richard Marsh, popular fiction and literary culture, 1890–1915: Re-reading the fin de siècle   Victoria Margree, Daniel Orrells and Minna Vuohelainen (eds)

Charlotte Brontë: Legacies and afterlives   Amber K. Regis and Deborah Wynne (eds)

The Great Exhibition, 1851: A sourcebook   Jonathon Shears (ed.)

Interventions: Rethinking the nineteenth century   Andrew Smith and Anna Barton (eds)

Counterfactual Romanticism   Damian Walford Davies (ed.)

The poems of Elizabeth Siddal in context   Anne Woolley

The penny politics of Victorian popular fiction

Rob Breton

MANCHESTER UNIVERSITY PRESS

Copyright © Rob Breton 2021

The right of Rob Breton to be identified as the author of this work has been asserted by them in accordance with the Copyright, Designs and Patents Act 1988.

Published by Manchester University Press
Oxford Road, Manchester M13 9PL

www.manchesteruniversitypress.co.uk

British Library Cataloguing-in-Publication Data
A catalogue record for this book is available from the British Library

ISBN 978 0 5261 5638 9 hardback
ISBN 978 1 5261 7453 6 paperback

First published 2021
Paperback published 2023

The publisher has no responsibility for the persistence or accuracy of URLs for any external or third-party internet websites referred to in this book, and does not guarantee that any content on such websites is, or will remain, accurate or appropriate.

Typeset by
Servis Filmsetting Ltd, Stockport, Cheshire

For Liv and William

Contents

Acknowledgements	viii
Introduction	1
1 The old, new, borrowed, and blue Newgate calendar	19
2 *Jack Sheppard*, the Newgate novel	47
3 Penny radicalism? *Sweeney Todd* and the bloods	86
4 Mysteries and ambiguities: G. W. M. Reynolds and *The Mysteries of London*	134
5 Distant friends of the people: *Howitt's Journal* and *Douglas Jerrold's Shilling Magazine*	175
Select bibliography	222
Index	230

Acknowledgements

Many thanks to the members of the English Department at Nipissing University for patiently tolerating me as I borrowed their brains testing out the ideas that led to this book. I would also like to thank the friendly 'periodical people' at the Research Society for Victorian Periodicals conferences over the last numbers of years where bits and pieces of this book were first publicly introduced.

Introduction

In the 'Prospectus' to *Politics for the People* (1848–49), F. D. Maurice, presumably speaking on behalf of his co-editors John Ludlow and Charles Kingsley, makes a startling observation, though in a roundabout way one that is frequently upheld by contemporary critics examining the first waves of Victorian popular literature. Less than one month after the 10 April 1848 Kennington Common 'monster meeting' and the last Chartist petition, Maurice claims that 'Politics have been separated from household ties and affections – from art, and science, and literature.'[1] Though he does not deny that party politics are rampant, Maurice insists that the politics that are 'human and universal' have subsided from these higher domains. *Politics for the People* thus sets out to return a non-partisan, generalised politics to the people, one that sympathises with working people but will not condescend to them through maudlin representations of poverty, a staple in both radical and reform literatures. The journal seeks to find ways that politics can be infused with Christianity: art and science and literature were to be bathed in the conflated religious, political mix. But the fact that politics had been excised from even just the literature of the age is a remarkable and rather conspicuous suggestion insofar as the 1840s began with *Guy Fawkes* and *Barnaby Rudge* in 1841 and 1842, for example, and produced *Mary Barton* in the very year Maurice made his observation. The literature of the 1830s and 1840s are saturated with politics, demonstrating a turn towards a broad politicisation of everyday life, something to which Kingsley, whose own *Yeast: A Problem* also came out in 1848, could bear witness. Perhaps the best way to understand Maurice's comment then is simply to understand that his journal was entering a packed field, set to be in competition with umpteen other *political* periodicals written or said to be written for working-class readers, and Maurice was trying to make room for a new brand, introducing Christian Socialism to the people.

Politics for the People had other objectives as well: above all it seems was to put a nail in the Chartist coffin after 10 April, largely by continuing the 'conversation' around franchise expansion (the paper was actually against expanding it) without input from Chartists. It is still worth imagining that, in addition to or as part of the spiritual regeneration they promoted, the editors might have had in mind the purported drift away from politics in the popular literature of the 1830s and 1840s, the massive wave of often violent, often sentimental literature focused on criminals and the 'low'. *Politics for the People* is preoccupied by politics and does not especially target popular literature, though it shares with many other middle-class periodicals of its time reaching out to an imagined working-class audience a message of education, improvement, and moral or personal reform.[2] Had Maurice been bemoaning the rise of the commercial presses and the sensational stories they produced, such as *The String of Pearls. A Romance*, aka *Sweeney Todd* (1846–47), because they lacked politics, because they were not producing 'politics for the people', he would be in rare company, but far from alone in criticising the rise of this kind of fiction and the periodicals that housed them. 'Cheap' fiction – the antagonist of improving, reform, or 'polite' fiction – was heavily criticised for pandering to the people's worst tastes, and though this line of criticism implied that it had no socially redeeming value, it was rarely said that the issue with the fiction was that it lacked political content. Today, this fiction continues to be criticised often enough precisely because it purportedly lacks political content, distracting readers from self-consciousness, from Chartism. *Penny Politics* is an examination of the political content in cheap British literature from the 1830s and 1840s. Challenging the idea that popular crime or 'low-life' narratives were bereft of politics, and of a politics that might appeal to working-class readers sympathetic to Chartism, it is an attempt to understand the way penny literature pinched political content from radical papers.

Popular literature from the 1830s and 1840s was mostly written for relatively poor working people, though it cannot be defined by its price. The literature was written to be easily consumed, with sensational and either gothic-like plotlines or crime-oriented ones, good or evil characters that often had corresponding appearances, lots of action, and isolated gags. With a history that can be extended quite far back, it was nonetheless recognised as an emerging phenomenon in the 1830s and 1840s, when British society was struggling with demands for political change that must have seemed to be coming from every possible quarter. Liberal and conservative advocates for reform, or just a more moral society, vied with political radicals for the attention and sympathy of 'the people'. Political lines were not always clear, and the very complexity of options – from piecemeal reform to Chartism to revolution – would only add to the politicisation of everyday social relations.[3] Far from offering itself as an 'escape' from politicisation, popular periodicals and popular literature could not and did not isolate themselves from the zeitgeist. Competing with relatively cheap reformist literatures and radical or Chartist literatures for working-class attention, they took up and reframed the political debates that were all around them. I argue in this book that popular fiction from this time experimented with incendiary and agitational materials, essentially capitalising on or taking advantage of the *popularity* of the radical or Chartist narrative. I do not deny that popular literature can be conservative or liberal-reformist in its messages, that it also took pages out of conservative and liberal playbooks, but I am focused on the way it looked to narratives 'from below' (which in this case might be better said to be 'from the side of') to capture a bigger part of the market. To be clear, I do not read the penny blood, Newgate calendars and novels, or melodramatic crime narratives as inciting revolution or promoting the Charter, but I do see them as inflected by radicalism insofar as they allow themselves to be used or understood as part of a movement, either local or historical. Neither an ersatz radicalism nor especially originative, popular literature was responsive, lending itself out to confirm the means to bring about radical change, though it draws short of directly advocating for change.

Though I see a form of fellow-travellerism in popular literature, I do not wish to treat it cynically as the product of morally or politically vacuous entrepreneurs exploiting honest attempts at amelioration to make a quick buck. I see this popular literature as both a genuine attempt to be on the right side of history and as evidence that radical politics was popular and commercially viable. Some of the authors in this study are genuinely liminal figures, caught between socially conservative, liberal/reformist, and radical or even revolutionary attitudes and agendas. That they would attempt to appeal to a public who they might have thought to mirror should not be written off as crass exploitation. The popular fiction I am looking at was primarily entertainment, but made entertainment out of the materials scavenged from the radical or Chartist press. I read in this imbrication a strategy to increase audience size, but representing popular grievances or demonstrating an openness to side with social unrest to the same imagined audience that might have been reading about working-class grievances and social unrest in the Chartist press is a radical act. 'Using' radicalism to court working-class readers can and will be seen as exploiting public anger, and critics have been quick to see popular literature as manipulative – more regulatory than subversive. But this only confirms a false polarity first established by middle-class Victorians. Exploiting anger, it also fed public anger, acculturating but also augmenting political dissonance and the case for extreme forms of remediation. Though the social anger or promise of revenge that popular literature hawks leads to something much less specific than the social anger harnessed in the Chartist press to further Chartism, for example, it nonetheless makes social anger available to a working-class audience – potentially Chartists or the same audience reading the Chartist press – for whatever purpose it might find. The representation of disenfranchised heroes, of underdogs vying against authority and martyring themselves for justice, of class conflict ending in a fantasy of violent vengeance, of the failure of charity and thus the need for agency, or of an elision in the lines between moral and physical activity (to be moral in popular literature is to physically act) could have politically mobilising effects, especially, again, if the audience is assumed to be the same audience also reading more directly political material. Popular literature follows the Chartist narrative: that until 'the people' become part of the process of change, change will not take place and life for 'the people' will be miserable and oppressive. The narrative implies that working-class agency is necessary for the progress of the working classes, and not just after they become educated but as part of the process of education. The Chartist narrative is not simply the representation of poverty and its effects; it is not a slightly re-accented 'condition-of-England' narrative. Neither can it be limited to mutual agreement over 'old corruption'; the antagonists in popular literature are especially not reducible to the aristocracy. Rather, it is a narrative that shows the failure of the moneyed classes to affect a better and more just world for 'the people' without first acquiescing to an initial redistribution of political power.

If, after Peterloo, a narrative persisted that the working classes were routinely subject to violence, a *Sweeney Todd* or *Jack Sheppard* (1839–40), encouraging in their own ways working-class audiences to meet violence with violence, begins to simulate political radicalism. Of course, the radicalism of popular literature is undercover, often concealed under 'cultural confrontations'. But attached to the undisguised fun it has going against the 'respectable' literature of social harmony is popular literature's conflation of cultural and political confrontation. In a large way, this book is meant to challenge the decoupling of cultural and political confrontations when reading popular literature, and to bring out the interplay between them. Separating out cultural and political hostilities is analogous to analysis that separates out the aesthetic and sociological: it is possible to do, but at the risk of marginalising one of the two. I am not arguing that cultural confrontations are inherently political – only that they are often enhanced by, or merge into, the political. Undoubtedly the two can be separated out, but they were used in popular writing in the 1840s to affect the same commercial and counter-bourgeois ends.

Instead of seeing popular literature as solely commercial or sensational, it is possible to see in it a provocative entanglement with the pervading spectre of political violence, even if such an entanglement was understood to be a commercial strength. Providing images of public outrage and working-class defiance enabled Chartism to appear as a threat, even while endorsing moral or constitutionalist arguments. John Walton points out that 'Chartism's characteristic weapon was the petition to parliament, which it was hoped would carry the day by the sheer moral force of its constitutional logic, without needing to be backed by the physical force of an outraged people, although this was a threat which could be held in reserve and alluded to in more or less veiled ways by Chartist orators.'[4] Contemporaneous cheap fiction also provided that backup by depicting an outraged and, perhaps more threatening, an outrageous people. As far as I know, to date, the complementarity between radical and popular fiction has only been approached from one side, with the Chartist press said to be adopting the melodramatic excesses of popular literature so as to reach the audiences that Edward Lloyd, for example, had captured. Late Chartist fiction – the longer, more sensational novels written by Ernest Jones and Thomas Frost – has been seen as capitulating to popular presses. Though G. W. M. Reynolds is often treated as exploiting radicalism, his market dominance is not typically explained by the popular appeal of radicalism. That popular fiction would look to the republican energies coming out of the Chartist press, and to the popularity of those presses, has not, as far as I know, been fully explored. If it can be agreed upon that popular literature attempted to reach as wide a working-class audience as possible, why would it not include material to attract the Chartist audience, the readers of the *Chartist Circular* (1839–41), or the *National* (1839)? Why would it not include the kind of political messaging that made the literature of the *Northern Star* (1837–44) reach 50,000 readers? I do not deny the great differences between popular and radical, specifically Chartist, often dividing along lines of education and improvement, family, a happy ending, and, importantly, the absence of the word 'Chartism' in popular writing. But I do see in popular writing a confirmation of some, however sporadic, radical narratives, especially given the complex and mutable nature of radical politics in the 1840s. Radicalism can take various forms. The moral of improvement, education, constitution, or reform mixed freely with an insistence on republican, revolutionary, insurrectionary, or Chartist militancy; differences between old and new corruption were often lost; and the hard dividing lines between moral and physical force were more likely to be reinforced in liberal, reformist literature than in radical writing. What popular literature took from radicalism it also took intermittently, often only for effect, but in doing so the texts popularised an image of defiance; the image is reconstituted but not decontextualised.

I am not precisely interested in returning to a discussion of hegemony, even with the sophisticated definitions of it that see 'popular culture as an area of domination, negotiation and exchange'.[5] I am more interested in the relationship between Chartist writing and popular writing, not between popular writing and the ruling groups or ideologies that purportedly insinuate themselves into popular culture. Just the opposite in some ways: I see Chartism or various strands of political radicalism as having an effect on popular culture, redefining and reshaping it as it in turn was redefined and reshaped. Instead of seeing the field of popular culture as 'one "structured" by the attempt to win consent to or compliance with dominant ideology', or even as 'forms of opposition to such attempts',[6] I want to examine the other side of the debate and take seriously the pressures that radicalism, democracy, or, specifically, Chartism had on popular culture. By adopting to the severe pessimism surrounding popular culture that emerged from Gramsci, Adorno, and Foucault – that sees popular culture as a means of social diversion at best, but in point of fact a means of social control – critics generally ignore the elephant in the room, leave it out of the equation. 'Hegemony' insists that the dominant ideology shaping popular culture is always the major, if not the only, player in the game. By looking out for the way mass culture was consistent with the interests of radicalism is not to ignore the way that mass culture was or was not resistant to middle-class forces, but to insist that the 'negotiations' that took place between popular culture's cultural confrontations and the hegemonic forces it did or did not perceive were complicated by a variety of agents. It is not difficult to find explicit moral lessons in the popular fiction of the 1840s that would confirm the social order. I am not rejecting the now somewhat orthodox though too-often presentist argument that popular taste is often tied to conservative politics, or that the popular in the 1840s did the work of the establishment. On the other hand, articulations of the conservative or regulatory do not preclude opposite articulations; consistency of messaging is especially alien with the popular. The overall effect of the narratives could also counter conservative messaging or at least create so much ambivalence that the story becomes available to audiences of all political stripes to do as they wish with it. I might reach the same conclusion that Tony Bennett does, and many before him, including and most importantly Raymond Williams, that in popular culture 'dominant, subordinate and oppositional elements are "mixed" in different combinations', but I do so by a very different route. Bennett in fact states that popular culture is 'an "area of negotiation" between the two within which – in different forms of popular culture – dominant, subordinate and oppositional elements are "mixed" in different combinations'.[7] I am simply insisting that the 'mix' is also the result of popular culture's eye on radical writing and not simply a negotiation between 'the two'.

Neither am I returning to the debate in cultural theory over what Juliet John defines as the 'tension between the goals of commercial culture and those of a genuinely "popular" culture consonant with the values and interests of the people, and of a more equal society'.[8] Rather I argue that the neat dichotomising of popular culture in this way accedes to the romantic notion that easily consumed, commercially successful enterprises must somehow be tainted, that there could not be a wide market for genuine radicalism. That culture migrates both up and down and innovation can come from below, above, and all sides was never more evident than with the explosion of periodicals in the 1830s and 1840s, emerging at the time that many saw Britain as verging on continental-style revolution. The upmarket could enjoy getting its hands sticky with downmarket reading and the downmarket could make copies of the upmarket material to sell, which it did. The appropriation of radical tropes and figures went up and down – 'up' to middle-class literatures and 'down' or around to popular ones; Chartism had its own 'arguments from culture'. Connections between liberal and Tory – Dickens and Carlyle – are clear and accepted. But it is less common for critics to countenance that popular literature would turn to radical literature, incorporate its forms and conventions, as if borrowing from radicalism would jeopardise its relationship with its audience, as if popular literature had to keep its filth pure. The mix of material in the Victorian periodical for working people almost assures that reading would have been both a social and a political activity. In 'the trouble with Betsy: periodicals and the common reader in mid-nineteenth-century England', Louis James says of Betsy, his nineteenth-century common reader:

> In one context, Betsy would have liked very much to consider herself a 'lady'; in another, she would protest against being considered middle-class. In imagination, she might wish to murder her mistress; in preparing an important dinner, she might take pride in making a good meal. A novel could not embody these conflicting structures of reality: a periodical, with its fiction, its different kinds of information, can reflect this diversity.[9]

James's insights here are wonderful, but it is not only in the sum of the periodical (or its readers) that we can find such diversity, it could also exist in its parts. The popular fiction the periodicals contained offered itself up to a variety of tastes, of moods, and of preferences as well.

A specific focus on gender is also beyond the scope of this analysis, though work on the intersections between gender, popular literature, and political allegiance needs to be done. Both Chartist and popular fiction are predominantly male, though they end up producing divergent images of masculinity. Working-class men in Chartist fiction are rarely violent or intemperate, unless the narrative explicitly attempts to outline how they became that way. Men in popular fiction are frequently 'toxic', damaging to themselves and others. Chartism's culture of respectability, promotion of temperance, and often inflated appeal to domesticity, as well as the tendency in the fiction for the male hero to be defeated or destroyed, generate questions around masculinity that are generally absent in popular fiction. In the context of Chartism's explicit rejection of *universal* suffrage, any complication of gender or entreaty to female audiences could resonate with a promise of a revised electoral platform. But popular fiction raises questions around gender as well, more frequently with female characters acting in ways that defy social orthodoxies and the pressures of respectability. Radicalism and popular culture were equally engaged in a complex set of negotiations, both imagining and constructing a broad constituency of audiences or 'structures of feeling' that might serve a specific end, political or commercial or both.

This study owes a great deal to critics of Victorian culture and the names of Louis James and Juliet John, as above, Rosalind Crone, Anne Humpherys, Richard Altick, Brian Maidment, and others come up as might be expected. I am, however, especially indebted to the work of Gregory Vargo, Ian Haywood, and Rohan McWilliam. Vargo has shown that liberal, middle-class, or reformist literature was aware of and, to a degree, influenced by radical and Chartist writing. In *An Underground History of Early Victorian Fiction*, Vargo demonstrates that:

> Radical writers closely followed the development of reform-minded fiction; they used popular literary forms for their own ends and recontextualised familiar genres in an oppositional print culture. Middle-class authors learned in turn from experimental writing that appeared in the radical press. Indeed, much of what was most innovative in social problem fiction of the 1830s, 1840s, and 1850s had its origin in the intersection and collision of these two literary nations.[10]

My work here builds on this paradigm of 'generative exchange'[11] by looking at another literary nation-state – the popular press. However, the transactions that Vargo finds 'between the working-class radical press and reforming novelists', that they were 'complex and contradictory, characterised by violent denunciations and significant borrowings',[12] hold true of the interaction between popular and radical literature, though I am not looking at the influence that popular literature had on radical literature.[13] While the platforms of 'education' and 'respectability' that often link Chartist and middle-class fiction together are no longer available, linkage is made through half-formulated but still threatening intimations of political destabilisation in the popular press. The traffic between middle-class, Chartist, and popular writing does not amount to any one of these literatures losing its characteristics or audience loyalties. As Vargo demonstrates, Chartist writers could be conscious of middle-class fiction and consciously in opposition to it, or aesthetically approving but still ideologically in opposition, or, intermittently, on the same page as their liberal counterparts. Popular literature can also share aesthetic and ideological habits with radical literature and wildly diverge from it as well.

Though I look closely at Lloyd and Reynolds, who emerge out of the radical tradition but are still often treated as less interested in radical than in commercial enterprises, I am primarily interested in genres that are not generally considered as responsive to radical arguments – just the opposite, such as Newgate writing, serialised crime narratives, and the penny bloods. This material has to be reassessed in light of work by Ian Haywood that shows a history of popular writing emerging out of the 1790s that earned its popularity in part because it was radical. Haywood looks at the intersection of popular enlightenment, popular politics, and popular literature. *The Revolution in Popular Literature* confirms links between popular literature and radical politics but demonstrates that the networking took place in a contested field, as innovations in popular literature emerged out of a struggle between radicals on the one hand and anti-Jacobin liberals (or conservatives) on the other, trying to contain 'the radicalised common reader' and his or her 'cheap' readings.[14] The popular literatures of the late eighteenth and early nineteenth centuries are thus constantly undergoing a 'process of continual appropriation and re-appropriation, of rapid response, innovation, imitation, assimilation and subversion'.[15] Haywood offers a history of the development of popular radicalism; my argument is an attempt to build on what he describes as the 'merging of the "Jacobin" periodical tradition of the 1790s and paradigmatic new forms of popular cultural pleasure such as cheap fiction'.[16]

Finally, I am also indebted to Rohan McWilliam's *Popular Politics in Nineteenth Century England*, which outlines a way to move forward from the opposition in cultural studies between old and new models of historical analysis. According to McWilliam's review, the 'old analysis' is class-centred, materialist, and intent on spotting how political (or cultural) discontinuities between classes emerge from economic ones, whereas the 'new', more postmodern analysis is concerned with the 'gap between social structure and political ideology'[17] and thus 'the relative autonomy of the political'. This division has far-reaching implications for my study insofar as the literature I am looking at is generally considered to be class-based (economic) but rarely treated as political. In looking at the intermittent use of politicised narratives that 'belonged' to radical epistemologies by both Salisbury Square and, in the last chapter, middle-class popular journals of improvement, I follow McWilliam in trying to find opportunities to negotiate the two poles and not to be confined by either of them. The old analysis by itself cannot fully answer why both popular and middle-class writing would incorporate the Chartist narrative, but the 'new analysis', for all of its insights, on its own would run the risk of starting 'to look as though we are simply left with a series of events, personalities and ideas that are typical of nothing but themselves'.[18] McWilliam's observation that 'Politics is about the distribution of power; therefore, social history cannot be complete without a political dimension whilst politics needs to be situated in social terms',[19] is precisely what the popular fiction studied here embodies and shows.

Writing against a literature (or culture or ideology or class) hardly precludes correspondences and overlaps between texts. Popular literature's use of the Chartist narrative intersects with its use of liberal or reformist and conservative discourses, as well as anti-Semitic, nationalist, familial, nostalgic, and constitutionalist expressions, for example. Confirming the 'relative autonomy of the political' in one sense, too much can be made of political divisions in the first place, as if a Chartist transforms into a liberal when seeking reform. In popular literature, what might be properly reformist or liberal or constitutionalist often becomes radical and revolutionary because it comes from below, because it is an expression of class anger, or because relatively minor political changes seem to need the threat of incendiary acts from below – or actual violence – to be considered or to come to fruition. The language of reform, or just discontent and dissatisfaction, can be simultaneously the language of social unrest and economic class when uttered by or put in the mouths of the poor. The political might have a dynamic of its own, but it should go without saying that its autonomy can be lost or at least complicated through representation. In other words, this study recognises that there is some danger in turning history into soup by constantly stressing the competing social identities of both the individual producer and consumer of culture. Political continuities between liberal, popular, Chartist, Tory, Christian Socialist, and so forth are notable often because of class-oriented and principled discontinuities, and I am not seeking them out so as to simply state that things were complex. Class or political identity can be fractured while class and political allegiances hold true, especially at times of perceived crisis. My argument is not intended to demonstrate the cultural or political fluidity of working-class audiences as the use of the radical narrative might not demonstrate fluidity as much as it demonstrates the dynamism and attraction of the radical.

Popular literature is non-party political, but it admits that its audience, 'the people', have political allegiances that they will not let go of, that have to be appeased. The perception that the audience would be thrilled by the hint of revolution, by the promise that insurrectionary instincts are almost always valid, suggests the limits of political fluidity insofar as popular literature invests in a stereotype of working people ready to grab their pitchforks. The insolent insubordinate living independently of middle-class respectability and middle-class laws, as if one was a corollary of the other, was a ready-made image. In a sense, I am less interested in the making of the common reader than in the way that the already-pegged common reader made for the fluidity of literature: the common reader was at least partly premade as a social and political malcontent. Patrick Joyce is certainly correct to argue that 'simply by receiving the conventions of melodrama those who received them were being constituted as political persons',[20] but audiences are not constituted out of thin air. I am not asserting that intermittent and casual images of political defiance or plebeian autonomy imply deep Jacobin designs or 'true' (or 'untrue') political allegiances. Rather, they should mostly be treated as signs of the public mood and public taste. An irreverent resistance to respectability, polite custom, established law, and representational propriety might define popular literature. But if cultural hostility is to be expected in popular writing as part and parcel of the commercial aspect of the enterprise, a political counterpart should not come as a surprise.

Seen against the literary products of the Chartist press, not much popular writing from the 1830s and 1840s would immediately strike the reader as insurrectionary. Chartist writing stressed education and self-help, working-class mutuality, temperance, self-culture, but also the urgent need for the Charter. It is generally written with the absence of the Charter in mind, and for that reason usually ends miserably with the death of the impoverished anti-hero.[21] Popular literature rejected the narrative of education and temperance, was most commonly understood as corrupting the minds of its working-class and often young readers, and always ends with justice and a happy ending for the good. The Chartist press generally looked down upon crime and Salisbury Square fiction, and the Chartist attitude towards Reynolds was mixed at best. Chartist periodicals were much more likely to reproduce Dickens, Kingsley, or stories from *Tate's* or the *Athenaeum* than *Jack Sheppard* or *Sweeney Todd*.[22] A narrative in which the popular culture 'industry' of the 1830s and 1840s rose out of, but abandoned, the radical politics of the unstamped papers, relinquishing it to Chartism, is possible, but even accepting such a bifurcation in reading choices for working people, the split could not be that clean. I admit I am looking at fragments of the radical tradition, but these piecemeal artifacts nonetheless betray an understanding of the importance of the tradition to its audience. I am interested in the very irregularity of radical tropes in popular literature, the contradictions in these texts between images of necessary rebellion and social harmony, between material that ignores politics, even conceals or belittles political causes, and the kind of inflammatory messaging that Chartist papers would only dare with caution. I am looking at popular literature that reflects popular opinion and mediates the political by running it through extreme social situations. Commercial activity, that is, was a location for extensive political engagement, and thus a fusion or confusion of political messaging was made available.

I focus on periodical writing, novels, and short stories, not the drama from the period that often went to further extremes than the novels on which they were based to make the most of a popular radicalism. The political content of melodrama has already been well argued. I mostly use 'popular fiction' to group together the literatures that are not Chartist or reformist/middle class; at the time, critics were more likely to call it 'morbid' writing, as in diseased. The difference between 'penny blood' and 'penny dreadful' is generally accepted, the 'dreadful' coming after the 'blood' and marketed primarily to a young male audience. 'Salisbury Square' identifies literatures coming out of a specific place at a specific time. The loose bag of terms I reach into so as to describe Victorian 'popular fiction' – cheap, low or low-life, street, crime, or penny fiction for example – is an indication of its rooting in class. Chapter 1 looks at the development of the Newgate calendar and its increasing politicisation as Chartism emerged as a social and political force. The ambiguity that marked early calendars, when rogues and rascals were both condemned and romanticised, continued when the calendars began reporting on Chartist trials, making the representation of the seditious rioter and Chartist agitator just as ambiguous as the representation of the romanticised thief, and the punishment dolled out to the rioter just as questionable as the punishment for the thief. I look at the politicisation of the calendars in the 1830s and 1840s, and see – however cautious, qualified, and couched – real support for the spirit of agitation and change voiced by the Chartist defendants, if not for Chartism itself. Chapter 2 traces the development of the calendars to the Newgate novel, focusing on William Harrison Ainsworth's *Jack Sheppard*. As with the calendars, the novel exploits its audience's desire for exciting political content and allows itself to be understood as willing to be part of a movement bent on changing the political course of the nation, however veiled and playful that willingness appears. I look to both its popularity among working people and to the criticism it encountered for not just its plot, but because of its popularity to support a reading of it as making itself amenable to a politicised audience, an audience feeling confined and powerless. Relocating history, *Jack Sheppard* is a story that mocks and defies the liberal debate over the licensing of freedoms.

Chapter 3 offers an examination of the penny blood, focusing on *Sweeney Todd* and two of Edward Lloyd's papers, the *People's Periodical and Family Library* (1846–47) and *Lloyd's Penny Weekly Miscellany* (1842–46). I ask if and how we should read the cultural confrontations of the novel given the political confrontations being waged at the time by radicals, especially Chartists. I also query if the penny blood can be read as enacting or engaging in a properly political confrontation, if it – however casually and sporadically – co-opted strains of radicalism simply because the authors of the bloods perceived a market for radical tenets and for broad social insubordination. Chapter 4 focuses on only one author, a central figure in popular literature, G. W. M. Reynolds. Instead of reading Reynolds as a commercial entrepreneur pilfering isolated idioms from the radical canon, I read Reynolds as a full-out radical attempting to increase the size of his audience by incorporating the non-radical into a hugely radical novel, *The Mysteries of London* (1844–45). In his own time and too often today, Reynolds's radical credentials are dismissed, often because his popularity is deemed as irreconcilable with a popular movement. But his radicalism, his proto-Chartism before he declared himself a Chartist, needs to be measured against a Chartism that itself was filled with ambiguities, incongruities, and differences. Unlike the often anonymous authors in Lloyd's papers who use radical narratives to profit off of the frisson of the revolutionary or insurrectionary threat, to augment the commercial enterprise, Reynolds is better understood as a radical who uses sensational content to expand and excite the political audience.

The final chapter switches gear to examine reformist periodicals of popular progress and improvement from the 1840s that were specifically addressed to the working classes, like *Politics for the People*, though I focus on *Howitt's Journal* (1847–48) and *Douglas Jerrold's Shilling Magazine* (1845–48). Competing with both 'cheap' and radical papers for working-class readers, they were nonetheless responding to, and – ever so cautiously – borrowing from the radical canon, though the attendant rejection of the popular press is noticeably pronounced. That the use of the Chartist narrative by these papers, however reluctant, was contingent upon the rejection of crime or 'low-life' narratives is indicative of a fear at the intersection between culture and politics established by those latter narratives. The chapter looks at the struggle these papers endured searching for a way to come to terms with the Chartist narrative.

Notes

1 F. D. Maurice, 'Prospectus', *Politics for the People* (6 May 1848), p. 1.
2 Maurice follows his opening 'Prospectus' with an article called 'Fraternity' where he celebrates the recuperative, 'national' literature of Charles Dickens becoming more popular than class-based literature, including 'low-life' literature written for the working classes (pp. 2–3).

Kingsley's first contribution to the journal as 'Parson Lot' is on the value of introducing working people to the National Gallery.
3 In Carlyle's footsteps, it was not unusual for newspapers and magazines in the 1840s to lament the number and variety of political voices surrounding John Bull. Before listing the demands made by labourer, farmer, manufacturer, poor man, artisan, and so forth, 'J. S'. tells the readers of *Douglas Jerrold's Shilling Magazine*, for example, to 'Look around! What a chaos of conflicting influences and movements are at work! Listen! What a hubbub of voices, each with its own peculiar burden, ascends from the tumultuously heaving masses of society!' J. S., '"Shadows" of "Coming Events"', *Douglas Jerrold's Shilling Magazine*, I, p. 22.
4 J. Walton, *Chartism* (London and New York: Routledge, 1999), p. 56.
5 O. W. Ashton, 'Chartism and popular culture: an introduction to the radical culture in Cheltenham Spa, 1830–1847', *Journal of Popular Culture*, 20:4 (2004), 62.
6 T. Bennett, 'Popular culture: history and theory', *Popular Culture: Themes and Issues* (block 1, unit 3, Milton Keynes: Open University Press), 31.
7 *Ibid.*, p. 31.
8 J. John, 'Reynolds's *Mysteries* and popular culture', in A. Humpherys and L. James (eds), *G. W. M. Reynolds: Nineteenth-Century Fiction, Politics, and the Press* (Aldershot: Ashgate, 2008), p. 163.
9 L. James, 'The trouble with Betsy: periodicals and the common reader in mid-nineteenth-century England', in J. Shattock and M. Wolff (eds), *The Victorian Periodical Press: Samplings and Soundings* (Leicester: Leicester University Press, 1982), p. 359.
10 G. Vargo, *An Underground History of Early Victorian Fiction: Chartism, Radical Print Culture, and the Social Problem Novel* (Cambridge: Cambridge University Press, 2018), p. 2.
11 *Ibid.*
12 *Ibid.*
13 The effect that popular literature had on radical and Chartist literature has been studied, for example, by Sally Ledger, Steve Devereux, and Jack Mitchell.
14 I. Haywood, *The Revolution in Popular Literature: Print, Politics, and the People, 1790–1860* (Cambridge: Cambridge University Press, 2004), p. 4.
15 *Ibid.*
16 *Ibid.*, p. 6.
17 R. McWilliam, *Popular Politics in Nineteenth-Century England* (London: Routledge, 2012), p. 33.

18 Ibid., p. 98.
19 Ibid., p. 99.
20 P. Joyce, *Democratic Subjects: The Self and the Social in Nineteenth-Century England* (Cambridge: Cambridge University Press, 1994), p. 179.
21 Contemplating middle-class literature, the literary critic of the *Northern Star* confirms what I refer to as the Chartist narrative by pointing out that 'the world of life is a very different world to that which poets and novelists dream of. We are conscious that in the world of stern realities it is too often the ... virtuous and good, and not the ... base and villainous, who come to a miserable end.' Anon., 'Reviews', *Northern Star* (29 March 1845), p. 3.
22 The *Operative* (1838–39) included reviews and excerpts from *Jack Sheppard*, as did the *Charter* (1839–40) as part of its review of *Bentley's Miscellany* (1836–68). I do not look at the work of John Cleave because I consider him unambiguously Chartist.

1

The old, new, borrowed, and blue Newgate calendar

This chapter argues that the criminal biographies or Newgate calendars of the Chartist period need to be reassessed in terms of their radical content and in light of their popular appeal. Because Newgate calendars are so often used only to introduce the Newgate novel, much of the criticism tends to sum up all eighteenth- and nineteenth-century editions as one and the same.[1] Without doubt, the formal and generic properties remain roughly constant from one volume to the next, and the calendars themselves seem to invite audiences to lump them all together by repeatedly reproducing cases from earlier editions. However, with the rise of Chartism in the 1830s and early 1840s, calendars became politicised in such a way as to make themselves available to an audience aware of, interested in, and even sympathetic with 'seditious' acts and class-based activism. That textual content would reflect the age in which it was produced should not come as a surprise. But by continuing and perhaps even amplifying the notorious ambivalence of the criminal biographies – the way they accommodate readers seeking a moral authority while at one and the same time accommodating readers who seek to thumb their nose at moral authority – in an atmosphere dominated by political upheavals, or simply by taking up the argument from reform, the calendars assembled in the Chartist years at the very least make political engagement as exciting as a highway theft.

Often in an eighteenth-century calendar, criminals are almost gleefully represented as folk heroes – scoundrels, but brave and talented or clever – and the law just as incapable, clumsy, or corrupt, though a morally didactic frame heavy-handedly informs readers that crime is bad and justice will be served. Despite borrowing material from Knapp and Baldwin's popular 1819 and 1824–28 calendars, *Martin's Annals of Crime* in 1838 and Camden Pelham's *Chronicles of Crime* in 1841 shift emphasis away from individual criminals towards distinctly political acts. The *Chronicles*, for example, adds multiple cases of riots, sedition, and treason. In doing so, it maintains an ambivalent attitude towards the subject matter, ostensibly condemning the rioters as earlier entries would have denounced a thief, while allowing readers to feel the frisson of the riot and celebrate the daring or skill – this time verbal – of the leader and his dedication to the cause. *Martin's Annals* is more explicitly radical, mixing essays on the rights of labour, including one by the Chartist J. R. Stephens, together with stories of intrepid pirates and highwaymen. As the number of violent demonstrations and sedition trials increased in the 1830s and early 1840s, notwithstanding the turbulence of the 1820s, more reports of social unrest might be expected; it was an established practice for calendars to include riots and politically oriented cases in their catalogues. But the way these calendars transpose a tradition of using affective discourses and hybrid utterances into an unstable social context creates potentially heroic narratives of political action. The ambivalent response to social unrest may simply illustrate commercial interests, a strategy to capitalise on what was seen as a popular, people's movement. But even if that were the primary reason for continuing with the dialogism of the earlier crime journals, it nonetheless demonstrates a readiness to be part of the changing political course of Britain.

    The history of Newgate calendars has been well documented and I will only briefly sketch out some of the salient features here. All the calendars are compilations, composites, written by anonymous contributors. Not all the represented criminals served time or were executed at Newgate, but naming a collection after the prison could function as a convenient way to tell audiences what was being sold, while also acting as part of the moral frame, a quick lesson in the probable destiny of the criminal. The very first reports were written by the chaplain or Ordinary of Newgate Prison in London. These seventeenth- and eighteenth-century broadsides, essentially single-page pamphlets that might later be collected into books, such as Richard Head's *The English Rogue* (1665), focused on the criminal's confession, uttered just prior to the scaffold. Maximillian Novak suggests that the 'first systematic collection of criminal accounts to be published in England was Captain Alexander Smith's *History of the Lives and Robberies of the Most Notorious Highwaymen*' in 1714.[2] Novak says that Smith's innovation was in recounting the personal history of the criminal, that Smith 'specialised in the brief account of the criminal's life, trial, and end: the pattern to be that of the Newgate Calendar'.[3] *The Newgate Calendar; or, Malefactors' Bloody Register* from 1773, the first to use the Newgate name, is widely thought of as the next most significant calendar until *The New and Complete Newgate Calendar* by William Jackson in 1795, which was issued in weekly parts to make up five volumes, with supplements later added. Knapp and Baldwin's 1819 *New Newgate Calendar* and their later four volume 1824–28 edition called *The Newgate Calendar* (the *New Newgate* is published prior to *The Newgate Calendar*, suggesting that the editors considered the latter volumes definitive) is an important milestone in the history of criminal biographies because, as Stephen Knight argues, citing Struan Sinclair, Knapp and Baldwin drop the religious language dominating earlier calendars and replace it with more legal and statistical frames of reference, ushering in a new legal and reformist perspective.[4] Novak calls this edition 'the most popular and enduring of the series',[5] in part because the authors of the Newgate novel – Bulwer, Ainsworth, and Dickens – used it as a source for their novels.

Generally speaking, each new edition would include a selection from earlier editions, sometimes edited and sometimes not, with additions from contemporary cases. The first volume of the *Chronicles of Crime* is almost entirely taken from Knapp and Baldwin's 1824 edition – approximately 250 of 275 cases are derived from the earlier calendar, though interestingly with more than a third of the new cases describing riots and other political 'crimes'. (Most of the first volume of the 1824 Knapp and Baldwin edition is taken from the earlier 1819 edition.) As the *Chronicles*, like most other calendars, proceeds chronologically, the second volume includes most of the new material, with only 46 of 203 cases derived from Knapp and Baldwin. In other words, individual volumes of a calendar are self-historicising, with a distinct character reflecting either the period represented in that particular volume or a new source for material used for that volume. Volume V of the 1819 Knapp and Baldwin somewhat strangely includes multiple cases of crime and conditions around Botany Bay, not to be found in the other volumes. Finally, it should be noted that the index of a volume might give a false impression that a particular kind of crime was increasing at a particular time: editors were in the habit of listing all the individuals involved in the same crime separately. Volume III of the 1819 Knapp and Baldwin, for example, seems to represent a huge spike in the number of riot cases, but only because the index lists one by one the many convicted individuals involved in the Gordon Riots.

Editors could also shape the overall meaning of their collections by the order they chose to reproduce the cases. Immediately following the story of a murderer born to a 'most respectable' family with the story of farmers executed for thievery (the cases of Mary Blandy and John McCanelly/Luke Morgan), the editors of the *Chronicles of Crime*, for example, potentially change the way both stories were read when they appeared pages apart in Knapp and Baldwin, though there is little chance of knowing if readers proceeded from first case to last. Certainly by the nineteenth century editors understood the collections as continuations and that their function was to select the most significant cases from earlier collections, adding in the most important present-day cases for the next generation of the collections. The calendars distinguished themselves from cheaper broadsides and contemporary newspapers – by the 1830s, many dailies and weeklies, appealing to many different audiences, were stuffed with crime reporting[6] – by promising to be shelf-worthy. Though George Borrow wanted to make a distinction between his collection of *Celebrated Trials* (1825) and the calendar genre, he says in his Preface to it that:

> One object was to form such a series as might serve for the basis of future continuations; for the cases recorded by the present activity of the ephemeral press and of society will be sufficient hereafter to fill a volume similar to one of the present in every seven or ten years; and partly with a view to such a series, this fundamental collection has been formed. A new volume as often as interesting cases have arisen sufficient to fill one, will confer on the present collection a perennial

value, and in another century the remarkable trials assembled in this British work may be expected to occupy as large a space on the shelves of our libraries as the French *Causes Celebres*.[7]

The main similarity of the calendars is structural. Many of the cases are represented straightforwardly, especially if the crime is violent, and the criminal is condemned both by the reporter and by the evidence or confession. In these cases, the calendars call for anger against the criminal, often representing the fury of the victim's community. However, framed by sermons on the ineluctable path of malfeasant crime to justified gallows and explicit denunciations of the criminal and the crime, ambiguity often emerges when the criminal is represented as an ingenious adventurer or a likable rascal, or pathetically repentant, or when the law is presented as inept or overly severe. Here editors often attempt to produce indignation against a restrictive or unfair social system or a flawed criminal justice system. Scholars have often recognised the double-voiced design of the calendars and in this way are justified to group them together.[8] Though the content cannot be ignored – the story of Jack Sheppard *is* terrible fun and the law could really be an ass – the frequent mixing of moral instruction and entertainment notoriously leads to a mixed message. This was well known before the Newgate novel popularised the debate over the representation of crime. Borrow states in 1825 that the 'Newgate Calendars as chroniclers of roguery and of vulgar depravity, in their various forms, have usually been compiled in language, which sympathised and accorded with their subjects.'[9] The calendars, that is, for all their high-handedness and higher-mindedness, regularly engage in less than subtle forms of cultural confrontation, undressing polite society by admitting a subculture of deviance and unruliness commonly or most easily associated with the working class. That William Campion in 1824, 'considering it to be an imperative duty of every man to resist oppression and uphold the oppressed',[10] would use the title *The Newgate Monthly Magazine* (1824–26) to publish not a calendar but a defence of radicals arrested for sedition suggests a consciousness that the Newgate tag might also imply an alignment of cultural and political confrontation.[11]

Explicit political content, however, is not common in calendars before the 1830s. Even in the 1840s, cultural confrontations are mostly represented by the actions of individual 'scamps' or reprobates such as 'Robert Taylor, convicted of bigamy'.[12] Taylor is a 'roguish adventurer' who defends his bigamy with bawdy humour and a laugh at authority on the grounds of society's avarice (multiple women marry him thinking he has money). Common criminals are frequently represented with enough personal detail to explain their motivations; in some cases readers are encouraged to consider how the criminal's sufferings led to crime. One of the most subversive aspects of the calendars is that they psychologise, attempting to provide a complicated internal narrative that fills out the external evidence. The story of George Griffiths in William Jackson's *New and Complete Newgate Calendar*, for example, is of a clerk who foolishly steals from his lover's father so as to make 'an appearance which he was unable to support, in order to secure the object of his wishes',[13] his lover's hand. Though the writers draw harsh lessons from the case about station, patience, and theft, they also insist that Griffiths truly loved his betrothed, ending with a fragment of verse that seems to honour his motivations and retract from an earlier statement that the crime constituted a capital offence:

> Reflecting on his fate severe,
>   We own that love has borne its part;
> A tale like this must draw a tear
>   From every tender, feeling heart.[14]

Against the unforgiving rhetoric condemning the already condemned is the humanising of the criminal. Perhaps feeding off the notion that life for the lower classes was unfair and becoming more and more prescribed from above, editors tend to juxtapose 'internal impulses of aggression' to 'the constraints of social reality',[15] both of which might be scrutinised and critiqued. So not only are the lowest elements of society sympathetically presented, but their actions were also attributed to a complicated interior life frustrated by a social reality that might very well be frustrating readers as well. Borrow includes a passage from Edmund Burke on his title page which is not only strikingly neutral, but makes the criminal the best model of real life:

The Annals of Criminal Jurisprudence exhibit human nature in a variety of positions, at once the most striking, interesting, and affecting. They present tragedies of real life, often heightened in their effect by the grossness of the injustice, and the malignity of the prejudices which accompanied them. At the same time real culprits, as original characters, stand forward on the canvas of humanity as prominent objects for our special study. I have often wondered that the English language contains no book like the *Causes Celebre* of the French, particularly as the openness of our proceedings renders the records more certain and accessible, while our public history and domestic conflicts have afforded so many splendid examples of the unfortunate and the guilty. Such a collection, drawn from our own national sources, and varied by references to cases of the continental nations, would exhibit man as he is in action and in principle, and not as he is usually drawn by poets and speculative philosophers.[16]

Stephen Knight neatly finds that the represented 'criminals are ordinary people who reject the roles society and their families offer them' and that 'Sometimes the criminal is led astray by another renegade from a life of integrated industry. Those who create crimes are not innately, incurably evil.'[17] Knight's point is that the calendars are dominated by an organic, Christian ideology, but it is also possible to use the same observation to argue that the reduction of the criminal to an antisocial misfit implies the failure of society, insofar as there is some fundamental reason why so many are led astray. Calendar criminals don't go around killing albatrosses; there is a reason they do what they do, and though not justified some criminal acts are presented as understandable. It is for this reason that they were such great material for the developing nineteenth-century novel, though this complexity unravels the simple morality so frequently evoked in the calendars themselves. The point I wish to make, however, is that this double-voiced narrative ambivalence continues with the calendars produced in the Chartist period, and with the representation of Chartist 'crime'.

On the other hand, as mentioned, some of the time the crime reports are straight and, as such, a 'despicable', violent criminal is simply caught, tried, and executed with great effectiveness, end of story. Heather Worthington is not wrong to see one type of story in the calendars as socially conservative: 'The confession, explicit or implicit, in the criminal's story served to validate the death sentence and demonstrate the efficiency of the penal system, reassuring the reader that crime could and would be contained and deterring the potential criminal with the apparent certainty of punishment.'[18] This is the case, except when it isn't. As Knight confirms, criminals are frequently caught only through 'pure chance'.[19] He notes that the most striking feature of the Newgate stories 'is the imprecise, unspecific, scarcely explained or motivated way in which' a criminal is recognised or brought to justice.[20] But his conclusion is similar to Worthington's, that this pattern assures readers that capture is 'inevitable', as 'the very community the criminal shunned can muster its forces and throw up the hostile body'.[21] But again, just as easily as it might be read that society fixes itself, it can be seen that society is fundamentally unfixable and the penal system an ineffective deterrent, as crimes keep on happening and no system is in play to prevent them from recurring. The sheer volume of the editions, despite the republishing, seems to imply that crime is rampant, various, transhistorical and anything but containable. The practice of publishing a calendar that begins with borrowed entries but then adds new reports based on the latest crimes proclaims that while crime may take different forms, it is an industry here to stay. In addition, the 'sheer luck' of the capture must have suggested to at least some readers the ineptitude, fragility, and chaos of the penal system, despite explicit assurances about the effectiveness of retributive justice.

The legal system, in turn, is frequently seen as inept or corrupt; the straightforwardness of the overall moral of the collection is especially subverted and a wholesale doubt as to the fairness or effectiveness of the law is suggested when heinous crimes are juxtaposed to trivial ones or mere social transgressions, especially when the punishment is similar. Knapp and Baldwin devote their Preface to a defence of capital punishment, but even they recognise that by being often repeated, 'the minds of the multitude are rendered callous to the dreadful example'.[22] Rayner Heppenstall notes that Knapp and Baldwin's works 'were among the first products of a reforming age which looked back fascinated at one during which too many were hanged for too little'.[23] The absurdity of the 'Bloody Code', where minor crimes were treated as a capital offence, seems to be the true narrative in the case of 'Fish-stealing out of a river or pond', set beside murderers, thieves, and rapists in Volume I of Knapp and Baldwin's 1819 edition. Similarly, stories where criminals insist on their innocence all the way to the scaffold, or are said to be innocent after having been put to death, something that happens more frequently in some calendars than others, are not easily reconciled with a reading of the genre as a staunch defence of the justice system. It is not at all unusual to come across a title such as 'An account of Richard Coleman, convicted and executed for a murder of which he was innocent.'[24] Nearly all calendars from William Jackson's on include the case of Margaret Dixon (or Dickson), who maintained her innocence and was suspected to be innocent, and who lived through her execution, and because she could not be sentenced twice lived for many years after her trial. It is a narrative of providential justice heaping scorn on a legal system that too often demonstrates its failures only after exacting capital revenge.

'Abraham Thornton, tried for murder' is another famous case that challenges the sanctity of the law. It appears first in Knapp and Baldwin before being reused in *Martin's Annals* (with an added Introduction and Concluding Remarks from a pamphlet written by the Rev. Luke Booker) and then entirely rewritten for Pelham's *Chronicles*. In 1817, Thornton was indicted for the rape and murder of Mary Ashford, and though he was clearly guilty in the eye of the public (and of the narrators) the judge's advice to the jury produces a verdict of not guilty for the murder charge and the rape charge is subsequently dropped. Because the public 'were far from considering Thornton innocent',[25] they raised money to pay for a new trial under an appeal of murder. It is important to note, especially in the *Chronicles*, that the authority figure, the judge, is deemed mostly responsible for Thornton's discharge; the 'people' know he is guilty and insist on trying Thornton again, a practice that was allowed at that time. Before the second trial can get underway, Thornton demands a 'trial by *wager of battle*'. The narrator and the public recognise this is absurd, a relic from a time way past, but the 'learned judges' disagree; and since William Ashford, Mary's brother in whose name the second trial was to proceed, was not prepared to fight, he has to withdraw his appeal and Thornton goes free. But again, the public shun Thornton, promising vengeful violence and forcing him to flee to America; the sailors on the ship he was scheduled to take will not let him aboard, and Thornton has to conceal his identity until he can escape. The law in this case, and its preference for its own formality over clear right and wrong, is patently at fault and, importantly, at odds with the common sense of the people. Thornton gets away with crime three times (twice on murder, once on rape). In 1818, the case drew attention to the way the law could be manipulated, leading to the end of both the appeal of murder and trial by battle; resurrecting the story in calendars might convey that improvements had been made to the legal system, but it also reminds readers that the experts often get it wrong. Knapp and Baldwin, two lawyers, state in their Preface 'that crime has always been followed by punishment; and that, in many instances, the most artful secrecy could not screen the offenders from detection, nor the utmost ingenuity shield them from the strong arm of impartial justice'.[26] But they too include the case of Thornton. Just as individual cases in the calendars might include a moral frame belied by the sympathetic treatment of the criminal, an unequivocal moral 'preface' to a calendar is often followed by content that fudges the matter.

Other calendars could be much more direct in their criticisms of the legal and court systems than Knapp and Baldwin. Introducing a declaration of bankruptcy case where a man was concealing money, *Martin's Annals* states, 'offences of this nature are constantly committed in the most clandestine manner, so as too often to escape detection'.[27] Borrow states in his Preface:

> It is difficult which to condemn the most, – the solitary murderer, way-laying and ensnaring his victim, or supple judges and tribunals, who commit legal murders with unblushing effrontery, to gratify a master, and promote their own personal aggrandisement. In one instance, every sentiment of virtue is set at defiance, while in the other, virtue is put to the blush, and sound axioms of justice dispensed with, or flagitiously compromised.[28]

Borrow pulls no punches when outlining the corruption of the legal system, characterising it as 'the pre-engaged servant of the long purse', as Wilkie Collins would later put it.[29] Borrow goes on to say that:

Examples of punishment may deter the solitary criminal, but retributive Justice is rare in regard to those who commit murders in ermine, and under the sanction of legitimate authority. The former have daily warnings, but the latter have received them but twice or thrice in our history; and they are such exceptions to the general course of events, that crimes have usually been committed by authority, in the confidence of perfect impunity.[30]

Though Borrow then goes on to explain how the British jury system can protect against abuses, quoting Phillips's *Golden Rules for Jurymen* at length, he ends his preface by outlining the shortcomings of that very jury system and the need to reform it. Conversely, Knapp and Baldwin affirm in their 1824 Preface that 'we may be thankful for laws ... which we find administered with rigorous impartiality, awarding the same punishment for the same offence, whether the culprit be rich or poor, humble in life or exalted in rank'.[31] And yet, the third case in the collection is of a nobleman murderer who escapes the scaffold, though we are assured that he dies a penitent (and wealthy) man. It also includes, for example, the case of 'George Alexander Wood and Alexander Wellesley Leith, indicted for manslaughter and slaying'. Here, two Eton boys brutally fight until the much smaller and younger one dies, the other and his backers plying the victim with brandy. Knapp and Baldwin conclude the episode with a startling tableau that leaves readers with an image of the wealthy being above the law and laughing at it. As the prosecution provides no witnesses, the verdict is not guilty and the Eton boys leave the bar 'attended by Lord Nugent, Colonel Brown, Sir Dashwood King, and other persons of distinction'.[32] The same case appears in the *Chronicles* but without a scathing introduction where Knapp and Baldwin blame the upper classes for their 'ungovernable' character, their 'blackguardism', and judge the Eton boys as 'most culpably'[33] responsible for the death of a young man, again, before reporting that they go free.

Worthington says that the criminals from the calendars 'tend to be from the lower classes'.[34] But the poorer classes do not monopolise the pages. Knapp and Baldwin directly appeal to 'respectable' audiences, contrasting them with 'the rude minds of the multitude',[35] though in the revised Preface of 1824 they add that

'The Newgate Calendar must prove highly acceptable to all ranks and conditions of men'[36] if it is to act as a deterrent to potential criminals from the lower classes. But the first case they reproduce is of a Reverend Thomas Hunter, 'Executed for the murder of two children'. The case begins with a reminder that criminals 'are generally confined to the abandoned and irreligious – the illiterate and intemperate'; yet the story is of 'a man of education and a minister of the Gospel'.[37] The second story is about the owners of a public house who murder a guest; this is followed by the case of the nobleman murderer mentioned above. It goes on: next a soldier; then a young man who 'received the education of a gentleman, was articled as clerk to an attorney of high repute';[38] then Captain John Kidd, the pirate; then an articling apothecary and surgeon. The point is that whether or not by design, even Knapp and Baldwin's collections offer a socially mixed collection of villains. Variety was the object of the calendars: as William Jackson states in his Preliminary Remarks to the 1795 *Newgate Calendar*, it is the 'professed intention of the Compiler of this Work to exert his utmost endeavours to unite *entertainment* and *improvement* ... [and] such *narratives* only as become *valuable* from the *singular circumstances* with which they were attended'.[39] Such incidental groupings are not criticisms of class systems, but they contribute to the steady slipperiness of the calendars, a deflation of the didactic message that allows for and encourages interpretive work.

Novak has noted that different editions will be more sensational or more factual, and have differing degrees of irony or religious reflection.[40] But calendars of the 1830s also differ from their predecessors by reflecting the politically charged atmosphere of the age. The calendars of this time were written in the heyday of the Newgate novel, when the debates it caused were peaking,[41] and when the Newgate label was being voraciously denounced for showing sympathy for criminals or glorifying them. Introducing calendars at this juncture, that is, would be to court controversy and to side with popular novels and drama against a haughty, indignant authority.[42] *Martin's Annals of Crime* was published weekly between March 1836 and March 1838, and collected into two volumes in 1837 and 1838. It is very different from Knapp and Baldwin's calendars, despite lifting a number of stories from them (or from the calendars Knapp and

Baldwin used to assemble their editions). As a penny weekly, the *Annals* was more affordable than Knapp and Baldwin's editions and likely had a different central audience. But the full name of the calendar might leave the impression that it would not be a departure from the established genre: *Martin's Annals of Crime; or New Newgate Calendar, and general record of tragic events, including Ancient and Modern Modes of Torture, &c.: comprehending a history of the most notorious murderers, traitors, highwaymen, pirates, burglars, pickpockets, adulterers, ravishers, decoyers, incendiaries, poachers, swindlers, and felons and rogues of every description.* In fact, the advertisement to the first volume of the *Annals* by 'A. M'. reads much like previous prefaces, insisting that the collection is written to convey 'the necessity of spurning the path of iniquity'.[43] The first few numbers also begin with commonly reproduced cases, such as one on Catherine Hayes, with an early four-part series on notorious highwaymen suggesting that *Martin's* panders to the public's desire for adventure stories even more than earlier calendars. But in the same number that introduces a new series on 'the most notorious pirates', Martin includes the first of six weekly columns on 'Naval and military tortures'. This is subtitled, 'Atrocious cruelty to an impressed seaman' and it begins with a condemnation of parliament much stronger than the words used to describe the notorious career of pirating:

> The expectations of the public have been again violently disappointed in the conduct of the *reformed* Parliament, with regard to the perpetuation of flogging in the British army, a mode of punishment which none but the most depraved and unfeeling minds can adopt, unless fatally misguided – not to say prejudiced – by some fallacious ideas on the subject; a mode of punishment which none else can attempt to justify, in the present day, on any tenet of morality, justice, common prudence, or rationality. Majorities of 212 to 95, and of 135 to 62, have decided upon its continuation, in disastrous opposition to the voice of the people – the voice of God; and it becomes a question of whether it will not be the righteous duty of the oppressed henceforth to resist the barefaced, beastly, and merciless cruelty ... A few manly resistances, – resistances even to death, if need be; for it is better to die struggling for freedom, than to die tamely submitting to the iron hand of oppression.[44]

Although Heppenstall notes that 'the tone' of the *Annals* 'was vigorous but not inflammatory',[45] it would not be an exaggeration to say that this editorialising is as provocative as what would come out of the Chartist press. In part because the working classes were particularly responsive to issues surrounding naval abuse, Chartist papers published numerous essays and stories against flogging, impressments (even after the practice had ended), and enlistment. For Martin to call state-sanctioned acts *torture* expands the reach of the calendars, but without changing the affective style. The fourth entry of 'Naval and military tortures' is from William Cobbett's February 1835 Letter to Robert Peel, part of *Cobbett's Legacy to Peel*, but most of the entries are original essays that are connected to crime only insofar as readers might conclude the state's 'oppression' to be criminal. If the Newgate calendar was expected to raise indignation and anger, officially against heinous criminals, the *Annals* transfers that energy to social crime, viewing 'HISTORY', in the words of Washington Irving that it quotes, as 'but a kind of Newgate calendar, a register of the crimes and miseries that man has inflicted on his fellow-man'.[46]

A similar set of essays focuses on 'Slavery in England: the factory system'. The first instalment is taken from the *Christian Advocate* of 2 May 1836 and is focused on child labour; the second is extracted from John Minter Morgan's 'Hampden in the nineteenth century' and is mostly on 'cruel and oppressive'[47] factory discipline. In introducing this material, the editors of the *Annals* state that their objective is 'to denounce the factory system as one of the most reckless and merciless ever devised by demoniac agency in human breasts' and to 'take our stand against the many-headed victimiser, with an indestructible determination to hold up to view, as far as our simple means will permit, the blood of the numerous martyrs to his insatiable thirst'.[48] The language of martyrdom, or what E. P. Thompson has called 'Radical martyrology',[49] is the same that would be used repeatedly in the Chartist press.[50] The next several numbers reproduce 'A memoir of Robert Blincoe', a famous exposé of the cotton mills. Finally, the eleventh and final instalment of the series reproduces in whole a speech given by J. R. Stephens, who would later be arrested for his involvement with Chartism on a charge of sedition, and would be subject to his own criminal biography in the *Chronicles of Crime*.

Martin's Annals is a completely different kind of calendar than its predecessors, and not simply because it does not proceed chronologically. Much of the material incorporates the same discourses found in Chartist periodicals or older unstamped newspapers, such as this short article titled 'Aristocrats':

> There is a set of men in all the states of Europe who assume from their infancy a pre-eminence, independent of their moral character. The attention paid them from the moment of their birth, gives them the idea that they are formed for command; they soon learn to distinguish themselves as a distinct species, and, being secure of a certain rank and station, take no pains to make themselves worthy of it. To this institution we owe so many indifferent ministers of state, ignorant magistrates, and unskilful generals.[51]

After an excerpt imported from Friedrich Von Raumer's 'England in 1835' called 'Picture of Irish misery', itself a strange addition to a crime calendar, where Von Raumer compares Ireland and England and states that the latter is much better off than the former, the editors add:

> The respected foreigner who penned the foregoing observations was, after all, but partially acquainted with England, what did he know, for instance, of the factory system? Evidently nothing. His delineation of the state of the Irish is by no means overcharged – it is pathetically true: but had he been acquainted with such scenes as are detailed in the 'Memoirs of Robert Blincoe', he would have been one of the last to speak in so unqualified language of the invariable happiness which awaits the denizen of England.[52]

In fact, some issues of the *Annals* have more in common with radical periodicals, or at least the more uncompromising reform journals, than with calendars, especially in the way they mix articles on the need for social reform with others on the need for working-class improvement. The 12 October 1836 issue includes a short report on a penitent thief returning from transportation to face execution, told almost entirely in his own sympathetic words (he is 'resigned to the will of Providence'[53]); a poem from the *Weekly Dispatch* as part of the 'Naval and military torture' series; a lengthy continuation of the factory system series; and finally a short concluding comment on the need to avoid gambling. The next number is mostly a continuation of the factory system series, followed by an old (1723), brief criminal case where a boy, 'abandoned to profligacy',[54] slips into a life of crime. The following number is entirely given over to the factory system series, save a short 'improvement' column, but nothing on Newgate-type crime; finally, the ensuing week only continues the factory system series. At this point in 1836, it is no more than the title – *Martin's Annals of Crime* – that is reminiscent of a criminal biography.[55]

The *Annals* was vehemently reformist, frequently including essays on the Corn Laws,[56] the excesses of punishment or the ineffectiveness and immorality of using torture to exact confession, and Richard Oastler's factory reforms. As with earlier calendars, it also included romanticised images of criminals and especially stressed the corruption of the law. In a short article called 'The Origin of Law', the authors treat dishonesty in the law as a fundamental part of the practice, stating, 'The profession of the law takes its origins solely from human depravity; and this being the case, it is no wonder that considerable abuses should always be found in it. Crafty and designing men are even attempting to enrich themselves at the expense of others, and never want professional assistants to gain their ends.'[57] The article ends by noting that 'perpetual reform' is needed because of the very nature of the law and lawyers. This is shortly followed by 'The melancholy case of Richard Coleman', who 'was as innocent of the crime for which he suffered as the babe unborn'. It begins with 'a striking caution to prosecutors not to be too positive in their identity of an accused party'.[58] Finally, 'The blood-money system' also represents systemic legal flaws, this time as a result of 'the mischievous principles of a law' that pays money to individuals who contribute evidence towards a conviction.[59] The editors suggest that this is a practice that overwhelmingly and negatively affects the poor. Placing the argument for legal reform in the context of class injustice, and surrounding it with articles on factory and military injustice, recognises class in a way often denied by earlier calendars. Though the case for legal reform is implicit in most of the calendars that precede *Martin's Annals*, the politicisation of this calendar indicates that it was alive to a new class-based political consciousness.

The *Chronicles of Crime*; or, the *New Newgate Calendar* does not share with the *Annals* an explicit reformist or radical agenda, but it is nonetheless socially and politically aware in a way that is not seen in earlier calendars. It was published by 'Camden Pelham' – a pseudonym – who claims to be a barrister and identifies himself as a member of the Inner Temple, but there is no record of a Camden Pelham as a member of the Temple. The collection is also of note because it includes fifty-two original drawings by Hablot Knight Browne, or Phiz. An American ad for it in 1843 suggests it was a popular edition, claiming 'Over Four Hundred Thousand copies of this far famed work have been sold in Europe, and the demand still increases.'[60]

The *Chronicles of Crime* is prefaced with the same kind of moralising seen in the calendars of the 1820s and earlier. It justifies itself by arguing that 'the more generally the effects of crime are shown, and the more the horrors which precede detection and the deplorable fate of the guilty are made known, the greater is the probability that the atrocity of vice may be abated and the security of the public promoted', adding that doing so with an eye to 'amusement', 'entertainment', and the 'interesting' can only recommend it the more.[61] Many of the cases, as Pelham admits, 'are derived from sources of information peculiarly within the reach of the Editor', while the later material 'is compiled from known authorities as accurate as they are complete'.[62] Distinguishing his collection, Pelham notes that the nature of crime has changed in recent years, as society has grown less vicious. He states that 'The comparison of the offences, and of the punishments of the last century, with those of more recent date, will exhibit a marked distinction between the two periods, both as to the atrocity of the one, and the severity of the other.'[63] True as his argument may be, it is conspicuously stressed; Pelham states that 'it cannot be denied that the general aspect of the state of crime in this country is now infinitely less alarming than formerly'.[64] Less alarming, that is, are the newer cases Pelham adds to the annals of British crime, which are, again, predominantly social and political, mostly concerning Chartist uprisings.

What primarily distinguishes Pelham's edition is four back-to-back essays on Chartism and numerous reports on contemporary riots, labour action, demonstrations, sedition, conspiracy, and treason, as well as a selection from earlier calendars that describe social protest, such as reports on the Gordon Riots and the Luddite struggles. These also tend to be grouped together, the case against Henry Hunt at Peterloo followed by the Cato Street Conspiracy, for example. Otherwise, cases are presented in chronological order. The new additions include burglary and murder trials, but reports on the 'Agricultural Riots', 'Reform Riots', 'Calthorpe Street Riots', 'Canterbury Riots', 'Dorchester Labourers', and 'Merthyr Tydvil Riots', as well as the essays on Chartist activity, give this calendar its character. The demonstrable shift towards political content in the calendars of the 1830s and 1840s is not only a response to the simple fact that there were more political trials taking place, but also to the popularity of Chartism and specifically the Chartist story of the martyr. Other new accounts, such as the one on François Benjamin Courvoisier, the valet whose alleged reason for murdering his master was his reading of *Jack Sheppard* (1839–40), are also distinctly class-oriented and political. The Courvoisier case became a touchstone for the class war that the Newgate novel was said to be provoking, and while the writer's closing comments downplay the idea that class resentment (or Courvoisier's reading of calendars) led to his decision to murder Lord William Russell – 'the dreadful crime of which he was guilty seems to have been rather the result of a sudden impulse than of pre-determined malice'[65] – presenting the murderer's long confession makes it clear that he was angered by Russell's continuous criticisms and that he had 'admired' the 'skill' and 'valour' of thieves and murderers he read about in the calendars.

Courvoisier is not represented as a folk hero; his confession nonetheless documents the passions that Newgate texts were accused of inflaming. Yet the same energetic rhetoric that allegedly provoked Courvoisier to murder Russell marks the reports on the riots: readers are told that rioting is a terrible act, but we learn of the rioters' frustrations, as well as their planning, skill, intelligence, daring, and most importantly, their honest motivations or belief in the rightness of their actions. Just as individual criminals are not presented as simply evil, but with a story that explains how they got to be criminals, readers are allowed to understand why the rioters and Chartists do what they do. Moreover, riots are often blamed not on 'the people', the rioters, but on the government's failure to properly prepare for protest or even its incitement of violence during peaceful demonstrations. The Calthorpe Street Riots are explained as the result of the government overresponding to a proposed demonstration by the National Union of the Working Classes, feeding public curiosity and provoking conflict by declaring the meeting illegal. The case is not a defence of the Union but a reproach of the government and police, whose overzealous activities only increased public interest and resentment. The authors are somewhat dismissive of the National Union, not mentioning the organisers of the protest until two pages into the article and arguing that the Union would never have been able to assemble such a large crowd if it were not for the authorities' mishandling of the event. Still, emphasis is placed on the orderliness of the people before the police became involved: 'The procession with these ensigns walked in good order to the spot at which the speakers had assembled; but they had scarcely taken up their position, when a body of police marched into Calthorpe-street.'[66] More importantly, the report gives voice to 'the people':

> A great number of witnesses were examined, many of whom declared, that the police had acted towards the people with unwarrantable harshness, striking and beating them with their truncheons; making no distinction between active parties in the meeting and defenceless women, but conducting themselves with equal and undue severity towards all; and that they had been guilty of this misconduct without any provocation being offered.[67]

Though the reporter also states that 'it was sworn, that the mob were violent, and that many of them were armed with formidable weapons', he mostly concedes 'that there was no disposition to riot among the people until the arrival of the police'.[68] The *Chronicles* does not support political activity in any direct way, but the instinct to defend the crowd, to agree with 'the people', on the basis that the agents of government must be able to 'draw the distinction between the intemperance of the few, and the usefulness of the main body',[69] implies allegiance with 'the people'. Whether the presumed audience were middle or working class,[70] or a mixture of both, the message is that 'mob violence' has its origins in the actions of the state, or at worst in the actions of miscellaneous ruffians, and not in the political reform sought by the Union. If the design of calendars is to generate emotion, this is a case that clearly elicits sympathy for those on trial and indignation against social authority.

The report on the 1839 Birmingham riots is of a slightly different character. At the outset the riots are called 'disgraceful'. But still in the opening paragraph the author explains that though the 'eventual estimation' of the Charter might be favourable, the Chartists must be checked only because of the 'violence of the views entertained by these persons'.[71] If 'these persons' include all Chartists, or just the 'physical-force Chartists' involved in the riot, the article does not explain, although it does later recognise and explain the differences between moral and physical forces. Though the article explicitly condemns Chartist agitation, it also raises questions about the actions of the police and magistrates, the neutrality of the juries, and even the desperate situation of the working people accused of rioting. And just as older calendars allowed rogue criminals to explain themselves in their own voice, the article gives readers the entire, unabridged two and a half pages of the 1838 national petition (in quotation marks). A letter from William Lovett is also given in full, ostensibly as evidence against him in a charge of libel, but in and of itself a hearty defence of Chartism. A similar treatment of a Chartist leader can be found in an article on J. R. Stephens, which is strikingly neutral and mostly matter-of-fact. Though the author raises concern about Stephens's 'dangerous powers of eloquence', and roughly characterises him as a demagogue seeking to gratify the tastes of his audiences, he also emphasises how Stephens earned his huge popularity; in addition to an honourable biography, readers are told of Stephens's calm intelligence, and the peaceable, reasonable nature of the crowds he attracted at his trials.

Immediately following the report on the Birmingham riots is a very comprehensive, twenty-one-page essay on 'The Chartist Riots, 1839–40', focusing on the case of John Frost and the Newport outbreak. It again begins with a declarative condemnation of Chartists, but then dives into the biography of Frost, outlining his devotion to justice, his work on behalf of social progress, and his well-deserved popularity. Though the article insists justice was done with the passing of the sentence, and that the proceedings were fair, it reports on the dignity of the accused (in addition to Frost, Zephaniah Williams and William Jones) in such a way that would at least allow them to be honoured by their supporters: 'The prisoners received the announcement of their fate with the utmost firmness, yet propriety of demeanour. They were the only persons in the crowded court whom the fearful nature of the sentence, and the low, solemn tone, in which it was pronounced, did not most deeply affect.'[72] Again, the article is in no way pro-Chartist, just as earlier calendars could never be called 'pro-criminal'. But when the author/narrator includes images of pathos – 'The prisoners were then removed from the bar, and the clanking of their chains was painfully audible'[73] – it gives licence to readers to make the text readerly, to debate it, and to make it their own, usurping judge and jury. Political violence, republicanism, and specifically Chartism were given passage into the public imagination as forms of political entertainment, not so as to question or undermine them but to allow readers to participate in the thrill of them. If Chartism was primarily 'constitutionalist', slow, and 'moral', as historians such as Miles Taylor and F. C. Mather contend,[74] it was making its way to larger audiences as something else.

Finally, the *Chronicles* concludes its section on Chartism with a report on Feargus O'Connor, 'Convicted of the publication of a seditious libel'. Once more it contains the direct words of Chartists, this time taking long excerpts from the *Northern Star* by William Taylor and Bronterre O'Brien. O'Connor's defence at his trial is then summed up in a page of argument that defends not just O'Connor, but the Chartist cause as well. O'Connor emerges as a victim, a martyr, a reconstituted folk hero struggling against faceless authority. The first three-quarters of the article are in fact handed over to O'Connor to make his case, and it is the same argument the writers of the *Chronicles* had used earlier in the 'Calthorpe Street Riot' to defend the people from accusations of unruliness:

> It was the act of the Attorney-general (with whom he [O'Connor] had once sat in the House of Commons), and of his party, who had turned the moral force Chartist into the Chartist advocating the use of physical force, and drove them to armed meetings by putting down the meetings where they 'morally' discussed their grievances.[75]

Naturalising the slippage of moral to physical force and pointing the finger for public violence at social authorities and the systems they confirm reproduces an argument customarily made by the Chartist press. But then the verdict of 'guilty' abruptly comes in without a single word from the attorney general. Including a lengthy defence of Chartism's actions and ambitions does not necessarily evoke the Chartist narrative legitimising the participation of 'the people' in bringing about social justice or amelioration, but at the very least it indicates that the monolithic, dull voice of authority does not adequately represent the people. Clearly, O'Connor would not want to be placed in the company of James Owen, George Thomas, alias Dobell, and others convicted of murder in the case which follows, but the *Chronicles of Crime* importantly allows readers to group him with the catalysts of cultural confrontation and equivocate in their judgement by making O'Connor appear as sincere, passionate for the cause, an underdog, and a victim against bureaucratic rule. Readers are told that O'Connor's 'speech lasted nearly five hours, and he concluded by declaring that he was, and always had been, a Chartist, and determined to have all the five points, but peaceably. He asked from the jury but justice; he asked not for mercy; and if their verdict should consign him to a dungeon, he would at least go there with his principles unsullied.'[76]

The *Chronicles of Crime* was the last calendar produced until the very sensational weekly *New Newgate Calendar* by E. Harrison in 1863, reprinted in 1886 and 1891. That there had been a new calendar approximately every five to ten years since Jackson's 1795 calendar, five multi-volume sets and one weekly between 1818 and 1834 alone,[77] and that Pelham's edition marked an end to this trend for twenty-two years suggests the possibility that potential editors were not entirely comfortable with representing popular political movements in the way they are represented in the *Chronicles*, though the debates over the Newgate novel undoubtedly played a major role in the temporary disappearance of the calendars as well. Pelham did not set out to radicalise the genre: he includes the case of Henry Hunt at Peterloo – only edited slightly from Knapp and Baldwin – which dismisses the idea that a 'massacre' took place in 1818, saying that this is simply radical propaganda. Hunt is irredeemable in the eye of the writer. But the case against Hunt, borrowed and blue, is not written in the same way as the case against O'Connor or Stephens; it is the exact opposite of the report on the

'Calthorpe Street Riot' which underlines police provocation and brutality. The later writer seems to be cautiously participating in a spirit of rebellion and change that is not typically seen in earlier calendars, which tend to focus on individual criminals. In fact, even in the article on Hunt in the *Chronicles* some ambiguity emerges

Figure 1 *Manchester Massacre* by Phiz (Hablot Knight Browne) for *The Chronicles of Crime* II, p. 29. By permission of World History Archive/Alamy Stock Photo.

through Phiz's illustration, depicting the demonstrators as fierce and brutal, but also depicting the hussars slaughtering women and children, something not mentioned by the writer. He titles his drawing 'Manchester Massacre', a word the original author refuses to use. Phiz was not a radical – his drawing of 'Unionists Being Initiated' expresses no subtle support for combination – but the two calendars produced in the Chartist years remain open to reform, to some kind of structural change, as if they wanted to be on the right side of history, but just didn't know for sure which side that would be.

Notes

1 Keith Hollingsworth's seminal study *The Newgate Novel*, for example, notes that *Martin's Annals of Crime* 'had its own significant character', but for his purposes he does not distinguish between calendars. K. Hollingsworth, *The Newgate Novel, 1830–1847: Bulwer, Ainsworth, Dickens, and Thackeray* (Detroit, MI: Wayne State University Press, 1963), p. 52. The distinct features of them, however, have been increasingly recognised. In *Form and Ideology in Crime Fiction*, Stephen Knight argues that calendar stories 'can be easily added or removed, their order can be changed and the whole is not in any real way different'. S. Knight, *Form and Ideology in Crime Fiction* (Bloomington, IN: Indiana University Press, 1980), p. 17. But thirty years later, he recognised that they 'are often substantially rewritten in the process of republishing, and the stories have no stability'. S. Knight, *Crime Fiction since 1800: Detection, Death, Diversity*. (Houndmills: Palgrave Macmillan, 2nd edn, 2010), p. 6.
2 M. Novak, '"Appearances of Truth": the literature of crime as a narrative system (1660–1841)', *The Yearbook of English Studies*, 11 (1981), 33.
3 *Ibid.*
4 Knight, *Crime Fiction since 1800*, p. 8.
5 Novak, '"Appearances of Truth"', 34.
6 For more on crime reporting in radical periodicals see A. B. Rodrick, '"Only a newspaper metaphor": crime reports, class conflict, and social criticism in two Victorian newspapers', *Victorian Periodicals Review*, 29:1 (1996), 1–18; E. Jacobs, 'The politicisation of everyday life in *Cleave's Weekly Police Gazette* (1834–36)', *Victorian Periodicals*

Review, 41:3 (2008), 225–47; and R. Breton, 'Crime reporting in Chartist newspapers', *Media History*, 19:3 (2013), 1–13.
7 G. Borrow, *Celebrated Trials, and Remarkable Cases of Criminal Jurisprudence from the Earliest Records to the Year 1825* (6 vols, London: Smackell and Arrowsmith, 1825), I, pp. v–vi.
8 For various interpretations of the dualistic tendency of calendars to moralise and sensationalise see, for example, K. Straub, 'Feminine sexuality, class identity, and narrative form in the Newgate calendars', in D. Todd and C. Wall (eds), *Eighteenth-Century Genre and Culture* (Newark, DE: University of Delaware Press, 2001), pp. 218–35; H. Worthington's 'From the *Newgate calendar* to Sherlock Holmes', in C. J. Rzepka and L. Horsley (eds), *A Companion to Crime Fiction* (Chichester, West Sussex: Wiley-Blackwell, 2010), pp. 13–27; and J. John's 'Twisting the Newgate tale: Dickens, popular culture and the politics of genre', in J. John and A. Jenkins (eds), *Rethinking Victorian Culture* (Houndmills: Macmillan Press, 2000), pp. 127–46.
9 Borrow, *Celebrated Trials*, I, p. iii.
10 W. Campion, R. Hassell, and T. R. Perry (eds), *The Newgate Monthly Magazine* (London: R. Carlile, 1825), p. 2.
11 The full title is *The Newgate Monthly Magazine or Calendar of Men, Things, and Opinions*; it was edited by William Campion and dedicated to Richard Carlile, 'the Republican Moralist'.
12 C. Pelham (ed.), *The Chronicles of Crime; or, The New Newgate Calendar* (2 vols, London: Thomas Tigg, 1841), II, pp. 594–9.
13 W. Jackson (ed.), *The New and Complete Newgate Calendar or Villany Displayed in All its Branches* (6 vols, London: Alexander Hogg, 1795), I, p. 28.
14 *Ibid.*, I, p. 29.
15 L. Gillingham, 'Ainsworth's *Jack Sheppard* and the crimes of history', *Studies in English Literature 1500–1900*, 49:4 (2009), 884.
16 Borrow, *Celebrated Trials*, title page for all six volumes.
17 Knight, *Form and Ideology*, p. 11.
18 Worthington, 'From the *Newgate calendar* to Sherlock Holmes', p. 14.
19 Knight, *Form and Ideology*, p. 12.
20 *Ibid.*
21 *Ibid.*
22 A. Knapp and W. Baldwin (eds), *The New Newgate Calendar* (5 vols, London: J. Robins and Co. Albion Press, 1819), I, p. iv.
23 R. Heppenstall, *Reflections on the Newgate Calendar* (London: W. H. Allen, 1975), p. xi.

24 A. M. Martin (ed.), *Martin's Annals of Crime; or, New Newgate Calendar* (2 vols, London: William Mark Clark, 1837 and 1838), I, p. 73. Reproduced from A. Knapp and W. Baldwin (eds), *The Newgate Calendar* (4 vols, London: J. Robins and Co., 1824–1828), II, pp. 52–5.
25 Pelham, *The Chronicles of Crime*, II, p. 20.
26 Knapp and Baldwin, *The Newgate Calendar*, I, p. iv.
27 Martin, *Martin's Annals of Crime*, I, p. 125.
28 Borrow, *Celebrated Trials*, I, p. vi–vii.
29 W. Collins, *The Woman in White* (Oxford: Oxford University Press, 1998), p. 5.
30 Borrow, *Celebrated Trials*, I, p. vii.
31 Knapp and Baldwin, *The Newgate Calendar*, I, p. iv.
32 Knapp and Baldwin, *The Newgate Calendar*, IV, p. 396.
33 *Ibid.*, p. 394.
34 Worthington, 'From the *Newgate calendar* to Sherlock Holmes', p. 16.
35 Knapp and Baldwin, *The New Newgate Calendar*, I, p. vi.
36 Knapp and Baldwin, *The Newgate Calendar*, I, p. iv.
37 *Ibid.*, p. 1.
38 *Ibid.*, p. 10.
39 Jackson, *The New and Complete Newgate Calendar*, I, p. 9.
40 Novak, '"Appearances of Truth"', p. 34.
41 *Bentley's Miscellany* published *Oliver Twist* between February 1837 and April 1839 and *Jack Sheppard* between January 1839 and February 1840.
42 Lord Melbourne's opinion of *Oliver Twist*, for example, is discussed in Chapter 2.
43 Martin, *Martin's Annals of Crime*, I, n.p.
44 *Ibid.*, p. 68.
45 Heppenstall, *Reflections on the Newgate Calendar*, pp. 52–3.
46 Martin, *Martin's Annals of Crime*, I, p. 208.
47 *Ibid.*, p. 150.
48 *Ibid.*
49 E. P. Thompson, *The Making of the English Working Class* (London: Penguin, 1980), p. 661.
50 The Scottish *Chartist Circular*, for example, produced numerous stories of martyrs, including 'The Republican: a tale of the French Revolution' (18 April – 9 May 1840) by 'Argus'. Here the hero 'suffer[s] martyrdom on the alter of blood-stained Mammon – a willing sacrifice in the cause of truth, justice, and universal mercy, that the seed of liberty might be planted, nourished, and reared in the blood of her martyrs'. Argus,

'The Republican: a tale of the French Revolution', *Chartist Circular* (9 May 1840), p. 135.
51 Martin, *Martin's Annals of Crime*, I, p. 120.
52 *Ibid.*, p. 256.
53 *Ibid.*, p. 258.
54 *Ibid.*, p. 271.
55 This goes on for a number of weeks. Though a later issue returns to traditional crime narratives, it is dominated by an article taken from the *Weekly Dispatch* on 'The private and personal swindling of the late king' ('The royal Jonathan Wild'). *Ibid.*, p. 289. The *Weekly Dispatch*, it should be noted, a favourite source for *Martin's Annals*, was, in the words of the *Epochs and Episodes of History*, 'Radical to the backbone', known especially for its 'vigorous denunciation of the police and the New Poor Laws'. H. W. Dulcken (ed.), *Epochs and Episodes of History: A Book of Memorable Days and Notable Events* (London: Ward, Lock, and Co., 1882), p. 203.
56 In one number the editors reproduce a pamphlet by Thomas Dixon called 'Criminal Legislation': 'BY whom are the taxes paid? By the artisan, the day-labourer, and the beggar; by duties levied upon the necessaries of life, such as tea, coffee, sugar, beer, and bread—ay, and beef and potatoes too, for the cruel Corn Law extends its baneful influence to every species of home produce'. Martin, *Martin's Annals of Crime*, II, p. 303.
57 Martin, *Martin's Annals of Crime*, I, p. 234.
58 *Ibid.*, p. 246.
59 *Ibid.*, p. 394.
60 T. B. Peterson, 'T. B. Peterson's lists of books', in *The Birthright: A Novel* by C. G. F. Gore (New York: Harper and Brothers, 1843), p. 19.
61 Pelham, *The Chronicles of Crime*, I, p. v–vi.
62 *Ibid.*, p. vii.
63 *Ibid.*
64 *Ibid.*, pp. vii–viii
65 Pelham, *The Chronicles of Crime*, II, p. 582.
66 *Ibid.*, p. 380.
67 *Ibid.*, pp. 380–1.
68 *Ibid.*, p. 381. The trial itself sets up the authorities, judicial and governmental, against 'the people' represented in the jury. Two of the rioters are accused of attempting to murder a sergeant and a constable. But the jury found 'a verdict of Justifiable Homicide on these grounds: that no riot act was read, nor any proclamation advising the people to disperse; that the government did not take the proper precautions to prevent

the meeting from assembling, and that the conduct of the police was ferocious, brutal, and unprovoked by the people; and we moreover express our anxious hope that the government will in future take better precautions to prevent the recurrence of such disgraceful transactions in the metropolis'. However, the 'law officers of the crown' overturn the jury's verdict. Eventually the assailants are found not guilty, but the *Chronicles* takes from this not that an attempted murder is excusable, but that 'the conduct of the mob can be justified only by the attack which it is clear was made upon them'. *Ibid.*, p. 382.
69 *Ibid.*, II, p. 382.
70 Heather Worthington argues that 'The Calendar anthologies were expensive, limiting their audience to the higher social classes.' Worthington, 'From the *Newgate calendar* to Sherlock Holmes', p. 15. Poorer classes would likely buy the cheaper pamphlets, though one cannot assume that they never bought a collection. Thomas Tegg, Pelham's printer, under 'Light reading & books in the Pickwick style', advertised the *Chronicles of Crime* (both volumes, new) for one pound 8 shillings in 1843. G. W. M. Reynolds's very popular *Pickwick Abroad*, also with plates by Phiz, sold for 14 shillings, exactly half the cost of the *Chronicles*, and it was only one volume.
71 Pelham, *The Chronicles of Crime*, II, p. 499.
72 *Ibid.*, p. 530.
73 *Ibid.*
74 M. Taylor, *The Decline of British Radicalism 1847–1860* (Oxford: Clarendon Press, 1995), p. 100. F. C. Mather, *Chartism and Society: An Anthology of Documents* (London: Bell & Hyman, 1980), p. 25.
75 Pelham, *The Chronicles of Crime*, II, p. 544.
76 *Ibid.*, p. 545.
77 A reprint of Jackson in 1818, George Theodore Wilkinson's the *Newgate Calendar Improved* in 1822, Borrow in 1825, Knapp and Baldwin in 1819 and from 1824 to 1828, and fifty-three numbers of the penny weekly, *The Annals of Crime and New Newgate Calendar*, in 1833–34. This list does not include Thomas De Quincey's 1827 'On Murder Considered as One of the Fine Arts' or the thirty-three volumes of *State Trials* by William Cobbett, F. B. Howell, and T. J. Howell published between 1809 and 1826.

2

Jack Sheppard, the Newgate novel

There is good reason to doubt both the generic and ideological coherence of a 'Newgate novel', let alone the number of writers needed to make a 'school'. A mere four novels unambiguously fit the bill: two by Edward Bulwer Lytton, *Paul Clifford* (1830) and *Eugene Aram* (1832), and two by William Harrison Ainsworth, *Rookwood* (1834) and *Jack Sheppard* (1839–40). Charles Dickens's *Oliver Twist* (1837–38) and *Barnaby Rudge* (1841) are often labelled 'Newgate', though they perhaps undermine some of the basic features of Bulwer's and Ainsworth's novels in more ways than they reproduce them, notwithstanding that both *Jack Sheppard* and *Oliver Twist* are supported by George Cruikshank's illustrations. Bulwer's *Night and Morning* (1841) and *Lucretia* (1843) are also generally thought to fit the Newgate pattern to some degree, and William Thackeray's *Catherine* (1839–40), despite being a parody of the criminal biography, is occasionally grouped with its targets. *Richmond; or, Scenes in the Life of a Bow Street Officer* (1827), usually attributed to Thomas Gaspey, is sometimes considered an early example of a Newgate novel, in part because the Bow Street Runner, Tom Richmond, begins his life on the wrong side of the law. Later in the 1840s, Thomas Peckett Prest would write perhaps the only self-consciously deliberate Newgate novel, *Newgate: A Romance* (1847). Attempting to capitalise on its most sensational features, and mixing in a wide assemblage of gothic tropes, Prest's reduction of the Newgate novel to a set of quick and easy conventions mostly demonstrates that the Newgate phenomenon had come and gone. At best, the Newgate name describes a very small, fuzzy set of novelists and novels.[1] The authors themselves go to great lengths to distinguish their works from each other's and to protest about the way they were being lumped together. Yet all this only makes the branding of 'Newgate' by critics in the late 1830s, and the fearful abjection in the responses, all the more remarkable.

Despite the relatively few Newgate novels produced in the 1830s and early 1840s, the grouping together and labelling of them after *Jack Sheppard* first appeared, starting with Thackeray in *Fraser's Magazine*, was widespread, overdetermined by the same literary and social history that shaped the novels in the first place. But before tracing the various and loosely counter-hegemonic strands that made the novel, leading to its rigid categorisation, it is worthwhile to stress the extent to which the Newgate novel as such represented less a stand-alone genre than a terrifying social phenomenon; critics reacted negatively to the phenomenon, the 'craze', more than they did to the handful of actual novels. In large part this is because the novels gave way to a huge number of stage productions, some based on the novels and some original, but all reproducing a basic Newgate interest in criminal biography, making the distinguishing feature of the Newgate novel, perhaps even more than with the sensation novel of the 1860s, the phenomenon of its reception, its extratextual life. To Ainsworth's delight and Dickens's chagrin, *Jack Sheppard* and *Oliver Twist* led to numerous plagiarisms. First serialised in *Bentley's Miscellany*, working-class access to the novels was prohibited by its half-a-crown cost. But it was assumed by nearly all the critics at the time that working-class audiences were accessing *Jack Sheppard* one way or the other, and for good reason today's critics do not disagree. As has been documented many times, the novels attracted a level of hostility that would have made Byron proud, and certainly exceeded the response given to their literary predecessors also gleefully representing forms of lawlessness. In other words, the anger directed at the Newgate novel had less to do with its flaunting of authority, which in many ways dominates literature even before the French Revolution, than with fear of its popularity in a climate that could only have been understood at the time as unstable, the people at the brink of outbreak. Given the reciprocity between the assumed audience and most of the heroes of the stories, that both were part of the same crowd, such popularity made the perceived cultural sedition of the stories politically as well as materially threatening. Aesthetic and moral criticism was directed at individual texts unevenly; greater antipathy was reserved for the cumulative and generative effect of the fiction, that it was productive.

In this chapter I examine *Jack Sheppard* as *the* Newgate novel, the only one of its set to demonstrate an openness to side with social unrest. I do not deny that in many ways the novel simply tells the story of Jack Sheppard or that the potentially incendiary content of his story is often treated ambivalently and non-politically. I am in fact interested in the way that the ambivalence made the novel so tantalising to some and so threatening to others.[2] Aside from nostalgia for the Jacobin rebellions, Ainsworth's biography includes little that would suggest he had radical sympathies.[3] But with Bulwer and Dickens, he was tuned into and highly responsive to developing reading markets and public debates – to the zeitgeist.[4] The novel's reception, that is, both its class-specific popularity and the criticism it faced, best argues that it made itself available to disenfranchised, angry men who could politicise it, read it as encouragement to express discontent, or develop an us-against-them class consciousness. That it can be read that way merely implies that Ainsworth had seen the sign of the times, glimpsed a tipping point, and was going to make entertainment of it. For those threatened by *Jack Sheppard*, it was far from an entertainment; it generated strangely emotional criticism, anger, and panic, mostly because it was thought to be influential, replicating itself and its morally ambiguous world. Behind the criticism was a fear that *Jack Sheppard* was producing active, sovereignty-minded readers half dreaming of ways and half planning ways to escape from the hard categories of their lives. Aside from confronting false authority and ridiculing the obstacles those authorities impose on their subjects, *Jack Sheppard*, with its heroically autonomous criminals, challenges hard, disjunctive categorisation, primarily by dismantling the division between good and bad. This was an acutely political act following the 1832 Reform Bill, where men who owned property worth at least ten pounds constituted a newly legitimised group: either you owned property or you didn't vote. It was not lost on the newly enfranchised middle classes, or those who enfranchised them, that for all of its fine points the Charter represented an opportunity for working people to control – increase, bend, or blend – the number of social and political categories any one person could belong to.

Thackeray was the most insistent and influential critic of what he was determined to label Newgate novels and novelists.[5] Setting out to categorise a Newgate novel in *Catherine* and elsewhere, he laments how the heroes of these novels defy hard categorisation, and rejects the figuring of autonomous and fluid self-categorisation they represent. The story of Jack Sheppard includes exactly what Thackeray finds impossible, amplified by Ainsworth's storytelling. Jonathan Wild *was* a thief-taker and a thief, a Jacobite and Jacobite-jailor; Jack Sheppard, beyond his ability to wear effective disguises, *was* a people's hero, a charismatic, skilled, and irrepressible but notorious criminal.[6] The story of Jack Sheppard is the story par excellence of the working-class body that cannot be contained or repressed, the historical Jack breaking from prison four times. Ainsworth develops this into the story of the thief that cannot be simply or rigidly categorised. On the one hand, Ainsworth depoliticises the story by making Jack's class position a complicated affair: Jack is raised working class and has working-class sensibilities, but his mother is the true sister of Sir Rowland. On the other hand, Ainsworth's defiance of established categories – Jack's moral and class position – adds to the indefiniteness of the story that Thackeray finds so impossible.

Thackeray mocks Bulwer's style and his pretensions, but Bulwer's novels are mostly criticised in the same way, for not being true to life insofar as they represent sympathetic criminals, a category for Thackeray that should not exist as it defies a more rigid category and allows for a more liberal process of categorisation. He is less harsh with Dickens and *Oliver Twist*, pointing to the workhouse scenes in particular as 'genuine and pure'. But when it comes to Dickens's representation of criminals, he returns to the same line of argument he uses against Bulwer, criticising the figure of Nancy the prostitute, for example, as 'the most unreal fantastical personage possible'.[7] Thackeray insists that there are unambiguous social groups to be deplored or ignored. Participating in a near mania for categorisation that is a central part of Victorian self-consciousness, from Mayhew to Ruskin, Thackeray considers the idea of a caring prostitute and gallant pickpocket absurd. Henry Mayhew, it may be mentioned, was as vehement in his criticism of the Newgate phenomenon, and specifically its popularity among working people, as was Thackeray.[8] Social categories had to be self-enclosing prisons from which not even a Jack Sheppard could escape, so as to explain how the nation was ordered. Behind the mask of the literary critic outraged by the artist's failure to achieve true realism is Thackeray's insistence that all criminals, like all Newgate novels, remain locked into labels, profiled, and thus deserving or undeserving of narrative space according to received categories. An individual can elevate themselves out of a group through effort, but if in a group the group defines.

Thackeray's definition of realism does not lead to the conclusion that literary criminals should be represented as vile, miserable creatures, representative of true criminals. Despite the story of *Catherine*, he maintains that criminals should not be represented at all: the thieves and rascals of *Oliver Twist* are 'not good company for any man' (*Catherine* 211). Thackeray was not alone in this line of criticism. As *Oliver Twist* is the only novel labelled Newgate with a contemporary setting, it repeatedly faced questions about the suitability of its subject matter. Famously, or infamously, Lord Melbourne tells young Queen Victoria, 'It's all among Workhouses, and Coffin Makers, and Pickpockets … I don't *like* those things; I wish to avoid them; I don't like them in *reality*, and therefore I don't wish them represented.'[9] Henry Fox, agreeing with Lady Carlisle, says much the same thing: 'I know that there are such unfortunate things as pick-pockets and street-walkers … but I own I do not much wish to hear what they say to one another.'[10] Thackeray's complaint is a bit different from Melbourne's and Fox's, who simply do not want to be confronted with wretchedness. Thackeray knows that any representation of thieves and rascals has the potential to entertain and that the line between feeling entertained by a character and feeling allegiance to a character is a thin and dangerous one. He would make a career out of it.

Thackeray rejects *Jack Sheppard* on the same grounds that he rejects Bulwer's and Dickens's novels, but Ainsworth's entertainment represents a different kind of contaminate as well – a capacity to produce. *Oliver Twist* is also guilty of a kind of productivity in that it apparently spawned an exaggerated version of itself in *Jack*

Sheppard, but it is mostly the later novel that represents the threat of productivity in the real world: 'And what came of *Oliver Twist?* The public wanted something more extravagant still, more sympathy for thieves, and so *Jack Sheppard* makes his appearance.'[11] So great is Thackeray's fear of Newgate literature as a force of uncontrolled generation that he deliberately confuses *Jack Sheppard* the novel and its eponymous character ('his appearance'), expressing with a wink the dangers of *Jack Sheppard* becoming a living thing. Privately, Thackeray made clear that a good part of his complaint with *Jack Sheppard* was its influence, the 'fact', for example, that there were four versions of it playing in London in 1839 (Keith Hollingsworth found that in the autumn of 1839 there were no less than eight different versions of it being performed in London, often in unlicensed theatres).[12] In a letter to his mother, Thackeray goes on to say that 'at the Cobourg people are waiting about the lobbies selling Shepherd [sic] bags – a bag containing a few pick-locks that is, a screw driver, an iron lever, one or two young gentlemen have already confessed how much they were indebted to Jack Sheppard who gave them ideas of pocket-picking and thieving'.[13] Earlier, before the 'craze' sets in, in 'Horae Catnachianae', he is willing to express 'the strongest curiosity and admiration for Mr. Ainsworth's new work, *Jack Sheppard*' (again with a wink, as long as such an opinion is kept '*private*. In public it is, however, quite wrong to avow such likings, and to be seen in such company'),[14] but like so many of his contemporaries he was worried about the material effects of it, that it might break free from its bindings, from its confinement as story. In its infancy as the 'craze' begins, Chartist fiction would soon adopt an extratextual narrative strategy, formalising the anxiety *Jack Sheppard* created as generative, bigger than itself. Full resolution in the Chartist story lies outside of the narrative as only the Charter could bring about true closure: reading was meant to be a productive act.

Criticism of the novel generally echoed this fear of the reproductive possibilities of such a popular, affective novel in the real world. An anonymous critic in the same issue of *Fraser's Magazine* which concludes Thackeray's *Catherine* (February 1840), for example, cutely argues that *Jack Sheppard* 'will tend to fill many a juvenile aspirant for riot and notoriety with ideas highly conducive to the progress of so ennobling a profession as that of housebreaking'.[15] The *Monthly Review* agrees with Thackeray about *Jack Sheppard*'s 'pictorial falsifications in the delineation of character'. But Ainsworth gets critiqued not simply for failing to be realistic, but for being *too* realistic:

> But independent entirely of this objection, we deny that it is wholesome to tell the whole truth, when the thing that is to be represented must tend to degrade the spectator or listener, and to infect perniciously the taste, which, unless diseased, or untutored, must revolt at the horrors, and the grossnesses, which the darkest passages in life, and the practices of the vilest, furnish. ... it is the morbidity and rude condition of the tastes and attainments of the multitude which has brought such works as Jack Sheppard [sic] into vogue, and to which tastes and attainments Mr. Ainsworth has so abundantly catered, and so successfully served to confirm and still further to lower ...[16]

Dickens's friend and biographer John Forster (and one-time friend, with Dickens, of Ainsworth himself) claims in the *Examiner* that he would ignore the book were it not for its potential to reproduce:

> Bad as we think the morals, we think the puffs more dangerous. Our silence would never have been broken if the book had been suffered to rest on its own merits. Little danger might then have been anticipated. Poisonous work is done by means of more cunning doses, nor are the ways of licentiousness, for those classes into whose hands such a book was in that case likely to fall, paved with such broad stones.
>
> The danger is in the resources that have been called in aid; in the paragraphs that with such nauseous repetition have drugged every town and country paper; and in the adaptations of the 'romance' that are alike rife in the low smoking-rooms, the common barber's shops, the cheap reading places, the private booksellers, and the minor theatres.
> [...] All the original insignificance of the thing is lost, in the pernicious influences that are set at work around it.[17]

The danger of *Jack Sheppard* was not so much that it has a greater spirit of lawlessness and defiance in it than *Oliver Twist* or *Eugene Aram*, or more politicisable content in it, or that it seems more tailored to an audience of disenfranchised, discontented youth than the other novels. The true danger was that it created a bona fide craze: it 'had given rise to a full-blown mania, generating a great wave of pamphlets and abridgements, plays and street shows, prints and cartoons, and related baubles and souvenirs'.[18] With reason, *Jack Sheppard* was singled out as *the* Newgate novel. It generated more criticism and fear than any other Newgate text, in part because it was more productive than any other Newgate story; not just more writerly in Barthes's terms or more carnivalesque in Bakhtin's, but more likely to make reading a materially prolific act. If it were read by the mass audience as a blueprint for action or as merely a snubbing of finer society is in some ways too barbed a question; that it was read by the classes fearing that the mass audience would read it as a blueprint points us to how close Britain was to a social war and how close *Jack Sheppard* came to egging it on.

With its elaborate descriptions of Jack escaping from prison time and again, the novel does have a certain handbook quality, in the same way that *Robinson Crusoe* would be smart reading material for someone stranded on a deserted island. But the way that critics saw *Jack Sheppard* crossing into reality and mobilising the public testifies to the panicked, divided, confrontational world into which it was received. Simon Joyce and others have documented the 'press campaign' that started after the Swiss valet B. F. Courvoisier claimed, in his second of several confessions, that the idea to kill his master was the result of reading *Jack Sheppard*.[19] Though Courvoisier later retracted his statement, newspapers such as the *Examiner* took to the story so as to underline the kind of productivity to expect from a *Jack Sheppard*: 'it is a publication calculated to familiarise the mind with cruelties, and to serve as the cutthroat's manual'.[20] In its July 1840 issue, the *Monthly Magazine* blamed the murder on 'the Sheppardism of the age'; when the critic says that 'it was the novelist who told him [Courvoisier] how to manage the execrable deed with safety and success',[21] he clearly goes too far. But *Jack Sheppard* made the perfect punching bag for a reason, not because it explains how to commit murder but because it allows itself to be read as promoting violent vengeance against anyone or anything that would deny sovereignty. In the 1830s, new industrial relations and demographic change could reasonably be blamed for working-class discontent, and they were. But there was little chance

Jack Sheppard, *the Newgate novel* 55

and perhaps even less will to put an end to the nation's main source of wealth, so it was easier to go after Jack.

Jack Sheppard's romanticising of crime did not generate panic. That it seemed to be spawning real world anger against authority did not in itself create panic either, for England in 1839 was already panicked. Though historians debate if the 1830s and 1840s, the years that see the rise and fall of the Newgate story, saw more social change than other decades in the Victorian period, it was undoubtedly a decade that witnessed increasing scepticism over of the legitimacy and stability of traditional authority, when Henry Worsley would bemoan that 'Insubordination to parental authority, leading to insubordination to all authority, is stated to be very general.'[22] After the satire-ready regimes of George III and George IV (and skipping over William IV's relatively short reign), a teenage Victoria ascends the throne in 1837, causing anxieties at every level of society over her readiness to lead the nation. Welcomed by poor harvests between 1838 and 1841, which help usher in what is now known as the hungry forties, and marrying the foreign Albert, Victoria would not come to stand for stoic stability for some time. The public also had to endure eight different heads of state between 1827 and 1841 – nine, if Peel is counted twice for his two different times in office – with the government changing seven times in those years. The Canadian Rebellions of 1837–38, the Rebecca Riots beginning in 1839, and the Newport Rising of 1839 presented an image of both colonial and domestic discontent and chaos, and the excessively violent response to the uprisings by the British army appeared to many, or at least to readers of the Chartist press, as a desperate need to maintain order. At the same time, 'radical', a word which denotes getting to the root cause of a problem, is claimed by several different classes of reformers as their own, from Benthamites to Chartists. The 1832 Reform Bill and the working-class disillusionment at its failure to achieve substantial political change did not bring about the 'first wave' of Newgate novels, Bulwer's and Ainsworth's *Rookwood*. But when the 'second generation' of Newgate novels arrive, if that was what *Jack Sheppard* and *Oliver Twist* signified, it was impossible for critics to ignore that it corresponded with the draping of the National Charter. Though political concerns help explain why the novels were grouped together,

Ainsworth's novel alone is written to take advantage of the social unrest Chartism came to represent.

Critics today generally agree that the *Jack Sheppard* phenomenon was understood at the time as being part and parcel of a revolutionary if not directly Chartist or 'physical-force' movement.[23] Discussing an 'assumed connection between Chartism and juvenile lawlessness', Geoffrey Pearson argues that 'an artful Chartist dodger' was seen, especially by well-meaning philanthropists, 'as some kind of embryonic revolutionary cadre'.[24] Correctly insisting on 'the erroneous identification of Chartism as a blind heathen force [and] the easy equation between crime and impending revolution',[25] Pearson concludes that the identification and equation was regularly made in part because of the moral slippage that novels such as *Jack Sheppard* were said to create. Simon Joyce confirms that 'contemporary reviews of *Jack Sheppard* consistently made reference to Chartism'.[26] Martin Meisel notes that 'For the alarmed, if the Jack Sheppard craze was not directly Chartist or republican, it responded to the same social distempers that generated those radical movements.'[27] Matthew Buckley agrees, adding that:

> In the summer of 1839, the working-class population had reason to be angered, and the *Jack Sheppard* mania offered a wonderful set of gestures and signs, attitudes and postures through which a servant, a beggar, or a petty laborer could make that anger evident. To the established organs of public order, and particularly those who recalled the not-so-distant and similarly disenfranchised mobs of Chartism and the Revolution, the *Sheppard* phenomenon appeared in that sense as a half-worn mask of insurrection – a theatrical pose, but one accompanied by a look in the eye that says one is not acting entirely in jest.[28]

Cassandra Falke notes that *The Times* rethought its attitude towards Bulwer's novels after *Jack Sheppard* was published (and after Thackeray's criticism); only at that point did the paper take the position that 'there can be no difficulty in tracing [to Bulwer's novels] the poison of an unhealthy tone of feeling upon the subject of crime'.[29] The 'unhealthy tone of feeling' is clearly a fear of unhealthy politics that *Jack Sheppard* had produced, the proximity between cultural and political confrontations. Referring to 'the apprentices of London' seeing a dramatic version of *Jack Sheppard*, the critic despairs that 'Socialism and Chartism have sprung up and become rank and thriving weeds.'[30] Socialism, Chartism, and murderous valets, that is, swirl together in *The Times*' panicked picture of 'public evil' overtaking a 'Christian nation'. Finally, Juliet John says 'that the controversial cult status achieved by Newgate texts and protagonists had very little to do with the ethics of character in the novel, and very much to do with anxieties about power – in particular the power of "popular" culture'[31] wresting power from traditional authority.

John is precisely correct to identify that the fight over power, free-floating in definition as it were, was thought to be at stake with the emergence of Newgate's popularity. Mary Russell Mitford, in her letter to Elizabeth Barrett, offers an excellent reading of the novel, but she is perhaps even more perceptive on the novel's affective, extraliterary push:

> I have been reading 'Jack Sheppard', and have been struck by the great danger, in these times, of representing authorities so constantly and fearfully in the wrong; so tyrannous, so devilish, as the author has been pleased to portray it in 'Jack Sheppard'; for he does not seem so much a man, or even an incarnate fiend, as a representation of power – government or law, call it as you may – the ruling power. Of course, Mr. Ainsworth had no such design, but such is the effect; and as the millions who see it represented at the minor theatres will not distinguish between now and a hundred years back, all the Chartists in the land are less dangerous than this nightmare of a book, and I, Radical as I am, lament any additional temptations to outbreak, with all its train of horrors.[32]

Mitford's fear that Jonathan Wild would be understood as 'a representation of power' and that audiences would then see Jack competing for that power, for freedom from Wild, and cheer on the hero against the 'incarnate fiend', nicely encapsulates a good part of the fear that the book generated at the time of its publication, but her insistence that the book's effect is almost in contradistinction from its design, that the effect can spread independently of its origin, reminds us that literature at the time was generally not read as mere entertainment, independent of the time. Indeed, this much-quoted letter continues to make clear that it was a working-class appetite to translate an aggregate Newgate experience into a political and social reality that was dangerous, and not individual works of fiction. *Jack Sheppard* again stands out as the text that scoffs at corrupt, cruel power, and that positions sovereignty or self-categorisation against an open-ended idea of authority – parents, headmasters, police, overseers, masters of valets, MPs, and so on:

> Seriously, what things these are – the Jack Sheppards, the Squeers's, the Oliver Twists, and Michael Armstrongs – all the worse for the power which, except the last, the others contain! Grievously the worse!
> My friend Mr. Hughes speaks well of Mr. Ainsworth. His father was a collector of these old robber stories, and used to repeat the local ballads upon Turpin, etc., to his son as he sat upon his knee; and this has perhaps been at the bottom of the matter. A good antiquarian I believe him to be, but what a use to make of the picturesque old knowledge! Well, one comfort is that it will wear itself out; and then it will be cast aside like an old fashion.[33]

Mitford's desire to see the stories contained as mere stories, narratives without extratextual effect, with a hint that novels might be better confined to the parlour room, again shows that the anxiety around the Newgate novel was that it was part of something else, and the special anxiety around *Jack Sheppard* was that Ainsworth knew it and exploited it: indeed, 'what a use to make of the picturesque old knowledge!'

From calendar to novel

Jack Sheppard was part of something else, something social and political, but as Lauren Gillingham makes clear in 'Ainsworth's *Jack Sheppard* and the crimes of history', something literary as well. Most ostensibly apparent in the multifarious origins of the Newgate novel, aside from the central image of the looming prison, were the calendars, with three of the four best-known and most distinctly Newgate novels pilfering characters and their exploits from the most popular stories. Before it is retold by Bulwer, the story of Eugene Aram, for example, is consistently reproduced in the calendars; though slightly adulterated from collection to collection, it is often described along the lines of 'the most remarkable and extraordinary trial in our whole Calendar'.[34] Without doubt, the familiarity of the Newgate calendar eased the way for the labelling of the novel. In his still central discussion of the Newgate novel, Keith Hollingsworth offers an explanation of its origins by defining a Newgate novel as 'one in which an important character came (or, if imaginary, might have come) out of the Newgate Calendar'.[35] As Hollingsworth implies, the distinction between imaginary and non-imaginary is not hugely significant, insofar as Bulwer writes both, for example, and equally pushes the boundaries of plausibility in both. *Oliver Twist* creates imaginary characters, but is so thoroughly grounded in social issues and reform that it is arguably less 'imaginary' than some of its novel or calendar counterparts. It is also important to remember that the calendars represent more than just lone thieves or rogues, and that they regularly report on political riots and demonstrations when these led to arrests. It was especially common in the late 1830s for calendars to switch back and forth between stories of individual crime and group action, making the reading public think in terms of both of them as Newgate material. The calendars, that is, blur the distinction between social rogues and political rebels; the coiner, footpad, murderer, moneydropper, or highwayman instantly acquires some association with the incendiary and rioter, beyond the 'underground' status that might be equated to both. They might equally represent an attempt at sovereignty or dissatisfaction with the polis, expressing what was already widely known, that society fails to satisfy all. In the novels, the criminals are merely social rebels, and association to political transgression would have had to be inferred by looking beyond the immediate text. *Jack Sheppard*, that is, has little in it that is directly or explicitly political, but the fear of 'outbreak' that it raised – as distinct from copycat burglary – has as much to do with a prior fear of outbreak as it does with a popular author stoking outbreak.

However, more and more critics today tend to deny a significant kinship between the calendars and novels, in part because criticism since Hollingsworth has had difficulty in speaking of the novel as a genre, given the differences among the novels. Whereas the novels are seen as diverse and polyvalent, 'so that any moment or character might be endlessly explored because that moment or character is as expandable as the language being used to create it', the calendars are seen as monolithic, reductive, and formulaic.[36] But the Bakhtinian privileging of the novel over other modes of writing ignores the way that the calendars differ from each other and that, with any of them, the accused do not invariably end up travelling to Tyburn. As with the Newgate novels, the calendar stories, individually and as a set, potentially elicit different kinds and different levels of reader sympathy, for both thief and rioter.

It is primarily this ambivalence, the possibility of a sympathetic or entertaining criminal that links the calendars and the novels and that distinguishes the Newgate novel from other social-problem fiction. The criminal is always central to a calendar story but is not always treated as psychologically or emotionally complex, which, as Jonathan Grossman suggests, the novel can clearly accomplish more thoroughly. But in both calendar and novel, despite the possible political reverberations, there is often some playful and irreverent rejection of 'personal responsibility', ambiguity over the causes of crime and recidivism, or just the promise of pleasure in bawdy, anti-establishment activity. Regularly, some attention is given to the criminal's redeeming qualities, palliating his or her crimes, and insofar as the fictional crimes represent any or all crimes, in the way that representation can always be interpreted as representational, liminal interpretive space emerges between right and wrong, or between just punishment and the possible legitimacy behind breaking the law. In *Oliver Twist*, when Bill Sikes aids in extinguishing a fire or attempts to shake Charlie Bates's hand, both times expressing a desire for community, Dickens raises doubts about the natural brutality of his worst villain and immobilises the reader's desire for vengeance that he so masterly creates in the first place. Nancy is both a prostitute and a missed-out mother; Fagin both the devil and a lonely, tortured soul. The category-challenging double readings made available in the calendars, where the criminal is reprehensible and deserving of the law's wrath, and thus held up for instructive purposes, but also individualised, a fox among sheep, perhaps exposing a greater social evil than his or her crime, and in any case the source of pure entertainment, has its counterpart in the Newgate novel, though instruction is not as explicit in the latter. The daring criminal act frequently creates a frisson of excitement that mocks the levity of judgement. Gillingham argues that though the novels demonstrate different levels of condoning and condemning crime, they are all absorbed 'in the agency and pleasure involved in social transgression'.[37] She notes that 'Newgate novels tend to accord a degree of primacy, licence, and pleasure to the exploration of criminality that exceeds that which is manifest in other fiction that was similarly interested in the force of the illicit, the enterprising, and the unconstrained.'[38] This is equally true of the stories in the calendars taken as a whole. Also in the footsteps of the calendars, and anticipating the sensation fiction of the 1860s, the novels offer the audience the vicarious pleasure of seeing the unfettered life, if not chosen then embraced. True, when Bill Sikes drinks he turns violent, but when Paul Clifford or Jack Sheppard drink, they sing fun, bawdy songs, conjuring up a carnivalesque defiance of propriety and decorum that makes the entertained reader complicit in a snubbing of the official culture, only half aware (or half unaware) that the uncritical enjoyment of unstructured practices is in itself unruly. Even the ostensible promotion of rowdyism, however, or of young men acting independently of parental, state, or moral guidance, is not likely to cause scandal unless there is first an audience imagined by both author and critic alike as susceptible, dissatisfied by their own lives.

The Newgate novel, to be clear, is not merely an extended, explicitly narrativised version of the calendar. In terms of its literary history, it also borrows from various forms of romance and melodrama that themselves treat commercial enterprise as synonymous with the voicing of the pent up and unfulfilled lives of readers. These include the historical romance, eighteenth-century rogue narratives, and urban (London) portraitures. The Newgate novel, that is, is also clearly related to other genres where authority and propriety are either directly or indirectly challenged, where ambition necessarily equals breaking rules, and where rattling the fragility of the social order is teasingly offered as the only means towards personal satisfaction, even when the texts have no obvious political content. As Alec Lucas says, 'The Newgate novel belongs, like the half-epical tales of Robin Hood or historical romances like *Rob Roy*, to fiction that seeks to vindicate lawlessness.'[39] The fiction in Chartist papers such as the *Chartist Circular* (1830–42) is dominated by historical romances in which rebels and revolutionaries fight corrupt authority and laws to bring about social and national good. In Chartists papers, representations of historical rebellions were part of a proleptic history designed to mobilise audiences by revealing how they fit into a universal, human need for freedom. *Jack Sheppard* has no such design, but it too, at least according to its critics, revels in the production of paratextual life.

The links between Newgate storytelling and its antecedents demonstrate an awareness of the marketability of rebelliousness, disorder, or cultural transgression in periods of heightened social tension. Freedom of movement is a central feature of romance and also of Newgate fiction, from the nostalgia of the highwayman to the claustrophobic imagery of *Oliver Twist*. The story of Jack Sheppard, of course, is the story of a man who cannot be imprisoned and contained, and of a thief who can effectively go anywhere he wants. More generally, the heroising of a charismatic rascal independently negotiating his way against all odds in a Newgate plot relates to the tendency of historical romances to position their heroes against privileged authority. One might even contend that romanticism, itself born of a surrounding revolutionary spirit, relates to Newgate lawlessness in certain ways, at least when it celebrates the outsider who shuns society's rules or when it embraces unconstrained emotion. The link, however, should not be taken too far. The high romanticism of a *Manfred* (1817) or even the low-high adventures of a Lord Ruthven, even if they share with some Newgate literature the absence of a middle class, do not involve the working classes, and so any antisocial or revolutionary energy evoked might only describe and promote personal and not group emancipation: the individual's release from society is often the precise point. A more direct connection might be between rogue novels before the Newgate story, such as Daniel Defoe's *Moll Flanders* (1722) and Henry Fielding's *Jonathan Wild* (1743) or William Godwin's *Caleb Williams* (1794), and the Newgate novel, as both associate a form of pleasure to the criminal's success. But in no way do these novels form a set, and they simply did not provoke the same kind of reaction as did the Newgate novels of the late 1830s. With the historical romance, however, they do have in common with Newgate literature the notion that the normal avenues for success in the modern world are at best dull, mechanical, and inauthentic (an idea William Morris would develop years later).

Juliet John notes that Pierce Egan's *Life in London* (1821) 'entertained more than inflamed', though it too is 'steeped in low-life criminality'.[40] In the prehistory of the Newgate story or label, Egan's popular representations of urban living, especially *Life in London*, deserve special attention as they share with the calendar and novel a defence of subcultural and counter-hegemonic, or notorious and low society. The same anonymous critic in *Fraser's*, complaining in tandem with Thackeray of the generative powers of Newgate fiction, asks, 'May we not expect a Jack Sheppard mania from the labours of Ainsworth, illustrated by the same artist, and dramatised for the same theatres, which twenty years ago resounded with applauses showered upon Wrench, Russell, and Jack Reeve, now, alas! no more?'[41] Egan repeatedly defends representing the people such as Jack Reeve who make up the crowd: 'Yes, my dear Coz. it is a motley group ... but it is a view of real life; and it is from such meetings as these, notwithstanding they are termed very *low*, that you have a fine opportunity of witnessing the differences of the human *character*.'[42] Tom and Jerry watch dog fights, visit a sluicery (a gin house), and eventually Newgate itself. Guided by a principle that there is an inherent value in encountering 'variety', for that in a word is for them 'LIFE', they meet with gamblers, smugglers, dustmen, and weavers, but also 'sprigs of nobility', swells, 'honourables', and MPs, '&c. all in one rude contact, jostling and pushing against each other'.[43] They socialise, that is, with anyone and everyone except the middle classes. In one scene that seems to mock the developing middle-class self-image as society's great benefactors, they meet beggars who fake being poor.[44] Egan and his illustrators, the Cruikshank brothers, duplicate the defence of human variety that was used in the calendars: in his introduction to the *Chronicles of Crime*, Pelham states that 'The study of life, in all its varieties, is one no less interesting than useful.'[45] Only the calendar editors feel obligated to underline 'use' or 'instruction' in a way that Egan goes out of his way to avoid.

Stephen James Carver further discusses the connections between Egan's *Life in London* and *Jack Sheppard*, addressing the thorny question of representational suitability.[46] The recognised danger of representing the 'very *low*' was that too intense a focus could lead either to envy of a lifestyle or sympathy for those locked in it, or at least to an interrogation of the social determinants that lead to social status and class divisions. If so, then the marginalising of the middle classes and emerging middle-class values in *Life in London*, *Jack Sheppard*, and other ostracised texts (which largely continue to be overlooked today) can be seen as at least semipolitical. Miscellanies such as Kenny Meadows' *Heads of the People* (1840) combine high and low, equally deserving of a 'portrait'. Picturesque idylls of humble, simple folk in Mary Howitt's short stories offer unabashed nostalgia for a time when working people enjoyed rural living, solving their problems on their own. *Jack Sheppard* for one – though certainly not *Oliver Twist* – continues to ignore the middle classes or their eighteenth-century counterparts, or at most treat them as the mere victims of crime and without agency. If it is true that after 1832 the middle classes of Britain became less a force of change and increasingly a source for the ascending novel, then the Newgate novel's inheritance of its subject matter, with the marked absence of the middle classes, was sure to be taken as politically provocative, as it was.

Finally, changes that were taking place in the penal system at the time help explain the emergence of the Newgate craze. Hollingsworth sees the demise of the 'bloody code' as initiating the positive, celebratory spirit that the novel is caught up in, as if Britain had left behind its barbarous past:

> The crudest terrors of Newgate, well enough remembered, could be thought of as safely in the past. Freedom and opportunity were in the air. A vast public could, at such a moment, permit itself to idolise a young thief – could see him as a victim of the old system or as a rebel against it ... This general high-spirited extravagance would not have been possible twenty years earlier; its *raison d'être* would have been lacking twenty years later. Ainsworth provided his novel at the right time. The Sheppard mania which followed was an uncalculated, uncalculating paean to the end of the bad old days and the arrival of a time like morning.[47]

In 1839, however, 'freedom and opportunity', at least for the novel's working-class readership, were in the air only insofar as Chartists were agitating for them. As Carver has noted, 'Despite a certain amount of reform of criminal law by 1840, hangings were still public and urban poverty and crime remained epidemic.'[48] In *Imagining the Penitentiary*, John Bender, taking a different view from Hollingsworth, looks at the way that the rise of the Newgate story corresponds with the reduction of public executions to argue that the Newgate story became a popular substitute for the spectacle of the execution, a mere transferral of an ongoing appetite for sensational stories of crime and justice. Grossman in some ways reverses the argument without overturning it. He looks at the way the emerging novel helped reinvent the criminal trial after it had succeeded the gallows as the final chapter in a crime narrative. Following Foucault's *Discipline and Punish*, the underlying assumption is that the movement away from the gallows produced a more hegemonic but less obvious form of social control or containment, what Foucault calls 'panopticism'. There is room between containment and freedom, more between regulation and freedom, however, and surely Newgate narratives themselves can be seen as debating or equivocating or playing coy with the energies they exploit.[49] More likely is it that the public appetite for crime narratives and the way they were interpreted continued to morph with the always fluid political context.

A reading of *Jack Sheppard*

The Newgate novel, however, is more than the sum of its literary and social (or judicial) parts. Aside from its representations of corrupt authority and heroically sovereign or sympathetic criminals, Newgate fiction, unevenly and to different degrees, opens itself up to politically radical if not revolutionary readings when it places its action, including the struggle between corrupt authority and heroic criminals, in the historical context of real reform movements or real revolts; when it excludes the middle classes as actors in the dramatic contest for power and insists that the 'people' are a natural force of action, change, confrontation, and history; when it documents a social villain as first or equally a social victim; when it lends the rogue ambitions that go beyond self-interest or self-preservation; and when it offers an image of the crowd as a purposeful, sincere, and structured grouping of the people, justified even when it riots. The Newgate story lends itself to radicalism, that is, when it demonstrates just, valuable violence. Finally, and most significantly, the Newgate novel allows for and even cultivates politically convertible anger when it creates and sentimentalises martyrs, evoking the 'radical martyrology' that E. P. Thompson identifies as a staple in the activist working classes from the eighteenth century onwards.[50] It is important to stress, however, that Newgate fiction as a whole represents corrupt authority and sympathetic or psychologically interesting criminals – that is its chief generic marker – and will include isolated plotlines or character developments that lend themselves to radical readings, but only *Jack Sheppard* brings together its political content in the form of a cultural provocation or challenge, rejecting any type of class reconciliation. All Newgate fiction, regardless of the historical displacements, shows an awareness of underlying public anger and even of the spirit of revolution that would manifest itself in Chartism, but only *Jack Sheppard* fully capitalises on discontent and the threat of revolution, contributing to the threat as well insofar as one is a corollary of the other.

Arguing *Jack Sheppard*'s flirtation with revolution, I find myself up against a number of contemporary critics who do not see the novel as political or politicisable. Critics may generally agree that *Jack Sheppard was* understood as politically threatening if not revolutionary in its day, but few read it now as having any substantive political content. Though very alert to the way it can and has been read as a dangerously political text, Matthew Buckley, for example, argues that the novel functioned 'as an exceptional mechanism of the period's rapid shift in collective consciousness – driving, and not simply describing or reflecting, the crucial shift from political to perceptual modernity'.[51] In other words, according to Buckley, the 1830s saw a shift away from understanding the city as a site for revolutionary activity or for a collective consciousness towards an appearance of it 'as labyrinths of crowded solitude and threatening anonymity', *Jack Sheppard* 'driving' this change. Simon Joyce sees Chartism as having at best 'a shadowy presence in the debates over the Newgate novel'.[52] Gillingham argues that *Jack Sheppard* was primarily a romance, and as such it positioned itself 'at some mediated distance from the real',[53] warning against readings of the novel that focus too stringently on the historical conditions in which it was produced. John agrees that 'Ainsworth's novel is lacking in any consciously political bias', saying that it 'avoids social comment; it purports to be nothing other than a novel of entertainment'.[54] Commenting on 'the difficulty of distinguishing unambiguously between "establishment" and "anti-establishment" forces at this time' (the forces that led to the Newgate craze), John joins Hollingsworth to argue that the 'Sheppard furore' had nothing to do with 'Chartist, anti-establishment, anti-hierarchical feeling'.[55]

Ostensibly, even *Oliver Twist* has more political content than *Jack Sheppard* and is much closer to the real. A thief like Jack Sheppard does not wish to overturn the state or challenge the status quo; thieves thrive on the wealthy to feed. The 'cops and robbers' narrative that Newgate tales helped establish has its own environmentalism, a mutually beneficial ecosystem. But it is this ambivalence that led at the time and should continue to accommodate a political understanding of the novel. *Jack Sheppard* does not plea for reform, though with *Oliver Twist* it represents a corrupt world. Unlike *Oliver Twist* and its engagement with poor laws, bastardy laws, and so forth, *Jack Sheppard* hardly advances social or humanitarian issues at all – it does not even give readers a firm, single answer as to why Jack turns to crime – leaving those matters in the hands of incendiary, potentially anarchic forces. *Jack Sheppard* provocatively opens itself up to radical readings by representing a broken world, but not identifying specific social problems to be addressed through rational, piecemeal reform. When it comes to addressing social issues or engaging in quasi-political criticisms – suspending for the moment that the celebration of working-class values was itself at this time a political act, and holding that Baptist Kettleby's aspirations for the Old Mint have more to do with working-class culture than actual reform[56] – *Jack Sheppard* provides only the image of destructive power and society as a contest between destructive powers. What comes out of the wreckage would be anyone's guess, but since 'context is everything', Ainsworth's contemporary critics guessed social and political chaos.

Looking at the novel from the point of view of its consumption, critics today are ready to agree that at the time of its release *Jack Sheppard* gave expression to a form of cultural dissatisfaction and resistance, if only temporary, but that in terms of its production, *Jack Sheppard*, and Newgate fiction more generally, was merely the effect of consumer capitalism. But one way or the other, points of consumption and production must meet: what sold was the image of cultural resistance, the possibility of belonging to an unofficial, unclassified people's movement with its own way of seeing and living, albeit spontaneous and sporadic. Ainsworth wrote an entertainment and his primary design was commercial success: what matters most is that he saw an opportunity in what we today call counter-hegemony. Does burglary (or highway theft) really figure as a redistribution of wealth? Does the image of a brave and talented criminal and a slovenly cruel or filthy rich victim really intimate the need to challenge hierarchy or rethink the franchise? Who is more likely to read a broad social metaphor – the censor, the would-be censor, and the ones with most to lose, or the disenfranchised member of the crowd? Does his Newgate novel know? Would it care?

Specific tropes, settings, and plot or character developments can be used, however, to create or promote the broad social metaphor, the generalised anger that is not to be appeased by a single reform or even a Charter. Most Newgate narratives are set during revolutions or attempted revolutions, for example, and if not the action of the stories will take place in politicised environments. Bulwer manufactures an imaginary hero in *Paul Clifford* and sets him in the time of the French Revolution; *Eugene Aram* is taken from the pages of the calendars, but Bulwer goes out of his way to legitimise Aram's participation in violent crime as a response to social unfairness and as part of a larger force of social change. The novel famously departs from its source to lend the Aram character virtuous, intellectual, and Byronic qualities that sentimentalise him beyond recognition (while also vilifying his victim). But most interestingly, Bulwer has Aram contemplating if a crime is truly a crime if it benefits society. Bulwer's interests are primarily in exploring the psychological and not the social aspects of the criminal, but the plot at points gravitates towards the way Aram participates in benefiting the world and bringing about social change, if indirectly, through the raw chaos of violence. After *Oliver Twist*, Dickens's second pseudo-Newgate novel, *Barnaby Rudge*, takes place during the Gordon Riots, but when 'no Popery' is misspelt to read 'no property', as Simon Joyce has pointed out,[57] the occasion for the riot can be read as being more about class discontent than religion. To be clear, however, Dickens's rioters cannot be read to be in the right or in any way sympathetic; the 'fearful amount of riot and destruction'[58] can only be read as explicitly condemned.

Like *Barnaby Rudge*, *Jack Sheppard* is also set in a time of rebellion and political intrigue, namely during the Jacobite revolt of 1715. The revolt corresponds with the years that the real Jack Sheppard operated, so Ainsworth, already finding success with the historical romance in *Rookwood* and *Crichton* (1837), is in his right to add the plotline into the background of his story. He is also most certainly in his element. The Jacobite revolt does not play a role in the Newgate calendar versions of the Jack Sheppard story, though the history of James Sheppard, the Jacobite executed in 1718 for plotting to kill the king, can be found in numerous versions. Years later Jacobin rebels would become one of Ainsworth's favourite topics for his fiction; he represents them in *The Manchester Rebels* (1873), *Preston Fight* (1875), and *Beatrice Tyldesley* (1878). Born in Manchester in 1805, Ainsworth knew the history of the city's Jacobite occupation in 1745 and was sympathetic to the cause. John Sutherland says that Ainsworth 'was indoctrinated by Jacobite ... beliefs which would remain with him throughout his writing career'.[59] Jeffrey Richards says that Ainsworth had 'developed in his youth a Romantic attachment to Jacobitism'.[60] It is difficult to place the novel's attitude towards Jacobites, however, insofar as William Kneebone, the woollen-draper Jacobite in the novel who does generally figure in the calendars, receives Mr Wood's and Thames Darrell's vehement condemnation for toasting King James (though later Thames turns Jacobite as well, when he finds out that he is a French marquis). But Jack, in the spirit of the 'general insurrection'[61] Kneebone promotes, and under the sway of spirits as well, joins in to toast 'King James the Third, and confusion to his enemies!'[62] Thames, noble and good, and a bit of a wet blanket, ominously says 'you deserve to be hanged for a rebel'.[63] Later,

Kneebone rages against Jonathan Wild, wishing him dead, and explains that 'Wild was formerly an agent to the Jacobite party, but, on the offer of a bribe from the opposite faction, he unhesitatingly deserted and betrayed his old employers.'[64] Kneebone unknowingly addresses a disguised Wild, and when the disguise is abandoned Wild hopes to bring Kneebone to Newgate saying, 'The Jacobite daws want a scarecrow.'[65]

Kneebone is introduced as a redeemable character: 'if it had not been for a taste for plotting, which was continually getting him into scrapes, he might have been accounted a respectable member of society'.[66] Eventually, the Jacobite is carefully but casually brought together with the thief, not because Ainsworth wished to resurrect a Catholic agenda or to justify the Jacobites – the aristocrat Sir Rowland Trenchard, Wild's partner, is hardly admirable, plotting to rob his sister Alvira of her estates, and he is also a hardened Jacobite – but as if in order to reinforce the novel's firmly undecided attitude towards civil disobedience. Ainsworth does not pass up the opportunity to point out that seven years before the historical Sheppard escaped from Newgate's 'Red Room' it had been used to house Jacobite prisoners after the Battle of Preston in 1716.[67] Such a connection also works, however vaguely, to broaden the metaphorical possibilities of the text, providing a larger scale of conflict that while also a failure (as the story of Sheppard is in a fundamental way) implies a political counterpart to bad behaviour. It is not pursued or developed and absolutely no direct comparison to contemporary political activity is assumed, as it likely would be in the hands of a Chartist writer, but such echoes are expansive, resisting interpretive containment. Ainsworth himself likely saw Jacobitism as nothing more than good material for storytelling, something 'magical and romantic' as Carver suggests.[68] However, recent criticism underlines that the rebellions involved class and social issues, that in the same way that the Gordon Riots were not simply about anti-Catholicism the Jacobite fight was not solely about advancing a Catholic agenda.[69] For Ainsworth to introduce an ambiguous Jacobite plot into his story a mere two years after the latest Hanover took the throne, no matter how much the rebellion was then considered part of history, in itself does very little, but it does add to the sense that every level of the social order can be held under threat.

Returning to the struggles around Jacobitism also links Ainsworth to Walter Scott. The Scottian historical romance is significant in the politics of the Newgate story mostly because of the way it tends to exclude the middle classes, or at least, as Georg Lukács argues in *The Historical Novel*, force middle-class audiences to accept that their primary source of ascendance, capitalism, was not always already dominant but merely a stage in history. As mentioned, Chartists in their turn would write numerous historical romances, again demonstrating world historical forces that existed without the middle classes. Of all the differences between *Oliver Twist* and *Jack Sheppard*, the role of the middle class, which hardly exists in the latter even symbolically, might be the greatest. Whereas Dickens gives us Losborne and Brownlow – good, generous, middle-class men – Ainsworth's Blueskin is as rough and tough as they come. But Blueskin proves to be as loyal to Jack as Brownlow is to Oliver. There is no Rose in *Jack Sheppard* to try to convince Edgworth Bess and Poll Maggot to change their lives. Dickens pushes boundaries himself by offering an image of Fagin and his gang welcoming Oliver into their 'home', offering him something to eat, perhaps not as a serious alternative to middle-class domesticity, but certainly as an alternative to the state's derisory social nets. But Ainsworth goes much further to undercut the burgeoning rise of domestic ideology by excluding the haven of the domestic altogether. Jack may sacrifice himself for his mother, but he is at home at the pub. Raymond Williams and others have chastised working-class writers who adopted the historical romance for the way they place the aristocracy or 'old corruption' and not the middle classes as the enemy of the people.[70] But to deny representation to the middle classes, and ignore their practices and values, can be seen as a form of criticism insofar as it accepts the idea of an independent working-class culture that does not need to get its identity in relation to the dominant group.

Jack Sheppard rubs in this heightened status of the underground class by playing up Jack's fame. As the calendars attest to, the historical Jack managed a level of fame, and not simply notoriety, almost as remarkable as his deeds. In the novel, Jack receives a visit from 'persons of consequence' – Sir James Thornhill, 'greatest artist of the day', a young Hogarth, the poet Gay, and the 'noted prizefighter' Mr Figg. The scene explicitly demonstrates the far-reaching impact of Jack's exploits and reputation.[71] He has made 'so much noise as to reach the ear of royalty'.[72] Ainsworth's version of the meeting is remarkable for its casual, warm and friendly sociability. Importantly, Jack is at home with artists, social commentators, and entertainers; he is presented as a brother among elites – Hogarth calls him a 'first-rate housebreaker'[73] and accidentally forgets one of his painting knives in Jack's cell – in a class that transcends neat economic divisions. Ainsworth may have been underlining that his protagonist is worthy of representation, anticipating some of the reaction his novel would receive. The historical Jack Sheppard had been admired by the general public and 'persons of consequence'. The novel asks, 'Why not now?'

With his two Newgate heroes, Sheppard and Dick Turpin in *Rookwood*, Ainsworth shows his attraction to the most famous criminals from the calendars (he had plans for a third Newgate novel on the life of Claude Duval, another legendary highwayman). But with Sheppard, a cockney from White Row in London's Spitalfields, Ainsworth stresses the way that the criminal might be first or equally a social victim. Most Newgate fiction includes some form of rationalising the criminal's criminality. On trial, the Dodger sounds like a jovial rogue right out of a calendar, speaking with 'great glee and self-approval'.[74] But given Oliver's experiences at court, readers have to accept his argument that it 'ain't the shop for justice',[75] arguably demonstrating that recidivism is a consequence of the state's legal system. But the matter of Jack's victimisation, and the almost supernatural ways he is fated to become a criminal, contrasts sharply with Oliver's exceptionalism, the way *he* is almost supernaturally able to resist corruption. Ainsworth's insistence that victimisation has consequences is not driven by a moralist school of thought; Jack embraces his fate, determined to 'own it' or make the most of it.

Gillingham examines the determinist society that victimises, but concludes that the novel demonstrates the way Jack defies victimisation:

> Jack appears simply a social underdog fighting to get out from under innumerable social and historical disadvantages. From infancy he is

hounded by his unfortunate lineage, constrained to an uninspiring range of future prospects and hampered by a wily visage that earns him little trust. The staggering weight of these social determinants occasions, nevertheless, one of the novel's most fascinating formulations: Jack's transgressions become signs less of a wholesale challenge to civil order, than of a mode of dealing with his own personal history, a defiance of the predetermination of his identity.[76]

The novel in this way accommodates a more individualistic ethic. Yet challenging the social order and defying a predetermined identity (or adopting a spirit of defiance that makes the most of it) are not mutually exclusive, and in fact making the personal political was exactly the way that Chartists were selling Chartism to the public – largely the same public to which *Jack Sheppard* appealed. Chartist fiction generally shows circumstance overwhelming unstained victims, not criminals, and though Jack also succumbs to fate, by dwelling on Jack's skill, success, and fame, Ainsworth allows him a kind of heroic agency absent in Chartist fiction (absent and impossible, for Chartist writers, without the Charter). Jack is also fully individualised, one of a kind, whereas victims in Chartist writing are often nameless, simply members of an anonymous working class. But *Jack Sheppard* shares with the radical playbook an instinct to manifest determinants as official agents of society, most notably Jonathan Wild. It is not uncommon for any Victorian novel to position the individual against society, but Jack, unlike the heroes of most Victorian fiction, does not attempt or want to join the society that challenges him,[77] and in this way brings to mind radical writing or the Chartist narrative that insists on society changing before its heroes can become successful members of it. Jack's heroic agency, however, is less successful than it is uncompromising; he remains loyal to his practices as he remains loyal to his associates, and they remain loyal to him. The degree to which the representation of a folk-hero outlaw is agitprop against law and order depends upon whether the outlaw defines the resilient character of a nation, like a William Tell, or remains firmly outside of regular society, like Jack. To some degree, both a William Tell and a Jack Sheppard will be appropriated by and into the mainstream, a process more easily accomplished with the national hero. But that process potentially has two very disparate effects. The first is the flattening out of history and containment of potential future energies, the subject marketed as a remnant of a time past to be consumed as memorabilia. The second is to create an alternative history, depending on the specific audience and the political moment. William Tell, an outlaw national hero, is after all appropriated repeatedly by Chartists as a model for just revolutionary action.[78] In other words, specific historical circumstances show how to read both the production and consumption of the text. *Jack Sheppard* solely as a product allows its energies to be taken in either direction. As an item of consumption it worked to amplify the politicalisation of the moment. But production and consumption always have a point of connection as one does not exist without the other.

Part of the novel's energy is located in Jack's instinct for life, but that instinct goes beyond self-interest and self-preservation. He is loyal to Thames, his mother, and Winnie, sacrificing his love for Winnie for both her and Thames's happiness, and mushily reserving his last words for his mother. Ainsworth has no difficulty matching this with thickness among thieves, a romantic stereotype Dickens goes out of his way to counter. Jonathan Wild, loyal to no one but himself, is Jack's opposite in almost all ways conceivable, aside from the thievery. Against the image of Jack's lithe, young body that impresses Hogarth so much, Wild's grotesquely mutilated one bears 'the marks'[79] of his encounters. Wild's body has a counterpart in the perverse collection of necrophilia that he hoards, from the weapons he had used to destroy his victims to their 'skulls and bones',[80] suggesting both a consumption fetish and a desperate need to maintain the world of violence in which he excels. In contrast to Wild's religion of death, Jack is associated with life, vitality, and a jouissance that was commonly linked with a working-class philosophy of life. Jack mostly craves the tools to do things, usually to break free from prison. Ainsworth focuses on Jack's jailbreaking, not his housebreaking. The money he gets he spends; the freedom he earns he devotes to others. Wild is vampiric, obsessive, capitalistic. He is Jack's would-be corrupter. Having persecuted Jack's father, he is irrationally driven to do the same to the son. In contrast, Jack's habits are romanticised to confirm a salt-of-the earth Britishness, a political designation insofar as the contest over defining working-class culture had political implications. *Jack Sheppard* caused such a stir not simply because Jack is a humanised criminal, like Nancy the prostitute with a heart of gold. More disturbing was the implication that the values that he holds were working-class values and that these were in fact the true values of old Britain. Chartists tended to make the same point when comparing the middle and working classes – working people, for example, marry out of love while the middle classes marry for money or status – except their working classes do not generally look like Jack. The point has been made numerous times that Chartists advocated a line of domestic normality that in some ways makes a plea for the vote, in that it shows that working people were just as culturally mature as the middle classes and not the drunken, abusive louts of the middle-class imagination. *Jack Sheppard* does not do this; Jack is often drunk and hardly seems to represent vote-readiness or the right kind of man to choose the nation's leaders. Jack does not want instruction, education, or improvement. His morality, like his abilities, is natural. He is trained to be a carpenter, which can explain part of his jailbreaking or house-entering skills, but he is mostly unguided and uneducated. The novel is never as provocative as when it holds that Jack does not need correction or instruction. This is far from the typical approach that most Chartists had towards working people. Though members of the working classes are mostly represented as down and out and in need of education (though not middle-class education), they are usually moral and decent, fully domestic and respectable. A Jack Sheppard in a Chartist story would be in dire need of improvement. Chartist writers had a specific goal: to advance the cause of the Charter. Ainsworth's novel does not have a concrete agenda, radical or reformist, but its emotional design is set to appeal to a raw, incendiary belief in the legitimacy of working-class energies, practices and cultures, notwithstanding the exaggerated contours the novel represents. By definition an opportunist, Ainsworth's Jack nonetheless makes a conscious decision to be a criminal of restraint, to act with design, to choose carefully what lines to cross, suggesting a hint of reason and reasonableness in his social transgressions. Bulwer elevates his Aram socially and intellectually to make him more sympathetic than the original; Ainsworth gives his Jack Sheppard romanticised working-class sensibilities to do the same. Jack is invested with a level of self-consciousness and autonomy that already makes him a full subject, a fully moral agent when it counts, exercising his will in every domain save the political. The political content mostly comes from the supplementaries of literature and the increased opportunity for inference in times of crisis.

Jack's untamed but moral instincts are complemented by the novel's crowds. The novel offers an image of the crowd as skilled, purposeful, and able to make justifiable decisions. The first depiction of a crowd comes early in the novel, when Mrs Sheppard and Wood are trying to protect the baby Darrell from Rowland and Cecil. The crowd at the Old Mint, made up from 'the lowest order of insolvent traders, thieves, mendicants, and other worthless and nefarious characters', unwittingly comes to the rescue when Wood shouts out 'Arrest'.[81] Most notable is Ainsworth's insistence on the crowd's organisational skills: 'A garrison called to arms at dead of night on the sudden approach of the enemy could not have been more expeditiously or effectively aroused.'[82] At this point, however, the crowd hardly knows right from wrong. It knows only its self-interest: 'deaf, as they had been, to the recent scuffle before Mrs. Sheppard's door, they were always sufficiently on the alert to maintain their privileges, and to assist each other against the attacks of their common enemy – the sheriff's officer'.[83] A little later the crowd is described as 'scouring the streets whose sole object seemed plunder'.[84] But at the end of the novel, when Jack has become a full-blown celebrity and is being taken to Tyburn to be hanged, the crowd redeems itself by finding its purpose, first to destroy Wild's power, and the symbols of his power, and then to burn down Newgate, another symbol of power. It mirrors Jack's own movement towards acting with a greater purpose, towards heroic sovereignty. The ensuing riot begins spontaneously but soon becomes a scene of social war, complete with barricades and a fight between the fully armed people loyal to Jack and the soldiery. To this point the state has been comically ineffective against Jack, and mostly absent. It is difficult to discern Jack's jailors from his accomplices, and Wild and his henchmen hardly represent the dignity of the state's authorities. Amidst the 'shouts of indignation'[85] the crowd becomes feral but deliberate, taking on a note of righteous vindication: Jack is a people's hero for defying the odds, but Wild's exploits generate most of the raw anger not just because he is Jack's corrupt pursuer, but because the crowd knows that justice must be served. Ainsworth was more or less obligated to depict a crowd at the end of his novel since 200,000 people came out to see the historical Jack Sheppard's final procession. But he makes it an image of an uprising, a rising against injustice, a riot that has a valid goal outside of rioting, very much in contrast to Dickens's crowds in *Oliver Twist* or *Barnaby Rudge*. Hardly the march of the intellect, the processional crowd would nevertheless appropriate the right the state has claimed to punish by death, and Wild is lucky to escape: the crowd, like Jack, becomes sovereign, reversing what is today called the necropolitics of the state.

Both challenging and complementing the biopolitics of Foucault, Achille Mbembe argues that it is mostly through death or the threat of death that the state achieves power, control, or sovereignty over its people. In this way he corrects Foucault's emphasis on a government's subtler but nonetheless 'numerous and diverse techniques for achieving the subjugations of bodies and the control of populations'.[86] Mbembe and Foucault would agree, however, that the right to take away life is the ultimate act of power and thus the decisive expression of necropolitics. This is the right that the state is exercising at the end of *Jack Sheppard*, and in some basic way Jack is going to give up his body or control over his body to the state. Wild is apparently waiting not just to see the execution but to collect a necropolitical trophy from it. Smart and fighting to be in control to the end, Jack predicts Wild will come for the bowl from which he was to have his last drink for that purpose.[87] It is also a contested moment insofar as the crowd too seeks destruction, the destruction of Wild, and in doing so it demonstrates that violence is *its* best tool by which to assert its power, expressing its own form of necropolitics. As Jack is executed he becomes a martyr, a sacrificial figure who refuses to allow the state's power of bodily destruction to act as a sign of its power, but he needs the crowd for this. Throughout the novel Jack refuses to be controlled or contained, resisting not only law and authority but the official morality, 'biopower' in a sense. At the end of the novel, with Jack's death pre-scripted by history, his fate inescapable, and his body hanged and shot, the state finally exercising its power, it is the crowd that emerges to assert its strength, and to lay claim to Jack's body, mocking the state's necropolitical power just as Jack had defied its biopower. Blueskin is also shot, but he 'was not unattended. A thousand eager assistants pressed behind him. Jack's body was caught, and passed from hand to hand over a thousand heads, till it was far from the fatal tree.'[88] Jack's body is given to the people: 'borne along by that tremendous host, which rose and fell like waves of the ocean'.[89] With the almost religious language of the everlasting, Ainsworth takes full advantage of inflated, romantic, and Christ-like imagery with a kind of flourish that readers must expect at this point in the novel. But the exaggeration, the appeal to popular taste, politicises insofar as the crowd has become meaningful and beautiful by becoming 'the people', a political entity acting with purpose as a whole. *Jack Sheppard* is casually, carelessly revolutionary insofar as Ainsworth, in 1839, when England seemed to be on the cusp of outbreak from its own prisons, seized an opportunity to enhance popular design and appeal by making the conflation of folklore culture and politics part of his Newgate novel.

Aside from confirming the value of the popular and of the crowd, even when violent, the final scene in *Jack Sheppard* mostly acts to ensure that Jack is seen as a martyr dying for the only cause he has truly ever had: freedom. The martyring of Jack is an assertion of his historical legitimacy and, as with all martyring, designed to invoke the idea of resurrection, a return. In this way martyrdom is not giving in but an alternative to despair. Popular taste is also satisfied as Jack engages in a final act of symbolic sovereignty, facing the executioner by maintaining his 'composure – a smile played upon his face before the cap was drawn over it'.[90] Earlier, when the procession began, the public gathering has an infectious 'festive character', with soldiers calling for drinks before they are 'immediately imitated' by others.[91] Jack as martyr is still productive, becoming the site where death and power and irreverent energies intersect; his body becomes even more physical and even more symbolic, not to show that resistance means destruction but to show that it means generation. The final image of a simple grave 'without any name or date' until 'some pitying hand supplied the inscription',[92] illustrated and not written out by the author's pen, and reproducing the way Jack had scratched out his own name into a beam of wood when a carpenter's apprentice,[93] makes Jack an emblem of reproduction, an example of writing your own history or way into history, and speaks of a refusal to disappear or to be forgotten.

Chartist writing was preoccupied with martyrs, especially in the early periodicals such as the Scottish *Chartist Circular*; later martyrdom was the image Chartist leaders such as Ernest Jones and Feargus O'Connor used to signal their authentic conversion to the people. Chartist fiction is the fiction of martyrdom as much of it martyrs itself, giving up its aesthetic intent for an extratextual message. This is the exact opposite of what we see with *Jack Sheppard*, which unapologetically seeks popularity, indiscriminately using sentimentalism or radicalism, or a combination of both, for commercial ends. In this way, the novel anticipates the direction Chartist fiction would take towards melodrama. But even when considering Chartism's evolving penchant for combining politics and sentimentality, there are more differences than similarities between Chartist fiction and *Jack Sheppard*, the greatest being that Chartist fiction always has a direct object, the promotion of the Charter, while *Jack Sheppard* refuses any directly political stance. In fact, Chartists did

Figure 2 Concluding illustration by George Cruikshank in *Jack Sheppard*. No known copyright restrictions. No known restrictions on use.

not like or endorse *Jack Sheppard*. In its opening issue, the *Chartist* castigates *Bentley's Miscellany* for catering to 'those who delight in murderous details, and all other things "horrid and barbarous"'.⁹⁴ *Bentley's* was of course running *Jack Sheppard* (but had also just run *Oliver Twist*). The *Chartist*, despite being full of crime reports, saw the need to instruct its audience, elevate it to the point that it could not be denied the vote. To this end it rejected 'merely amusing and useless' literature: 'Wholesome mental food is now more scant in the dwelling of the mechanic than is the food for the body.'⁹⁵ But *Jack Sheppard*, at least according to its critics, did what much Chartist literature and historiography sought to do: make representation generative beyond mere imaginative acts, making texts produce not just more texts but more history as well.

Notes

1 Lesser known novels such as Charles Hooton's *Colin Clink* (1841), serialised in *Bentley's Miscellany* at the same time as *Jack Sheppard*, with illustrations by George Cruikshank and John Leech, were not often grouped together with Bulwer's, Ainsworth's, and Dickens's novels by contemporary critics. Hooton was Ainsworth's friend and, it might be mentioned, for a time a sub-editor of the *True Sun* (1832–37), a radical paper that covered meetings of the National Union of the Working Classes. See W. H. Ainsworth (ed.), 'Sketches of Charles Hooton', *New Monthly Magazine: Part the First* (London: Chapman and Hall, 1847), p. 397. Plagiarisms such as G. Purkess's *The Life and Adventures of Jack Sheppard* (1849) or penny-a-liners such as *The History of Jack Sheppard* (1839) by John Williams were again not generally in the critics' frame of reference.
2 Buckley notes that 'While Sheppard's popularity spanned a broad working-class audience, his most numerous and fanatic devotees were, as one would expect, the young, 'masterless' men who constituted much of the city's growing industrial labor force.' M. Buckley, 'Sensations of celebrity: *Jack Sheppard* and the mass audience', *Victorian Studies*, 44:3 (2002), 427.
3 Ainsworth was born and grew up in early nineteenth-century Manchester and was fourteen at the time of Peterloo, but that did not lead to radical tendencies. Stephen Carver notes that an early

attempt at contributing to a political pamphlet with John Ebers, called *Considerations on the best means of affording Immediate Relief to the Operative Classes in the Manufacturing Districts* (1826), 'abandons the radical call for state intervention he appears initially to be suggesting in favour of rather insipid suggestions involving charity'. S. J. Carver, *The Life and Works of the Lancashire Novelist William Harrison Ainsworth, 1805–1882* (Lewiston, NY: Edwin Mellen Press, 2003), p. 97.

4 As George Worth says, 'much in Ainsworth's novels that seems to us puzzling or annoying can be understood only if we know something of the size, the composition, and the tastes of the public which he was clearly anxious to please'. G. J. Worth, *William Harrison Ainsworth* (New York: Twayne Publishers, 1972), pp. 22–3.

5 Perhaps betraying a frequently expressed canonical preference for Dickens over Ainsworth, John Russell Stephens complains that Thackeray 'insisted on linking *Oliver Twist* and *Jack Sheppard* in his condemnation of the whole Newgate school'. J. R. Stephens, *The Censorship of English Drama, 1824–1901* (Cambridge: Cambridge University Press, 1980), p. 66.

6 The calendars offer a detailed life of Jack Sheppard as a people's hero, often dwelling on his legend as much as they explain his exploits. Ainsworth is frequently said to have taken Hogarth's *Industry and Idleness* (1747) as inspiration for his version of the story, with Darrell standing in for industriousness and Jack for idleness. After all, like Tom Idle, Jack proceeds to Tyburn to hang. But Ainsworth's Jack, like the Jack from the calendars, is anything but idle, and the main opposition in *Jack Sheppard* is not between Darrell and Jack but between Jonathan Wild and Jack.

7 W. M. Thackeray, 'Going to see a man hanged', in *The Works of William Makepeace Thackeray. Vol. XIV* (London: Smith, Elder and Company, 1884), p. 446. Dickens responded to the criticism in the Preface to the third edition of *Oliver Twist* by insisting that his project was to show criminals 'as they really are'. Regrettably, Dickens here accepts Thackeray's twisted definition of realism by saying that he represented 'them in all their deformity, in all their wretchedness, in all the squalid poverty of their lives'. C. Dickens, *Oliver Twist* (Oxford: Oxford University Press, 2008), p. liv. In the novel, and this of course is Thackeray's complaint, he also shows them in all their humanity, if inconsistently.

8 See H. Mayhew, 'The literature of costermongers', in *London Labour and the London Poor* (London: Penguin, 1985), p. 25.

9 Quoted in F. B. Schwarzbach, 'Newgate novel to detective fiction', in P. Brantlinger and W. B. Theising (eds), *A Companion to the Victorian Novel* (Massachusetts: Blackwell Publishing, 2002), p. 227.
10 Quoted in N. Page, *A Dickens Companion* (Houndmills: Macmillan, 1984), p. 85. Again in his third-edition Preface, Dickens responds to this line of criticism, this time lashing out at the 'people of so refined and delicate a nature, that they cannot bear the contemplation of these horrors'. Dickens, *Oliver Twist*, p. lv.
11 W. M. Thackeray, *Catherine: A Story. Fraser's Magazine*, Vol. XXI (London: James Fraser, 1840), p. 211.
12 K. Hollingsworth, *The Newgate Novel, 1830–1847: Bulwer, Ainsworth, Dickens, and Thackeray* (Detroit, MI: Wayne State University Press, 1963), p. 139.
13 E. F. Harden (ed.), *Selected Letters of William Makepeace Thackeray* (New York: New York University Press, 1996), p. 49.
14 W. M. Thackeray, 'Horae Catnachiannae', *Fraser's Magazine*, Vol. XIX (London: James Fraser, 1839), p. 408.
15 Anon., 'William Ainsworth and Jack Sheppard', *Fraser's Magazine*, Vol. XXI (London: James Fraser, 1840), p. 228.
16 Anon., 'Art I', *Monthly Review* (December 1839), p. 459.
17 J. Forster, 'Review', *Examiner* (3 November 1839), p. 691.
18 Buckley, 'Sensations of celebrity', p. 426.
19 S. Joyce, *Capital Offenses: Geographies of Crime in Victorian London* (Charlottesville, VA and London: University of Virginia Press, 2003), p. 95.
20 Quoted in Joyce, *Capital Offenses*, p. 91.
21 Quoted in L. L. Panek, *Before Sherlock Holmes: How Magazines and Newspapers Invented the Detective Story* (Jefferson, NC and London: McFarland and Company, 2011), p. 34.
22 Quoted in G. Pearson, *Hooligan: A History of Respectable Fears* (New York: Schocken, 1983), p. 166.
23 Modern criticism tends to reproduce the obsession with what *Jack Sheppard* generated, as distinct from reading the novel closely, by focusing on the craze and on contemporary reviews. To some degree I follow suit in this section of the chapter, as the response to the novel is central to my argument, but further analyses of *Fraser's*, the *Monthly Chronicle*, the *Examiner*, and the *Athenaeum*, among others, and their responses to the novel, can be found in Hollingsworth and nearly every other interpretation of *Jack Sheppard* that follows.
24 Pearson, *Hooligan*, pp. 161 and 163.
25 *Ibid.*, p. 178.

26 Joyce, *Capital Offenses*, p. 92.
27 M. Meisel, *Realizations: Narrative, Pictorial, and Theatrical Arts in Nineteenth-Century England* (Princeton, NJ: Princeton University Press, 1983), p. 265.
28 Buckley, 'Sensations of celebrity', p. 431.
29 Quoted in C. Falke, 'On the morality of immoral fiction: reading Newgate novels, 1830–1848', *Nineteenth-Century Contexts*, 38:3 (2016), 187.
30 *Ibid.*
31 J. John, 'Twisting the Newgate tale: Dickens, popular culture and the politics of genre', in J. John and A. Jenkins (eds), *Rethinking Victorian Culture* (Houndmills: Macmillan Press, 2000), p. 126.
32 M. R. Mitford, *The Life of Mary Russell Mitford, Told by Herself in Letters to her Friends* (New York: Harper and Brothers Publishers, 1870), II, p. 218.
33 *Ibid.*
34 A. Knapp and W. Baldwin (eds), *The New Newgate Calendar* (5 vols, London: J. Robins and Co. Albion Press, 1819), III, p. 12.
35 Hollingsworth, *The Newgate Novel*, p. 14.
36 J. H. Grossman, *The Art of the Alibi: English Law Courts and the Novel* (Baltimore, MD and London: Johns Hopkins University Press, 2002), p. 35.
37 L. Gillingham, 'Ainsworth's *Jack Sheppard* and the crimes of history', *Studies in English Literature 1500–1900*, 49:4 (2009), 883.
38 *Ibid.*, p. 885.
39 A. Lucas, '*Oliver Twist* and the Newgate novel', *The Dalhousie Review*, 34:1 (1954), 382.
40 J. John, 'Introduction', in *Cult Criminals: The Newgate Novels, 1830–1847* (Abingdon: Routledge, 2000), p. vii.
41 Anon., 'William Ainsworth and Jack Sheppard', p. 228.
42 P. Egan, *Life in London* (Cambridge: Cambridge University Press, 2011), p. 222.
43 *Ibid.*
44 *Ibid.*, pp. 343–7.
45 C. Pelham (ed.), *The Chronicles of Crime; or, The New Newgate Calendar* (2 vols, London: Thomas Tigg, 1841), I, p. vi.
46 Carver, *The Life and Works*, pp. 199–203.
47 Hollingsworth, *The Newgate Novel*, p. 141.
48 Carver, *The Life and Works*, p. 197.
49 Foucault in fact appreciates that 'the song of crime', the generative aspect of Newgate fiction, would 'travel from singer to singer; everyone

is presumed able to sing it as his own crime, by a lyrical fiction'. Quoted in P. Joyce, *Visions of the People: Industrial England and the Question of Class, 1848–1914* (Cambridge: Cambridge University Press, 1991), p. 87.
50 E. P. Thompson, *The Making of the English Working Class* (London: Penguin, 1980), p. 661.
51 Buckley, 'Sensations of celebrity', p. 426.
52 S. Joyce, 'Resisting arrest/arresting resistance: crime fiction, cultural studies, and the "turn to history"', *Criticism: A Quarterly for Literature and the Arts*, 37:2 (1995), 331.
53 Gillingham, 'Ainsworth's *Jack Sheppard*', p. 882.
54 John, 'Introduction', p. xxxix.
55 *Ibid.*, pp. xii and xli.
56 Though Kettleby longs for the day 'when Tyburn and its gibbets shall be overthrown – capital punishments discontinued', his desire to see all London become 'one Mint' suggests he is thinking in terms of cultural and not practical change. W. H. Ainsworth, *Jack Sheppard* (London: Penguin, 2010), p. 211.
57 Joyce, 'Resisting arrest', p. 318.
58 C. Dickens, *Barnaby Rudge* (Harmondsworth: Penguin, 1977), p. 598.
59 J. Sutherland, 'Harrison Ainsworth, 1805–1882', in *Lives of the Novelists: A History of Fiction in 294 Lives* (New Haven, CT and London: Yale University Press, 2012), p. 89.
60 J. Richards, 'The "Lancashire novelist" and the Lancashire witches', in R. Poole (ed.), *The Lancashire Witches: Histories and Stories* (Manchester: Manchester University Press, 2002), p. 166.
61 Ainsworth, *Jack Sheppard*, p. 105.
62 *Ibid.*, p. 114.
63 *Ibid.*
64 *Ibid.*, p. 121.
65 *Ibid.*, p. 127.
66 *Ibid.*, p. 104.
67 *Ibid.*, p. 446.
68 Carver, *The Life and Works*, p. 80.
69 See, for example, G. Rudé, 'The Gordon Riots: a study of the rioters and their victims', in *Paris and London in the 18th Century: Studies in Popular Protest* (London: Collins, 1970), pp. 268–92.
70 See especially R. Williams, 'Forms of English fiction in 1848', in Francis Barker *et al.* (eds), *Literature, Politics and Theory: Papers from the Essex Conference* (London: Methuen, 1986), pp. 1–16.

71 In a particularly rich moment of metafiction, Ainsworth implies that Jack here inspires Gay's *Beggar's Opera* (1728) and Hogarth's *Industry and Idleness* engravings (1747), teasing the audience with the generative features of the Jack Sheppard story.
72 Ainsworth, *Jack Sheppard*, p. 429.
73 *Ibid.*, p. 433.
74 Dickens, *Oliver Twist*, p. 357.
75 *Ibid.*, p. 356.
76 Gillingham, 'Ainsworth's *Jack Sheppard*', p. 891.
77 See R. Williams, *Modern Tragedy* (London: Chatto and Windus, 1969), pp. 190–204.
78 The history of Tell figures prominently in Chartist fiction. A version of his story inaugurates the *Chartist Circular* and another can be found in an issue of the *National* that focuses on wealth. Anon., 'William Tell, the Swiss Patriot', *Chartist Circular* (28 September 1839), p. 4. Anon., 'William Tell', *National* (10 April 1839), p. 226.
79 Ainsworth, *Jack Sheppard*, p. 155.
80 *Ibid.*, p. 228.
81 *Ibid.*, pp. 17, 24.
82 *Ibid.*, p. 24.
83 *Ibid.*, p. 25.
84 *Ibid.*, p. 78.
85 *Ibid.*, p. 532.
86 M. Foucault, *The History of Sexuality, Vol. 1, An Introduction*, trans. Robert Hurley (London: Penguin, 1979), p. 140.
87 Ainsworth, *Jack Sheppard*, p. 528.
88 *Ibid.*, pp. 531–2.
89 *Ibid.*, p. 532.
90 *Ibid.*, p. 531.
91 *Ibid.*, p. 527.
92 *Ibid.*, p. 532.
93 *Ibid.*, p. 87.
94 Anon., 'The Magazines', *The Chartist* (16 February 1839), p. 3.
95 Anon., 'To our Readers', *The Chartist* (16 February 1839), p. 1.

3

Penny radicalism? *Sweeney Todd* and the bloods

Penny bloods did not appear overnight. They came about when a variety of romantic formulas were mixed together by enterprising men in what might be called the absolute realism of early nineteenth-century history. A messy bricolage of inflated Newgate storytelling, 'low-life' and highwayman adventure narratives, gothic fiction, and any other affective discourse that indulges in depictions of frustrated love, madness, violent villainy, and so forth were merged together just as an urban working class was hardening into a semi-self-conscious class; though it can be overstated, the penny story of the 1840s has been seen as playing a significant role in the development of a new working-class culture defining itself against the developing new middle-class culture (defining *itself*, of course, against the emerging working-class one).[1] Less noted is that penny literature also emerged just as Chartism was establishing itself and defining its strategies. The dissolution of penny bloods in the early 1850s also corresponds almost exactly with the demise of Chartism. Whether penny bloods are part of the history of Chartism – or at least the aura of mass violence and revolt that many associated with it – or if Chartism is part of the historical context that sees the genesis of the bloods are not questions that are often asked directly, and when they are, they are usually dismissed. Certainly the main figures behind the penny bloods, with the exception of G. W. M. Reynolds, were not fully fledged members of the political tribe, though E. P. Thompson notes that Edward Lloyd (like William Howitt, John Cleave, William Chambers, and Reynolds), the most significant figure in the development of the bloods, came from a 'Radical background'.[2]

Critics instead debate whether the bloods are escapist; whether the 'mass culture industry', or popular culture as a whole, at the time but certainly with an eye on contemporary history, produces 'instruments of mass deception and manipulation'.[3] Or, as John Springhall phrases it in his study of *The String of Pearls* or *Sweeney Todd*, are those products the sign of a

> genuine people's culture, opposing and resisting the dominant elite culture – the basis for cultural renaissance? In other words, does commercial entertainment present us with socially conservative fables, thus acting as an agency of social control by the dominant culture, or do penny dreadfuls represent 'a symbolic form of class conflict', subverting authority and challenging middle-class norms?[4]

To go further, one might ask: what would be the significance of engaging in a culture war under the clouds of a political war? Does *Sweeney Todd*, the most famous of the bloods, and often treated as representative of the genre, really do anything more than create the frisson of urban terror? If so, were strains of radicalism co-opted to demonstrate the dangers of politicising the carnivalesque spirit when approaching it too 'seriously', or were they used to help sell the product because there was a market for radicalism, a penny radicalism?

Jonathan Rose argues that the politics of popular culture 'has become an obsession in academic literature departments and cultural studies programs'.[5] On the one hand is a 'left'-leaning school that clearly desires to see an intersection or even a dialectic between popular and radical expression. Bakhtin's carnivalesque and dialogism or de Certeau's practice of everyday life, for example, give us brilliant insights into the way 'subversion' or 'resistance' thrives in forms that do not appear obviously political. On the other hand is a 'left' leaning school that sees hegemony in popular expression. Horkheimer and Adorno's 'culture industry' or Foucault's self-discipline, for example, are equally brilliant arguments about the way people and their true desires are controlled and contained. But popular culture is often able to position itself in and exploit spaces not so much in-between as outside of hegemony and counter-hegemony. *Sweeney Todd* takes up the radical mantle, echoes the Chartist cause, or just subverts and resists, except when it doesn't.

Rose, however, complains that the 'failure' in the effort to ascertain whether popular culture should be understood as subversive or regulatory 'is methodological: with some exceptions, it ignores actual readers. In this terrain, critics repeatedly commit what might be called the receptive fallacy: try to discern the messages a text transmits to an audience by examining the text rather than the audience.'[6] Content analysis, it seems, can only hint at whether there was an appetite for pseudo-seditious fiction. But even with this approach we might see a similar need for a definitive, consistent answer. I want to avoid this dichotomising not by attempting to examine how the fiction was received by individuals or groups, as if reader response would be more consistent than the fiction itself, but by accepting that this fiction can have its cake, or pie, and eat it too. Historians who avoid interpretive work run the risk of not being able to recognise the interpretive work they do. The separation of culture into either resisting or oppressing forces is ideally challenged by de-dichotomising 'culture' and 'politics'. But this will not lead to a final pronouncement on the ideology of penny fiction, its politics, or even its 'cultural politics'. With literature coming from below one might expect to see representations of dire poverty, callous employers, class conflict, and what is found in contemporaneous Chartist fiction in cheap publications intended for working people, roughly the same audience that Chartist publishers wanted to attract. And while all of this is to be found, a little bit here and a little bit there in what is often incredibly stretched-out fiction, the political content certainly will not overwhelm readers and there is very little evidence that it did. Penny-issue fiction is stuffed with arranged marriage plots, drunken fathers, squeaky-clean lovers, and interminable representations of some aristocrat plotting to keep his illegitimate identity hidden from the world. If Chartist fiction is Chartist because it looks to the Charter to resolve the conflicts it represents, because it seeks an extratextual resolution, nothing remotely like this happens in the cheap romances and bloods of the 1840s. But penny literature from the same years can casually and sporadically – not necessarily ingeniously, but arguably with deliberation – take advantage of, attach itself to, or attempt to profit off of Chartism, the Chartist threat, or the Chartist frisson. As James notes, Lloyd and other publishers 'felt their way into the field by trial and error'.[7] The flirtation with Chartist narratives of class identity and rights, with Chartist arguments for full citizenship, or with Chartist attempts to elide or end the separation between physical and moral force, may have simply been part of that process of feeling out what was popular and preferred.

Chartist scholars generally agree that radical fiction shifted from a satiric to a melodramatic mode after the 1834 New Poor Law. In fact, both liberals and radicals alike essentially saw the New Poor Law as criminalising poverty and punishing the poor, and with the political change in the approach to poverty, stories came out that generally included sympathetic or perhaps pathetic treatments of poverty, outlining as well the crime, treachery, and violence that came with the dissipation of the old paternal order. From that point on, it is generally held that fictional modes of political radicalism gradually went from satire to melodrama in order for Chartists to reach the broadest audience possible, one that would include, for example, Lloyd's readers. Sally Ledger argues that 'Chartism's turn to the popular was inspired by the need to compete with the new commercial popular press that developed in the 1840s and whose political clout among the masses was to become nothing less than awesome.'[8] As Iain McCalman has shown, radicals even resorted to pornographic production in the hope of attracting more working people to the radical cause.[9] (On the other side of the coin, that the Chartist press often reproduced Dickens or Charles Lever in their papers suggests that the editors were aware of and encouraged the audience's amenability to respectability and 'respectable fiction' as well.) In a sense, I am looking at the attempt to reach wider audiences from the other point of view: what did popular literature – the bloods – do to attract the Chartist audience? What political content is added to penny literature to entice or accommodate the working-class readers who were more likely to pick up the *Northern Star* than *Lloyd's Penny Weekly Miscellany of Romance*? What is then the relationship between the production of violent entertainment and the rise of Chartism, especially as prominent Chartists more and more rejected the split between moral and physical force?

In this chapter I am looking at penny literature from the 1840s, before it was conscripted for juvenile entertainment (before the penny blood became known as the penny dreadful) and I am not tackling the work of Reynolds, which warrants its own chapter. My argument is partly indebted to Michael Denning's work on the American dime novel. Denning argues that cheap literature should 'be understood neither as forms of deception, manipulation, and social control nor as expressions of a genuine people's culture, opposing and resisting the dominant culture' but as 'a contested terrain, a field of cultural conflict where signs with wide appeal and resonance take on contradictory disguises and are spoken in contrary accents'.[10] Most Chartist scholars today, such as Owen Ashton, here quoting Stuart Hall, agree that popular culture should 'be viewed as "one of the sites where a struggle for and against a culture of the powerful is engaged"'.[11] I am also following the work of Richard Altick, who argues that 'The men behind the leading popular weeklies, most notably Edward Lloyd and G. W. M. Reynolds, were active in such current radical causes as anti-Corn Law agitation and Chartism, and it would have been remarkable if their papers had not voiced their personal views. But they were also shrewd businessmen, well aware of the commercial value of radical propaganda.'[12] Ian Haywood has also situated Lloyd (and Reynolds) within 'the longer, "Jacobin" revolution of popular literature which begins in the 1790s', though he also is careful to point out that Lloyd 'tended to keep literature separate but related'.[13] Some critics read penny literature as unambiguously subversive. Sara Hackenberg argues that the penny-fiction trope of the coffin-breaker or body-snatcher was not only a response to the 1832 Anatomy Act and the 1834 New Poor Law, but also 'represents the return of the politically repressed, shaded with radical and republican energy'.[14] Louise Creechan states that *Sweeney Todd* includes a 'scathing proto-Marxist critique of the workings of early capitalist society'.[15] No one would deny the commercial motivations of the penny press, but no one should imagine that having profitmaking motivations nullifies the possibility of having genuine political sympathies.

However, I am also mindful of other critics, such as David Vincent, who do not see much resembling a political imaginary in penny literature. Rather, Vincent says 'The dimensions of the new aesthetic were determined less by the absolute level of hardship and more by the character of the expanding centres of population, where the bulk of the literature was produced and sold.'[16] This echoes Louis James, who noted in his pioneering work, *Fiction for the Working Man*, 'how directly these periodicals were the expression of the new life of the towns'.[17] Though some cheap literature such as *Sweeney Todd* tends to conflate hardship and urban living, Vincent is right to develop the argument that the new urban dweller demanded a different kind of literature to match something in their own experiences, and that would not be restricted to the pursuit of good employment or the goal of full citizenship, even in the 'hungry forties'. Vincent argues that 'The heightened sense of drama which pervaded the penny fiction, the speed with which the new material was written, produced and presented, seemed appropriate to the accelerated existence of the towns.'[18] Again, this is true, though one could point out that the content of the material being produced, as distinct from the way it was produced, suggests that something else must have been in play as well. Certainly the length of serialised penny fiction is not built for speed, and a large number of the authors, such as the authors of the most significant and read penny stories – *Sweeney Todd*, *Ada, the Betrayed*, or *Varney, the Vampire* – frequently go out of their way to remind audiences that the action of the story takes place in the past. *Varney*, for example, takes us to gothic castles, removing readers from the urban reality surrounding them. In step with Vincent insofar as she is doubtful that penny literature has direct political correlatives, Rosalind Crone also notes that the fiction frequently avoids the life of the city, and that that avoidance is in fact a sign of the conservative politics of the authors. Quoting Rohan McWilliam, Crone says, 'Melodramatic plays and penny bloods were dominated by a sense of nostalgia and promulgated myths of a past golden age. This theme was central to the inherently conservative outlook of early Victorian popular culture as the simplicities of past or village life were "preferred to the city where order was overturned and custom replaced by lawlessness."'[19]

Crone is among a number of contemporary critics who sense that the fiction reflects the social experiences of its audiences, but is nonetheless not quite politically radical.[20] Non-dualistic readings of penny bloods and other forms of penny literature, where the texts are treated as both resistive and capitulating to the cultural status quo, have become more common. Speaking on the violence that inheres in penny bloods, Crone points out that in the sense that violence was a part of working-class culture, from social upheavals to sport:

> it did become a form of protest by the labouring classes, or by those who continued to make up the audience for these various genres. Extreme violence was a useful way in which to assert the place of popular culture within the mainstream, flying in the face of an increasingly prominent or even hegemonic culture supported by the new middle class and characterised by restraint and respectability.[21]

The extent of the class-based subversiveness, however, is generally limited, as it is here, to culture wars. Representations of violence, rowdiness, or lower-class rabble in cheap literature are frequently seen to be challenging the culture of respectability that the middle classes were solidifying for themselves, but the politics of the plot, with some reason, are seen by the same critics as highly conservative.

The concept of a culture war is hugely significant and must be examined carefully, but doing so should not take the place of close content analysis because it is in the latter, as I will argue while examining *Sweeney Todd* and a number of other stories from 'Salisbury Square', home to the cheap presses, that flashes of political radicalism are found, despite being mixed up in a good deal of 'conservative' content, making cultural assertions much more meaningful. Still, there undoubtedly is something counter-hegemonic, defiant, even rebellious, in the very establishment of a cheap press that confirms a separate reading class and attempts to monopolise the category of 'the people', even when representing the trials and tribulations of non-working classes. Literature explicitly produced for underprivileged, urban people announces its own culture, denouncing the putatively calming idea espoused more and more regularly after the 1832 Reform Bill of mutual interests: the notion that the middle class could lead working people on a march of the intellect that would guarantee they would come to understand that their interests were the same as the class now representing them in parliament. Though penny papers from Salisbury Square frequently include 'educational' material, the romances can be seen and were seen as undermining any effort to 'improve' their readers.

Lloyd may have absorbed some of the practices popular in the publications of the Society for the Diffusion of Useful Knowledge (SDUK) or the Society for Promoting Christian Knowledge (SPCK), but that his periodicals were designed to satisfy popular tastes as distinct from refining them almost goes without saying. That there was 'moral panic' over this emerging working-class culture has been well documented,[22] though the conservative nature of so much of the content suggests that it was less a moral than a cultural panic. This too has political overtones and might even have caused some political panic, insofar as the fiction seems to express dissatisfaction with the idea that middle-class production would be the same as working-class production, implying not only that middle-class tastes were not universal but that the middle classes were unable or unwilling to speak for working people.

Still, Charles Knight's complaint that penny literature was 'diffusing a moral miasma through the land'[23] seems a bit disingenuous in that a story like *Ida Walton; or, a Tale of Trials* by Ellen Barton, from the *People's Periodical and Family Library* (7–14 April 1847), confirms, not confronts, the official morality of the day. After their father loses his hard-earned fortune through speculation, Ida (who is eighteen) and Lizzy (fifteen) become factory girls, as the usual occupations available to women such as sewing, governessing, and schoolteaching, are unavailable. The story exists mostly to demonstrate the ideal quaintness of a well-run factory town, how beautiful it is because the factory owner, Mr Ellison here, will be a kind man, and loved by all his workers. Ida and Lizzy start to work in the factory and are the happier, the more rosy-cheeked for it.[24] Ida's 'trial' is not poverty, not working in a factory, which 'brought with it a feeling of strength and independence',[25] but the 'unkindness' of a suitor and frustrated true love. Knight may have had the bloodier fiction of the cheap presses in mind, but Ida shares the page with *Sweeney Todd*, as do countless domestic romances such as *Rose Summerville* or morality allegories such as 'The history of a dime; or a peep into the world' (9 January 1847).[26] The *People's Periodical*, much like Lloyd's other publications, includes a great deal of fiction, and perhaps that in itself could raise Knight's chagrin, even if much of it is unambiguously 'wholesome'; but it is not surprising to find in cheap periodicals both fiction and non-fiction representing working people (or peasants as the case may be) in need of education and sobriety, and the top levels of society in need of financial and sexual morality, messages not unlike the take-aways from more than a few middle-class productions.

The understudied Thomas Frost reminds us that most of the cheap literature of the 1840s was not in fact 'bloods' but highly moralistic domestic dramas. His divide of the fiction barely has space for the bloods: 'The Salisbury Square fictions may be divided ... into two classes, one consisting of romances of the kind made popular by Anne Radcliffe, the other of the sentimental novels purveyed to our grandmothers by Anne of Swansea and Anna Maria Jones.'[27] Frost insists that 'The moral tone of ... most of the tales issued by Mr. Lloyd, was unexceptionable, virtue being set in as bright and beautiful contrast to vice as in any of the novels on the shelves of Mudie's library at the present day. It is doubtful, indeed, whether the comparison would not be in favour of the former.'[28] Louis James also notes that the bloods do not dominate the cheap periodicals: 'The "domestic story"', he says, 'lies at the heart of almost all the penny-issue fiction published during the 1840s.'[29] These may not be very realistic attempts at realism, with seduction plots, inheritance plots, madness plots, and so forth driving the interminable action, but despite the gothic textures, the gypsies and the drawn-out chase scenes, they do not indulge in carnivalesque celebrations that evoke cultural war. Though Rosemary Crone notes that 'Serial domestic romances were almost always very bloody romances',[30] at least some of the shorter stories were not. 'The lesson: a tale of domestic life'[31] has a wise father teach his daughters the difference between a husband chosen for character and one chosen for wealth. 'Economy' by 'the author of Rose Sommerville', published during *Sweeney Todd*'s original run, follows an upper-middle-class couple as they spend too much money. The wife, who is said to be mostly at fault, eventually learns 'a right appreciation of the true value of money, and the consciousness of being able, by self-denial, to contribute to the comforts of others through her own industry'.[32] The bloodier tales themselves convey explicitly wholesome morality, even if they do not do so in an acceptably moral manner for the day. The point is Knight's complaint is really about something else.

The material produced in middle-class periodicals is not always especially distinguishable in its morality or ideology, nor even in its style, from the narratives produced in Lloyd's papers. To the degree that this is true – contestable because penny literature also includes, as I will argue below using the example of *Sweeney Todd*, a good deal of gratuitous violence and startling overtures to radical politics – the emergence of the penny press simply underlines a bifurcated marketplace, and a split nation which is in itself an assertion of working-class practices in a public space. The rise of the cheap press represents a 'cultural confrontation', in part because it announces working-class economic power as a form of capital looking to expand and as a form of social currency looking to spend, a consciousness of an independent consumerist power willing to be exploited.[33] The split in reading groups would not necessarily increase class consciousness in the way that Chartist fiction attempted to do, given that so much of the cheap literature coming out of Salisbury Square barely represents a working class beyond the pitiable poor or the derisibly drunk rabble-rouser, but it does 'make' or confirm an audience as it competes for market share. It must also be remembered that Knight – and later the Howitts or Douglas Jerrold, for example – produced papers specifically for the working classes as well, attempting to make or remake an audience from roughly the same public. To the degree that the fact of the cheap press represented a symbol of cultural unification and resistance, economic independence, or marketplace competitiveness standing ground against the forces of middle-class production, it paralleled itself to a form of Chartism's 'cultural confrontation'. It is well accepted that Chartism was not simply a political movement, that it produced alternate social identities and cultural preferences as well, and that Chartist 'cultural experiences represent an important arena for class struggle'.[34] In other words, there were various avenues for cultural confrontation available in the 1840s, and if they do not always present themselves as oppositional, their separateness itself, and their size, indicates at least a point of potential opposition. Chartist and cheap presses vied for the same public that the middle-class papers of cultural harmony sought out,[35] competing against each other but cooperating or blurring into each other as well as they observed each other's successes.

Focusing on what makes the cheap press notorious (the blood), Owen Ashton, however, is very correct to point out that between the cheap and the Chartist press we have 'a real conflict of values between aspects of two plebeian cultures. On the one hand we have noted the culture of the fair, the street-life and the public hanging, which was Hogarthian, riotous and semi-pagan; on the other there was an improving culture of the sober, self-educated and politically conscious workman.'[36] If the bloods signal a cultural assertion insofar as they demonstrate a rejection of the middle-class culture of respectability, it is also then the case that they demonstrate a rejection of the Chartist claim that the working classes were respectable, could be respectable, or desired respectability, a claim especially pronounced by moral-force Chartists in the late 1830s.[37] Chartist fiction, howsoever melodramatic it became, is serious and sombre, very rarely Hogarthian, and it mostly represents working people who are or would be vote-ready if they did not have to deal with the effects of poverty, a consequence in this fiction of not having the vote. *Sweeney Todd* revels in representing the 'scampish'[38] or unworthy poor, thieves' dens and a public always ready for pugilistic confrontation; the Chartist poor are overwhelmingly 'worthy', hardworking and teetotalling when conditions are right.[39] For many Chartists, this was the real cultural confrontation. Between the two forms of cultural confrontation that the cheap press represented – the exploitation of violence that seems to fly in the face of middle-class culture or the very act of establishing autonomous cultural products – it is most directly or obviously confrontational when it implies or 'makes' a distinct audience in the image feared by the middle classes, as violent or attracted to violence. But again, this is only part of what is found in penny papers; flip the page and find the staidest, most sedate and sober morality tales you will ever want to read. At the very time when Chartists were publicly debating the value of moral force, increasingly attempting to abandon the distinction between moral and physical force, penny papers were in their own way obscuring the lines between morality and violence.[40]

Popular fiction is excessively violent and excessively moralistic, and it includes instructional or educational discourses that are frequently the bread and butter of the Chartist press. To be sure, some Chartist fiction, Reynolds's novels for example, enjoyed drifting into the street. It is improbable, however, that the simultaneous emergence of a penny literature both moral and violent and a redefinition of Chartism as something both moral and physical was part of an elaborate, coordinated strategy. The overlap was more likely the result of palpable working-class frustration over the binary construction of its identity. However, Chartism as a whole benefited from the image of a culturally uncompliant working class, and the frequently attendant image of an excitable, streetwise, unruly, angry, agentic public, whether acting independently or in a crowd. John Walton explains that for all of its constitutionalist morality, Chartism 'also had an insurrectionary mode of expression, especially at times of maximum frustration and economic hardship'.[41] He points out that 'It is not helpful to analyse the movement's activities and internal divisions solely in terms of a dichotomy between "moral force" and "physical force" because "moral force" always needed the threat of insurrection in the background to give it credibility, while "physical force" needed the legitimisation which could only be provided by the visible exhaustion of all alternative routes.'[42] Cheap fiction acts in the same way, offering an image of an impulsive, irrational, and violent public easily angered and moved to action – a boon to Chartists teasing the threat of insurrection should the Charter continue to be rejected – but also a morally sweetened public, instinctively knowing right from wrong. The popularity of the fiction itself announced that the audience enjoyed narratives of violent vengeance or justice through vigilante vengeance, such also is morality. If the cheap press primarily represented a cultural contestation and the Chartist press primarily a political contestation, the former can be understood as ensuring the chasm between radicalism and liberalism remained deep.

Again, I am not suggesting anything like a coordinated strategy between penny publishers and Chartist agitators, only that the former were aware of the ever waxing and waning popularity of the latter. A more deliberate cultural provocation on the part of the penny press was in placing among all the dull, conservative, 'proper' material the occasional *Sweeney Todd* with its occasional intimacy with the Chartist narrative or republican politics. Part of the energy of the cheap press is in its political unpredictability and ambiguity. Beyond, and even more daring than the declaration of a culture war through its mass production or its unsavoury populism, is the irregular but recurrent commitment to radical thinking – a political confrontation – whether through the simplified language of 'us against them' or something more specific. Salisbury Square fiction does not shy away from establishing the value of working-class agency, showing working people as rational decision makers even as the mob is represented as irrational power, and it frequently insists that violent rebellion is the only response to violent repression. The material is rarely political in the sense that we understand Chartist writing as deeply, directly political, but a story such as *Sweeney Todd* revolves around the problems arising when workers have no rights, when the relations of production match the political landscape. If the bloods reflect the social experiences of their working-class audiences, and if Lloyd wanted to tap into the criticisms that were making Chartism a popular movement, it would be greatly surprising if the fiction did not comment on labour relations and the relations of production, or perhaps more imprecisely, voice discontent over instrumentalism, subordination, and the forces of heteronomy. The political confrontation, however, is not political in the way that Chartist fiction is political, but constructed as part of and inseparable from the cultural confrontations.

None of this is to suggest that Chartist fiction and Salisbury Square fiction, aside from their melodramatic leanings, have sustained content in common. The greatest point of difference might be found in the consolation for suffering that penny literature nearly always provides and Chartist writers refuse in their own material. As James says, 'popular fiction cannot allow a sad ending'[43] whereas the typical Chartist story ends with piled-on suffering or death for the good, honest, working-class characters. Chartist fiction, deeply realistic, generally does not allow the problems it narrativises to be resolved, given that the political structures of the represented world are the same as the real one. Vincent points out that in penny literature, 'What was required was a form of expression which would reflect their own lives in their own circumstances, yet provide a dramatic working out of the moral dilemmas which they constantly faced. It was not enough to describe. As social relations came under increasing pressure, intractable problems had to be simplified and displaced to a realm in which there was always a resolution.'[44] This should not suggest that penny fiction is necessarily 'escapist', even if all romances by nature express an element of dissatisfaction or frustration with everyday reality. Richard Altick stresses the 'escapist' appeal of *Varney* and other gothic-related fiction from the Salisbury Square publishers: 'Life was much easier to endure when one could read, with mounting horror, of the evil deeds of werewolves and vampires, spectres and hags.'[45] But escapism hardly seems like the fitting term, and not only because politics itself might also be called escapist, in that so much of it consists of making promises for a better future. Romance, it has been noted frequently now, does not insist on disengagement; rather, it opens up the mind to new, seemingly impossible worlds. As Patrick Joyce says, 'Older, and palpably inadequate, notions of popular art and popular attitudes as "escapist", evasive or parochial' deal 'in a false polarity of protest and consolation',[46] and it is not my intention to revive that split. Rather, in the following reading of *Sweeney Todd*, I want to demonstrate just how engaged the novel is and just how amenable it allows itself to be to politically radical readings.

Sweeney Todd

Sweeney Todd is not Chartist fiction, not radical fiction: far from it. But its representation of hostile labour relations is also not just incidental to the gruesome business of making pies from human flesh. Its success may mostly have to do with its twisted violence, but it hints of public dissatisfaction with relations of production, the most personal point in which economic power becomes political and social domination. Its critique of the lack of political or social agency that is naturalised in standard conditions of employment, making the workplace ground zero in the struggle for class rights, is unorganised, sloppy, and secondary. While it insists on the same kind of class-based 'us against them' binary Chartism itself worked to establish, *Sweeney Todd* largely confines itself to representing class through employer/employee relations that speak little to politically redressing those relations, except through unorganised, personalised violence. A workplace drama that critiques contemporary practices of labour discipline, the regulating of workers in the name of a productive labour force, it refuses to go further than to exploit a working-class grievance. This is nonetheless significant, since it implies that that appeal to radical idioms, howsoever tangential, had commercial benefits. After briefly introducing the novel and surveying a number of quasi-radical readings of it, I will offer a reading of it not specifically in relation to Chartism, but in relation to the social problems the passing of the Charter was promised to address and resolve, focusing on the relations of production that dominate not just the main plotline, but the minor ones as well. Historians and literary critics have thoroughly explored the impact that industrialisation and urbanisation had on popular culture; looking at *Sweeney Todd*, I am looking at the impact radicalism had on the character of popular culture. I also compare the original serial to the longer novel in order to surmise what was deemed most successful in the initial run at capturing the appetites of the working-class audience. Finally, at the end of the chapter, I briefly discuss two other serialised fictions coming out of Lloyd's periodicals, as well as a number of shorter narratives, in order to demonstrate a pattern in the way that Lloyd's papers exploited the political.

The String of Pearls. A Romance or *Sweeney Todd* first appeared anonymously in a weekly penny paper published by Lloyd called the *People's Periodical and Family Library*. It was printed in eighteen Sunday instalments from 21 November 1846 to 29 March 1847. There is no debate over the intended audience. As Altick says, 'What Ainsworth brought to the drawing-room audience, the hacks of Salisbury Square manufactured for the tenements.'[47] Whether the novel was written by James Malcolm Rymer or Thomas Peckett Prest, or both of them, or someone else, is not for me to debate here; anonymous publication is not unusual in nineteenth-century periodicals and is in fact the standard in papers published for working people, both Chartist and Salisbury Square. The *People's Periodical* did not primarily produce bloods like *Sweeney Todd*. The magazine includes long domestic romances, short advice columns and anecdotes, numerous illustrations, and plenty that might be deemed to promote rather standard Victorian confirmations of respectability. Column-filling articles on 'Industry and Integrity' that recount the way utterly destitute boys make their way successfully through the world, not by changing the world but through, yes, industry and integrity, are not unusual.[48] The first issue, 'For the week ending October 10, 1846', includes an excerpt from *Dombey and Son*, a report on the activities of the Duke of Wellington, quips from *Punch*, and a Table of Years for helping readers figure out any day of the week in any year of the nineteenth century. If the articles surrounding the fiction reproduced in Chartist periodicals help shape the meaning of the fiction, the mostly unadventurous, uncontroversial material that surrounds *Sweeney Todd* could only return readers to dull reality. Lloyd likely crammed in his paper a mash-up of material to appeal to as diverse an audience as possible; this is also a standard Victorian aesthetic.

Following David Vincent's reading of Victorian popular culture, many interpretations of *Sweeney Todd* quite rightly focus on its most immediate social context, the way the novel represents the anxieties of urban life, though whether this participates in a form of populist agitation is another matter. Pursuing arguments made by Sally Powell, Crone suggests that 'By drawing upon a range of themes in working-class life, including changing work patterns, food adulteration, neighbourhood dislocation and urban mortality, the story of *Sweeney Todd* provides a useful window onto the fears of the urban masses.'[49] But for Crone, this does not extend into the political. She writes, 'However, the method of presentation used to tell this story, namely melodrama, meant that the overriding tone was highly conservative. Like other genres in the culture from which it emerged, its interest was not in promoting social reform but in protecting and asserting the position of popular culture in the face of competition from a potentially hegemonic respectable culture.'[50] As a story that flies in the face of polite society, *Sweeney Todd* expresses and may have produced vague social discontent, culturally disruptive exhalations against the official culture, but for anti-bourgeois populism to be meaningfully political it would seem that it must do something a bit more, even though that does not need to take the form of a clear reformist agenda.

Rohan McWilliam also situates the original serial primarily as an urban tale. Describing the social chaos that emerged out of the 'hungry forties', including Chartism, he agrees that, 'The horror fiction that filled the streets of the mid-1840s was the product of an age of anxiety.'[51] This inches closer towards the political. Chartists in the late 1830s and early 1840s were doing their best to channel the anger generated by the Corn Laws, for example, towards the Chartist cause, politicising hunger in a way that could attract supporters.[52] The gross abundance of pies in the novel reflects on industrial manufacturing practices, but it is not out of step with anxieties surrounding food shortages as well, given that the consumption of human meat is not a great alternative to hunger. When Mark Ingestrie, beginning his masquerade as Jarvis Williams, takes the job of pie-maker at Mrs Lovett's, it is because he is starving, and he eats twelve pies before he ever makes one. But again, if the author was tapping into emotions raised by the Corn Law debate, at its height when the first instalments of the serial emerged, the political content is easily lost, and not only because the typical consumers of the pies are not starving men and women, but glutinous office clerks and students of the law. Sweeney only murders the 'better-dressed' people who come into his shop (or at least, that is, when he sends Tobias away). Though the novel exploits working-class fears to some extent, the horror tends not to involve the indigent as much as it involves the 'better-dressed', except in their capacity as workers. While it is true that Tobias enjoys a pie and that 'High and low, rich and poor, resorted to it',[53] working people are often on the margins of the story, peripheral or merely working in the system to allow the middling classes to go on about their dog-eat-dog business.

As with so much of the cheap literature of the 1840s that eschews psychological complications for plot, and where ample metaphorical content is conveyed through plot, *Sweeney Todd* opens itself up to a profusion of meanings. The cumulative effect of these half-baked themes reproduces or reinforces the urban feel of the story; London in the 1840s, as with any major city today, was a place where many different things were all taking place at the same time. The other perhaps more significant cumulative effect of the multiplication of meanings is that the story allows itself to be felt as something it probably is not, a full-out politically radical confrontation, or at least a form of radical populism that could lend itself to agitational forces. Here are some of those meanings. Sharing the image of a 'repurposing' of the dead with a number of penny bloods, it has been read as commenting on the commodification of working-class bodies that so angered the poor when the Anatomy Act of 1832 was first introduced. Again, Prest or Rymer merely tease readers with this possibility: the pies are generally made with the bodies of the fairly well-to-do who go to the barber shop for a shave, not paupers. Closer to the point, then, is the way Sweeney '*smugs*' his customers, 'Uses 'em up', which is reminiscent of the way employers such as Lovett treat employees, as mere means to wealth, a product, raw material.[54] Relatedly, the story explores a shift from a world concerned with production to one preoccupied by consumption, even if it is not a complete shift as one cannot be divorced from the other. But the story comments on consumerism and the bad business practices that develop when consumer desire overwhelms production ethics and the welfare of workers are ignored in the quest for cheap, abundant pies. Equally, the story comments on the rise of advertising; from the outset we read of large yellow letters advertising Sweeney's shop. A simpler and rather common moral might be self-control, both in terms of the public's vulnerability to the consumption of pies and the seduction of advertisements. Certainly the pies distract customers from work, 'endangering – who knows to the contrary? – the success of some lawsuit thereby'.[55] The serial opens by demonstrating the seduction of the consumer, not only through the savoury smells of the pies but through Mrs Lovett's perfectly calculated flirtation with her customers. Clearly it says something about the loss of better, humane instincts (like Hector the dog has) when capitalist consumption practices are left unchecked. In Lovett's shop we see the dissolution of the family and home – a customer explains he used to eat with his uncle, but when the uncle disappeared (Sweeney's victim), he now eats at Lovett's.[56] The story also hints at the problems with the unchecked growth of capital: 'Lovett's pie manufactory'[57] is constantly expanding. Not satisfied with a shop, pies are sent in carts all over the suburbs of London to the point that more of them are sold outside of the shop than in it. It is not precisely the story of working-class body consumed by middle-class hunger, but it states that the capitalist/colonial promise of lower prices guaranteed by greater market size is a swindle. In what follows, I read the story as commenting on labour relations, but even if this qualifies as a sustained theme it should be understood in relation to all the other meanings the story generates, all the other political axes grinding away. As we will see in the fiction of G. W. M. Reynolds, the overstuffing of popular fiction creates an aggregate effect whereby generalised discontent is promoted or exploited.

Finally, as a populist story, it flippantly comments on the inability of the ruling class to rule. The author goes out of his way to illustrate that this world is full of violence, endless threats, disguise and trickery, secrets, and greed. Sweeney is motivated by 'love of money' and he blends into the world that has accepted the 'sport' of greed.[58] Tobias stumbles upon all the accumulated prizes – walking sticks, watches –[59] of Sweeney's killings: the barber is a hoarder like Jonathan Wild, suggesting the deep pathology behind capitalism's need to maximise. The modern world is antagonistic at every level, everyone is cheating everyone else; young lawyers are learning the trade not only in the Temple but on the streets as well. Employers and employees are scheming against each other; producers and consumers are at each others throats; husbands and wives are natural enemies; British sailors battle 'natives'. Violence is everywhere – urban, domestic, workplace, colonial. At some level this is simply the overloading of plot to make the resolution grander. In another way, the exaggerated rottenness of the world implies that reform is not a solution, that the problem is deep and demands radical responses. Except, of course, resolution happens without a radical response or even reform.

Set in 1785, the story begins by noting that barbers 'of the old school'[60] like Todd, and unlike the barbers circa 1847 when the novel was written, were apolitical. As Kathryn Hughes confirms, Victorian barbers had a reputation for radical politics,[61] splendidly configured in Thomas Cooper's 1845 short story, 'Kucky Sarson, the barber; or, the disciple of equality', where Kucky shouts out his opinions to clients nervously aware that he wields a razor in his hand, even though the barber himself is unconscious of his violently threatening position. Does Todd's political neutrality tell readers that *The String of Pearls* is not going to be political? Is the implication that the violent Todd would be a radical in 1847? Or is his rejection of the political intended to establish his self-interest, that he is a party of one? He is also described from the outset as freakish looking and 'considering his trade, there never was seen such a head of hair'.[62] Before readers find out that he is a murderer who robs clients of their walking sticks and jewellery, or learn about his underground operations, they learn that he 'did a most thriving business' and is 'evidently a thriving man'.[63] His success is only partly attributed to advertising (the 'extremely corpulent yellow letters over his shop window'),[64] and if the point is that people should know better than to visit a barber with 'such a head of hair', a Bluebeardian moral, it pales in comparison to the threat of urban randomness in the novel: Sweeney's random clients, the random violence, the random ingredients in the pies, the random employment (Ingestrie stumbles on his appointment), and so on.

However, the introduction of Sweeney's apprentice, Tobias Ragg, brings something much more predictable and familiar. The abusive relationship between the employer and employee is explained at length in the first chapter; like Jack Sheppard, Tobias is essentially indentured, though without any overtones of a paternal bond: 'you will remember, Tobias Ragg, that you are now my apprentice, that you have of me had board, washing, and lodging, with the exception that you don't sleep here, that you take your meals at home, and that your mother, Mrs. Ragg, does your washing'.[65] Todd makes a mockery of indenture, but he also has successfully expanded its definition to go beyond the legal binding by contract of an individual to work for a specified period of time so as to include anyone who is bound to work for another because of any agreed to arrangement. Tobias is a modern-day 'slave' bound to Todd because if he leaves Todd promises to have his mother punished for a crime that he has told Tobias she committed. Remarkably, after Todd horribly beats up Tobias, still in the first chapter, old Mr Grant from the Temple, Mark Ingestrie's uncle, replies to Todd's confession that he was teaching 'my new apprentice a little bit of his business', by merely remarking that 'I know what it is to let young folks grow wild.'[66] Todd is a violent criminal, but Grant, a lawyer who had wanted his nephew to follow in his footsteps, accepts and helps normalise the employer's use of violence. Grant, and not only Todd, acts as if an employer's authority has no bounds.

Todd had beaten up Tobias because the boy had corrected Todd in front of Mr Grant, pointing out that they *had* had a customer lately. As we see later with Mrs Lovett and Mr Fogg, the madhouse man, employers demand that their employees turn a blind eye to their practices. Todd tells Tobias, 'I'll cut your throat from ear to ear, it you repeat one word of what passes in this shop, or dare to make any supposition, or draw any conclusion from anything you may see, or hear, or fancy you see or hear.'[67] The passage was used on the frontispiece when the book was rereleased in 1850. Beyond the violence that Todd accepts is the prerogative of the employer, endowed by virtue of the employer/employee relationship, is the insistence on a vertical division of labour, not unlike Ruskin's division of the workplace into masters doing the brainwork and workmen doing the handwork. The novel exaggerates the way employers carefully restrict employees from knowing how the business operates, an exaggeration of Marxian alienation that lays bare the relationship between knowledge and power, and recognises that knowledge is a form of capital under capitalism. When Sweeney advertises for a new 'lad', after having disposed of Tobias in the madhouse, he states his preference for 'One of strict religious principles' because 'They are much easier managed, for the imagination in such cases has been cultivated at the expense of the understanding.'[68] Mrs Lovett also keeps her cooks ignorant of the intricacies of the production process. Of course, *Sweeney Todd* dramatises not only the horrible consequences of 'not knowing' but additionally the relationship between the forced ignorance of the worker and the degraded product or service.

Sally Powell has written of the way that Lovett's bakers are imprisoned in their place of employment, used up, and alienated from the product of their work. The novel gives us a very Marxian description of the production process: the better the equipment, the more 'miserable' the worker. It also narrativises the Marxian concepts of 'commodity fetishism' in the consumption of pies and in Sweeney's hoarding, and of 'false consciousness' insofar as we see both Jarvis and Tobias struggling to recognise the true nature of their employment. Mostly, the personal interactions between employer and employee replicate the relations of domination that employees accept because they are employees. Relations of production or the social relations of production are what Marx thought of as the 'real foundation' or economic structure of society, the way that economic relations extend beyond workplace or production relations. The definition Marx supplied has been rightly critiqued as economistic and deterministic, but I use it here simply to underline the vast implications of representing employers who assume that workplace dominance justifies complete dominance over their employees:

> In the social production of their life, men enter into definite relations that are indispensable and independent of their will, relations of production which correspond to a definite stage of development of their material productive forces. The sum total of these relations of production constitutes the economic structure, the real foundation on which rises a legal and political superstructure and to which correspond definite forms of social consciousness.[69]

Though it represents a world largely organised around the economic, production and consumption, claiming that *Sweeney Todd* exposes the relationship between the economic base and the superstructure would go too far. The novel represents relations of production only at the level of employer/employee relations, novels as a whole tending toward personalised microcosms of social theory. But by representing the ideological control that Lovett and Todd assume they have over their employees, the novel not only locates social class as originating in work relations, it echoes the Chartist mantra of 'slavery in England' or 'white slaves'. Reproducing material from the *Savage*, the *Chartist Circular*, for example, asks, 'What injustice is discoverable in the conduct of the southern planter, which is also not found in the practices of the northern farmer?'[70] or claims 'The laws and the progress of civilisation have made the indigent labourer a slave to every man in the possession of riches ... and his reward is the reward of every other slave – subsistence. The situation of the white slave is often more unfortunate than that of the black.'[71] For some Chartists, as in *Sweeney Todd*, the devastating consequences of employment are as bad, if not worse, than unemployment.

Todd is testing the amount of power the relations of production grant him when he tells Tobias that 'You may think what you like, Tobias Ragg, but you shall say only what I like.'[72] Understanding his boss's threats, Tobias thinks to himself, 'I will say nothing – I will think nothing.'[73] Demanding of his employees 'a wholesome fear of me',[74] Sweeney blatantly attempts to reproduce a master/slave relationship, and is largely successful.[75] Knowing Sweeney is a murderer, Tobias stays silent because of Sweeney's threats against his mother. Martyred, he reproduces the role of the poor in Chartist fiction, where sacrificing oneself for a vulnerable family member is commonplace. But his relationship with Sweeney is marked by the employer's fetish for total domination, perversely requiring Tobias, for example, to look 'cheerful' even in the barber's absence. He repeats his desire to hire only 'boys of a religious turn' so as to master and dominate them more easily.'[76] When Johanna, dressed as a boy, takes the position, he threatens her as well if she 'presume[s] to listen to what I say!'[77] Once more, the radicalism of the novel, its insistence on divesting authority and empowering the disenfranchised, can and should be tested. It is possible to read that the novel imagines the alternative to a master/slave relation as a master/dog relation. The relationships between employers and employees are without any of the loyalty and devotion that man and dog share for each other: the loyalty and devotion that Hector has for his missing owner, Thornhill, is made to contrast Sweeney's relationship with Tobias. The 'mutual ill-will'[78] between Hector and Sweeney, and Sweeney's attempt to kill the canine, suggests that the new form of worker/employer relationship is to be antagonistic, but the paternalistic, Carlylean alternative is at best radical conservatism. However, its proximity to the radical message, and even its mutation of that message, can be understood as a sign that the author knew of radicalism's commercial value.

As an employer, Lovett is also a tyrant, establishing an unmistakable pattern of workplace abuse that resembles captivity more than 'employment'. She insists on controlling every aspect of Jarvis's life, reducing his existence to his employment where she is always his superior. Knowing he has no money, she echoes Sweeney's mockery of indenture, saying, 'remember that you have to live entirely upon the pies, unless you like to purchase for yourself anything else, which you may do if you get the money. We give none, and you must likewise agree never to leave the bakehouse.'[79] That the terms of the relationship between employer and employed are solely the privilege of the employer is something even Jarvis recognises, promising to be subservient as an employee: 'My poverty and my destitution consent, if my will be adverse.'[80] He realises that he has to allow Lovett to set all the conditions of employment because working is a 'price paid for his continued existence'.[81] But Jarvis thinks he can maintain something approximating autonomy insofar as he can quit his job: 'if I should feel dissatisfied with my situation, I will leave it and no harm done'.[82] Of course the story demonstrates that he is wrong here, that the assumption that workers might have that they can be independent of the relations of production, independent of need or independent of the capitalist system, is a fraud (Lovett promises that the position can be terminated, but not in the way Jarvis imagines). As long as he makes pies, he will be allowed to live, reasons Lovett, and that should satisfy him. When Mark Ingestrie first comes to ask for employment, losing his name in the process and becoming Jarvis Williams, Lovett tells him to 'Go away, we never give to beggars.'[83] She then thinks twice because the current pie-maker had 'grown insolent, and fancies himself master of the place'.[84] That baker then becomes part of the product he once produced in a strikingly clear if ghastly expression of surplus value, or a macabre reversal of alienation (the baker is not alienated from the product he produces, he becomes it), or simply being worked to the bone. Jarvis Williams himself explains that he was once Lovett's frequent customer and would receive his fair share of flirtatious smiles from her, but when the consumer becomes the producer the latter can expect to be reduced to his or her function. This is part and parcel of the same system, for the novel makes clear that Lovett treats both the consumer and producer in terms of her own self-interest.

For Jarvis, 'At first everything was delightful.'[85] Interestingly, he only recognises his workplace as a prison when he is full of pies, suggesting hunger stupefies; and then he understands his position even better – that he 'is condemned to such a slavery'[86] – when he reads a note from the previous baker, suggesting that a full working-class consciousness is a collective process. Jarvis is not born of the working classes and only finds himself working as a cook because of his misadventures at sea. But he becomes working class when forced to capitulate to the relations of production, standing in for working people, or at least in the way the working classes were commonly represented, insofar as he expresses an instinctive desire to define himself outside the role of producer/consumer, saying he needs more than work and pies (Jarvis's predecessor wanted to return to nature).[87] Jarvis thinks his lowered class status should end at the end of the day, but Lovett knows that the workday, as well as the subordination and dependence it symbolises, only ends with her employee sinking gruesomely deeper into his work. Lovett nonetheless complains that he is most 'troublesome' because he is well educated.[88] When he then 'defies' her – he prepares for a violent confrontation to earn his 'freedom' – he is energised by drinking porter. The drink is emphasised as enabling his 'grand effort at freedom': 'This is nectar for the gods. Oh, what a relief, to be sure. It puts new life into me.'[89] Though Chartists tended towards temperance, British working people have a long history of politicising themselves over beer, from the Malt Tax Riots of 1725 and 1806 to William Cobbett's association of home-brewing with plebeian independence. Through Jarvis, the author signals an allegiance with a folk tradition that implies more than just a cultural war, for the porter emboldens Jarvis to physically confront his boss and adversary.

Other employers and employees are constantly at odds in the novel as well. Overturning a case of spectacles, Sam Bolt, Mr Oakley's shopboy, says, 'I'll try the old dodge whenever I break anything; that is, I'll place it in old Oakley's way, and swear he did it. I never knew such an old goose; you may persuade him into anything; the idea, now, of his pulling down all the shutters this morning because I told him my aunt had the toothache; that was a go, to be sure.'[90] Sam seeks 'revenge' because he thinks Mr Oakley is frustrating a potential relationship with Johanna, but this undeveloped plotline also helps establish the nature of labour relations. Mr Fogg, who runs the madhouse that incarcerates Tobias, and his employee, Mr Watson, are also hostile to each other.[91] Though I argue that bad labour relations are used to exploit the working-class mood in the way that Chartists had constructed it, one might also conclude that *Sweeney Todd* comments on Lloyd himself as an employer hiring and using up 'hacks' to anonymously produce mass amounts of consumable fiction. James notes that Lloyd either paid his contributors a meagre fee or, when possible, none at all.[92] Rymer had financial difficulties in the late 1840s and went bankrupt midway during the writing of the serial.[93] If Rymer or Prest engage in this line of criticism, it is done lightly, as there is not much in the novel that is told without some level of jocularity, from the names – Ingestrie – to Mr Oakley owning a spectacle store but not seeing the chaos that surrounds him.

Whatever political content *Sweeney Todd* includes to attract a politicised audience, or an audience ready to be provoked by class-based political matters, it is not pursued consistently. Jarvis voices working-class grievances by saying, 'I cannot be made into a mere machine for the manufacture of pies. I cannot, and will not endure it.'[94] Though this sounds very rebellious, just earlier we read that 'human nature is prone to be discontented',[95] confusing the motivation for his rebellion by making it sound as if he suffers from a victimisation complex. He of course is a true victim, but the novel constantly distracts from its would-be radicalism. The story of Mr and Mrs Oakley and their violent power struggle diverts from the power struggle between employers and employees. Mostly serving as comic relief, when Mr Oakley teams up with Big Ben the beefeater to assert his 'rights'[96] in the Oakleys' marital relationship, with the novel implying that the struggle for power is the result of the wife's natural deviousness (she pretends to poison Mr Oakley and Ben), the dog-eat-dog world is seen operating outside of employer/employee relations, naturalising conflict between perceived opposites. Equally, when Sweeney is repeatedly called something along the lines of 'the arch enemy of all mankind',[97] the novel is depoliticised as he becomes simply evil incarnate, an inexplicable serial killer, not a representative employer. The story at intervals expresses the exact opposite of what one might expect from a radical publication. Speaking on the British navy, the narrator engages in a species of nationalistic flag-waving that belies the corruption that seems so ubiquitous on British soil: 'no other nation has ever attempted to achieve a great maritime existence without being most signally defeated, and leaving us still, as we shall ever be, masters of the seas'.[98] In the hands of a Chartist writing about the British navy in 1785, surely the emphasis would be on impressment or flogging. Earlier in the story the narrator pokes fun at the beadle of St Dunstan's Church for attending a mechanics' institute, 'where he learned something of everything but what was calculated to be of some service to him'.[99] In this way the novel frequently winks to its primary audience, mocking the educationalist ambitions and seriousness not only of middle-class reformism, but of Chartism as well; Chartism was, after all, as serious as any Victorian expression of the compulsory seriousness of character. In this way the novel subtly assumes, rightly or wrongly, it also knows the essential conservatism of it audience, saying '*we* know there is actually only one way to get ahead – cheat, lie, steal, deceive'. Morality is so middle class, and Chartist.

The 1850 novel

The success of the serialised story led to an immediate remake that is roughly three times the length of the original.[100] Much of what is added – such as numerous long chase scenes – does not act to advance the main plot or themes, and might be described simply as 'action', though comedic 'B-plots', violent encounters, and secondary romances augment the original as well. The added material was clearly written to satisfy a branded taste, an attempt to reproduce the kind of action that led to the initial success of the original serial. Significantly, the later 1850 novel includes more direct and explicit condemnations of bad labour practices. For example, the first chapter that differs from the periodical, Chapter 30,[101] begins with the following:

> THERE are folks who can and who will bow like reeds to the decrees of evil fortune, and with a patient, ass-like placidity, go on bearing the ruffles of a thankless world without complaining, but Mrs. Lovett's new cook was not one of those. The more destiny seemed to say to him – 'Be quiet!' the more he writhed, and wriggled, and fumed, and could not be quiet. The more fate whispered in his ears – 'You can do nothing' the more intent he was upon doing something, let it be what it might. And he had a little something, in the shape of a respite too, now, for had he not baked a batch of pies, and sent them up to the devouring fangs of the lawyers' clerks in all their gelatinous beauty and gushing sweetness, to be devoured. To be sure he had, and therefore having, for a space, obeyed the behests of his task-mistress, he could sit with his head resting upon his hands and think. 'Thought! What a luxury! Where is the Indian satrap – where the arch Inquisitor – where

the grasping, dishonest, scheming employer who can stop a man from thinking? – and as Shakespeare, says of sleep,

> 'From that sleep, what dreams may come?'
> so might he have said of thought,
> From that thought what acts may come?'

Now we are afraid that, in the first place, the cook, in spite of himself, uttered some expression concerning Mrs. Lovett of neither an evangelical or a polite character, and with these we need not trouble the reader. They acted as a sort of safety-valve to his feelings, and after consigning that fascinating female to a certain warm place, where we may fancy everybody's pie might be cooked on the very shortest notice, he got a little more calm.

'What shall I do? what shall I do?'[102]

The chapter then proceeds to describe Jarvis's failed attempt to break out of his place of employment by including a note about his imprisonment with the pies, only to have Sweeney intercept it. The scene does not advance the plot, but it does suggest that the image of the disgruntled worker plotting escape and revenge was thought to build identification and attract readers.

The extended novel especially plays up the antagonism in relations between Jarvis and Lovett. His insubordination and defiance of her assumed superiority is sharper here than in the serial, as he frequently talks to her as if he were her superior: 'Again there was that tone of sarcasm about the cook's voice, which created a doubt in the mind of Mrs. Lovett if, after all, he was not merely playing with her, and in his heart utterly disregarding all that she said to him.'[103] Lovett herself is cast as if she were Sweeney's employee, saying at one point that 'I have sold my soul to you, but I have not bartered myself.'[104] On occasion, passages from the longer novel are more directly critical of English society than the serial, such as when Johanna, dressed as a boy, is described as destitute:

> The crowd in that dense thoroughfare passed on, and no one took heed of the seeming boy as he wept and sobbed in that doorway. Some had no time to waste upon the sorrows of other people; – some buttoned up their pockets as though they feared that the tears that stood upon that pale face were but the preludes to some

pecuniary demand; – others again passed on rapidly, for they were so comfortable and cosy that they really could not have their feelings lacerated by any tale of misery, not they. And so Johanna wept alone.[105]

However, it is difficult to say that the 1850 text defies the established social order more than the original serial, as so much clear filler – love affairs between Tobias and Minna Gray or between Arabella Wilmot and Colonel Jeffrey – has a depoliticising effect. By 1850, after the Kennington Common demonstration of 1848, Chartism had suffered its greatest embarrassment with its last petition to parliament including so many forgeries, making the demonstration seem more merely carnivalesque than forthrightly political, as sketches from *Punch* capture and celebrate. The crowd in the 1850 novel plays a much bigger role than in the original serial, either seeking justice or social revenge, but as with so many other representations of crowds from the period, it acts recklessly. The first crowd that forms serves to protect Hector the dog from the murderous Sweeney, after the canine is initially saved by an ostler and a butcher's boy: 'The people took the part of the dog and his new master, and it was in vain that Sweeney Todd exhibited his rent garments to show where he had been attacked by the animal. Shouts of laughter and various satirical allusions to his beauty were the only response.'[106] But later the crowd is depicted as viciously animalistic in its attempt to seek justice: 'the people that were in the shop have spread the news all over the neighbourhood, and the place is getting jammed up with a mob, every one of which is mad, I think, for they talk of nothing but of the tearing of Mrs. Lovett to pieces. They are pouring in from Fleet Street and Carey Street by hundreds at a time.'[107] Though the mob has every right to its anger, its irrationality, foolishness, and instinct towards violence is censured. Ingestrie places faith in the law, a career he had once rejected: 'I will go with you, and implore the people to let the law take its course upon this woman.'[108]

The image of the mob is central to a good deal of cheap fiction and so it is not surprising that the novel is extended in this way. In *Varney, the Vampire*, the mob functions as one of the main characters. However, especially after 1848, the addition of an unruly mob that is nonetheless justified in its anger underlines the political ambiguity of the long novel and certainly an ambivalent attitude towards popular justice. Images of a villain such as Sweeney or Mrs Lovett being pursued might hint at communal solidarity, communal instincts, and popular justice, but when the crowd 'speaks' as if only semi-literate, when it is drunk and reckless, and easily riled up by a sort of plebeian demagoguery, the message is clear. The mob also does not catch Lovett and later is equally hopeless in its attempt to capture Sweeney, just as the mob in *Varney, the Vampire* fails miserably in its attempts to capture the vampire or, as in *Ada, the Betrayed*, is ineffective in catching the villains therein, all of which renders *Jack Sheppard*'s final procession scene even more remarkable. What Edward Jacobs argues in the context of cheap periodical crime reporting is as true in the fiction produced by the same press: 'the cheap Sunday papers published by Edward Lloyd during the 1840s artfully manipulated and intensified the standard narrative conventions of Victorian crime reporting by dramatising the legal system as a paradigmatic instance of the tension between the practical need of the British people to be institutionally governed and their cherished belief in the right to evade institutional discipline and to live "free-born."'[109] Representing a rioting crowd expresses both dissatisfaction with having to wait for justice and defiance of the state's systems of order and control, but representing the failure of the crowd, especially after Kennington Common, casts doubt over the ability of the people to act on its own.

Varney, *Ada*, and the Salisbury short story

Troy Boone argues that James Malcolm Rymer's *Varney, The Vampire* 'seeks to forge agreement, among working-class readers, regarding the value of sustained but moderate political agitation' by raising readerly interest in violence only to shift attention to something else, thereby demonstrating 'that power is gained specifically by not carrying out the bloodshed of which one is capable'.[110] *Varney* was serialised between 1840 and 1842 before Lloyd published it in book form in 1847. It is an incredibly sprawling text, and by the third volume Rymer is trying out every staple in the repository of cheap fiction at a truly torrid pace. As the chapters become increasingly shorter we move from a forced marriage plot to a Jack Sheppard break-in, to murder, to more loveless marriage, more murders, 'Count Pollidori's palace', gothic monks, shipwrecks, bandits, highwaymen, even a vampire blood orgy. The themes of the novel become as difficult to follow as the plots. In one chapter Varney impresses by giving alms to a poor woman whose son was press-ganged. Moments later he is a common murderer. Boone's reading of the novel is based on the action in the first two volumes, where there is a sustained representation of the crowd. Boone reads the crowd as provoking the audience to contemplate 'excessive agitation' and to choose 'moderate agitation' after witnessing a mob so base, vile, and comically vicious as imaginable, thereby allowing working-class readers 'to maintain a critical distance'[111] from it. Boone's reading is convincing, especially as it situates cheap fiction in the debate over moral and physical force Chartism.

More generally, the novel warns against 'the wildest vicissitudes of passion'.[112] Though the message to working people might be to increase their power through slower, 'cooler' ways, it is nonetheless a very middle-class message. Representing 'the populace, or, perhaps, the townspeople, [as] extremely pugnacious',[113] undermines the basic fact that Chartism was not an individual's movement but a popular one. Rymer is blunt:

> This was a mob's proceeding all over, and we regret very much to say, that it is very much the characteristic of English mobs. What an uncommonly strange thing it is that people in multitudes seem completely to get rid of all reason – all honour – all common ordinary honesty; while if you were to take the same people singly, you would find that they were reasonable enough, and would shrink with a feeling quite approaching to horror from anything in the shape of very flagrant injustice.[114]

Varney is not a book to be read aloud, and in this passage one can see both a rejection of Chartism and an appeal to individual members of the Chartist audience. Though the descriptions of riots read as if Rymer was well versed in middle-class accounts of the Newport Rising, it is not necessarily anti-radical. The sensible 'Mr Leigh' fails to grab the attention of the crowd,[115] suggesting that working people had to pay closer attention to the true leadership provided by, say, Leigh Hunt. Rymer refers to 'the misguided, or rather the not guided at all populace', but by constantly referring to 'the superstitious fury of the populace'[116] he rather cleverly muddies the narrator's superior attitude towards the crowd. Varney *is* a vampire, and though he is often drawn sympathetically, the mob's instincts are not unjustified. Though it seems Louis James is correct to say that Rymer's 'ambition was to be a middle-class writer',[117] he surely was not writing for a middle-class audience, and *Varney* thus appeals to both popular reading and disparages it, something that James and Boone note as well. Rymer overuses the word 'popular', especially when describing the riotous crowd: 'popular disease', 'popular tumult', 'popular riot', 'popular resentment', 'popular feeling' (twice), 'popular violence', 'popular mind', 'popular vengeance', 'popular education', and 'popular superstition'.[118] After describing the furious savageness of the mob, he states 'but such is popularity'.[119] Rymer's suspicion of the popular, while playing a role in the creation of a popular press, is emblematic of his ambiguous relation to radical discourse and radical thought, as a sense of what the populace wants competes with a rather stuffier sense of what it needs.

Rymer's clear unease with the popular movement of the day does not prevent him from randomly espousing the language of the popular cause. Calling 'a rich man' a 'nabob',[120] the narrator comments:

> It is astonishing, as a general rule, what people will submit to when it comes from those who have riches at command. That fact alone seems to stamp all that is foolish and absurd, coming from such a quarter, with sense and worth.
>
> It is in vain for any one not blessed with property to talk; his talking is nothing in comparison with what falls from the lips of the man who has property. You are talked down, and if you are obstinate, and won't be talked down, why, you are a disagreeable fellow, a dissatisfied man, and your neighbours ought to set their faces against you.
>
> Thus, through life, he who does not submit to the wealthy, is always run down, and there is every disposition, if possible, of running him off the road altogether, no matter how great the injustice against him, and the enormity of the conduct of others; they are, as

they think, justified, because he is not a genteel person; in fact, he is not evangelical.[121]

John Springhall is correct to ask if the 'frequent recourse to the antiquated figure of the corrupt and dissolute aristocrat', such as Varney, 'reinforce[s] rather than subvert[s] existing social and political structures'.[122] But popular writing is not experimental beyond its inclination to conflate genres; it taps into a generic zeitgeist, into successful literary tropes and forms, and aristocratic villains are a standard trope likely because the middle classes had a hardened reputation for being too dull for good villainy. Yet it is important to attend to the specific content of popular fiction such as *Varney*. '[T]hose who have riches at command', 'blessed with property to talk', who are 'genteel' and 'evangelical', are not the Varneys of the world, an 'anti-hero' according to James,[123] but the respectable bourgeoisie apparently still puffing over their acceptance to full citizenry in 1832. In no way does *Varney, the Vampire* develop or sustain this language, but in the very intermittent, random use of working-class politics we see the same thing as when we see the tired aristocrat, a crowd-pulling enticement to a familiar talking point.

Rohan McWilliam wisely reminds us that 'When the relationship between liberalism and popular culture has been discussed, it has usually been in terms of the rupture between respectable, nonconformist, and pro-temperance liberalism and the bawdiness of popular life with its fondness for beer and flag waving, a divide that afforded the Tories a point of entry into the world of demos. Yet liberalism did have a purchase on popular culture.'[124] What distinguishes Rymer's critique of middle-class snobbery from the self-critical middle-class critique of the same – it is far from absent in the Victorian 'canon' – is that Rymer's smear is *not* part of a reformist strategy, not a humanitarian effort to correct a classist fault but merely a minor ploy to touch base with the readership. Another of his serialised novels, *Ada, the Betrayed, or, The Murder at the Old Smithy*, also successful,[125] engages in the same type of identification strategy. It was first serialised in *Lloyd's Penny Weekly Miscellany* in 1843, divided into fifty-six parts. The most interesting aspect of this story is that it includes three distinct villains, Jacob Grey, Squire Learmont, and Andrew Britton, who roughly represent the middle, upper, and lower classes. Not only are they all rather horrible to the young Ada, concealing her identity and inheritance, and always seemingly on the verge of murdering her, but they are constantly plotting against each other as well. They are also in cahoots with each other: the suggestively named Britton, a blacksmith, murders Ada's father under direction from her uncle, Learmont, while Gray witnesses the crime and keeps it concealed by bribing Learmont, which Britton does as well. Its politics are hardly Jacobin, though like *Varney* it sporadically includes scenes or statements that belie the ostensible theme that villainy knows no class (our heroes are also drawn from across the social spectrum). Late in the novel, for example, Sir Francis, who helps Ada and her true love Albert find justice and each other, visits the Home Secretary and tells him that Learmont is a murderer. The sudden politicisation of the scene is surprising: "'Dear me,' said the Secretary, 'he [Learmont] might as well have waited till the general election was over. It is really such a very awkward thing to hang a man who can command several votes in the commons.'" At this point the Secretary convinces Francis to put off arresting Learmont until Learmont's upcoming ball is over, and then concludes by saying:

> 'By the by, I quite forgot to ask you who he had murdered. It's nobody of any consequence I presume?' 'He certainly had no vote.' 'No vote?' 'No, nor was likely ever to have one.' 'Indeed. Well I do hate people who have no vote most cordially, and I should say there can be only one class of people more abominable, and that is the class which votes against one. I don't at all see the use in this world of people without votes. How uncommonly silly Learmont must have been really.'[126]

The novel does not have a radical or reformist agenda; the scene is gratuitous, secondary, included it appears for a sort of working-class inside joke acknowledging the reading public, declaring identification, and offering something to satisfy the prejudices of the audience. There are not many moments in the novel that do this, but Rymer does go far out of his way, for example, to explain Britton's malice, his immorality or Godlessness, in terms of class: "'Recollect you forced me to it. What was I? The smith of Learmont. I toiled day and night; and they called me 'a savage', and why? because I was in your toils – I did a piece of work for you that –" "Hush! hush!" gasped Learmont. "Oh, you are delicate, and don't like it mentioned. I am not so nice – I murdered for you, squire, and you know it. What was my reward? Toil – toil – and you know that too."'[127] A Dickens or a Gaskell might do something similar, but generally as part of a deep humanitarian effort to forward a programme of reform. That's clearly not Rymer's objective. His appeal to working-class identity or politics works, disturbingly, exactly like his anti-Semitism or family-value conservatism, to satisfy an assumed market.

Noting the 'sickly sentimentality' of *Ada*, and also its enormous success, Thomas Frost states its 'moral tone' was 'unexceptional', meaning virtue is rewarded and vice punished.[128] *Ada* typifies the Salisbury School of writing by dwelling on vulnerability or the victimisation of the helpless, nearly always a woman. Women here generally represent a lack of agency: beautiful daughters are usually the victims, often forced into loveless marriages, such as in the very gothic, 'The old monastery; or, the deed of blood',[129] and fathers, brothers, or potential husbands have to rescue them. In 'Janet; or, the persecuted', a young woman is hounded, kidnapped by an ardent admirer, and would have fallen victim to him had her true lover not returned in the nick of time to rescue her from a horrible marriage by giving her 'a natural and legal protection'.[130] 'The Abduction' features the Lord of Ellerby Castle, a 'bad man' who, because of his 'violent passion', a standard motivator in these stories, abducts a young, helpless, destitute woman named Mary, but is caught and killed in the ensuing struggle, Mary marrying her rescuer, a soldier.[131] The inherently conservative material is not anti-radical because it is insipidly traditionalist. Chartists at the time also represented women as weak and vulnerable, largely in order to insist that men be empowered – given the franchise – so as to rescue the helpless damsels. It is unlikely that Salisbury had a similar strategy, but it is tantalising to consider that the helpless woman may have been thought to represent more than simply the natural position of women, but of the disenfranchised as well. 'Mary Evans; or, the maniac mother' concerns 'the daughter of the people of limited means' who becomes a fallen woman owing to the treachery of a 'gentleman' who had been her rescuer from a 'ruffian'.[132] The story seems to demonstrate that the 'ruffian' and the 'gentleman' have different ways of seeking the same ends, implying that Mary has to get herself empowered. Even in *Sweeney Todd*, Johanna, mostly involved in a romance plot, dresses as a man to get employment with Sweeney in order to find out more about the shop and her lover. A woman and an employee, she is doubly without agency, but recognising that the only way to advance her interests, as they are, is to go on a gender-bender is to expose that passively accepting a subordinate social position is for both the woman and the employee tantamount to failure. The furthest away from full citizenship, Johanna attempts to have some agentic effect. She rarely adds to the political content of the serial or the longer novel, but her attempt to take matters into her own hands at least exposes the frustration both women and employees feel by being rendered helpless. Chapter 30 of the serial includes an interpolated story titled 'The madwoman's tale'. It is 'a catalogue of wrongs'[133] – 'wrongs', as in 'Woman's Wrongs', was a word used frequently by radicals from Mary Wollstonecraft to Charlotte Elizabeth Tonna to Ernest Jones – experienced by a girl abused by her parents, who want her dead so as to have the girl's inheritance. The servants are generally kind to her but have to treat her harshly because of the parents' orders. She suffers the same fate as Tobias and one symbolically experienced by Jarvis, the two main workers in *Sweeney Todd*: she is thrown into a madhouse. The madhouse is a common destination for innocent victims in cheap periodical fiction, feeding off and feeding into the idea that accepting one's powerlessness is a sort of madness.

The short fiction appearing in Lloyd's periodicals, taken as a whole, parallels the political ambiguity of the longer, serialised novels, significant insofar as the anonymous authors of the short fiction were frequently working people, not professional 'hacks', and likely the very consumers of the papers in which they were attempting to publish. 'The highway robbery; or, the first crime' is very much like a Chartist story of the broken artisan, such as 'Will Harper'. A respectable, family-loving, pleasant farmer, Mortimer, suffers a bad crop and bad luck, at which point the callous landlord evicts him and his family. Ruined, he cannot keep work as a labourer, so to keep his family from starving he robs a coach.

Condemned, he dies in jail of a broken heart.[134] 'William and Mary Ann; or, the press gang' by Thomas William Allen also reads exactly like a Chartist story. Here an industrious, working-class man is press-ganged, dies in battle, and then his betrothed dies as if from his absence.[135] This is very similar to the stories in the Chartist press, from the shortness of the story, to representing an issue such as impressment that was fundamentally class-oriented, to the horrible death-filled conclusion, as if to suggest that the resolution to working-class issues needs to be extratextual. It is unlikely that Lloyd saw this material as 'political', however, saying in his correspondence to 'An Unitarian – We never insert articles relative to religion, or politics.'[136] Some of the short fiction, such as 'The contrast: or, the gentleman and the itinerant' is as anti-Chartist as imaginable. A man born poor, but who raises himself to a position of wealth and power through ambition and effort, is not as happy as an itinerant tinker because the latter has a 'contented disposition'.[137] 'The soldier and his wife' is another example where the moral works against the typical moral of Chartist fiction. It is simply about the rotten luck some have; full of affect, a soldier and his wife are separated and both die.[138] As mentioned at the outset of this chapter, a good deal of the short fiction in Lloyd's papers can be morally sentimental and socially conservative. Finally, 'The double murder' about a nasty well-to-do couple who have affairs before murdering or being murdered, even murdering an infant, has no ostensible working-class message, except insofar as it anticipates the sensation novel rather closely by locating the heinous crimes and 'vice' in the homes of the wealthy.[139]

Still, it is important to note before ending this chapter that short stories are essential to Lloyd's periodicals, for they allowed the working-class audience a chance to publish and, perhaps more significantly, to define through production and not just consumption the cultural confrontation. Lloyd's papers were not a vanity press, but they approached something like reader-based fiction. We do not know much about the writers of the short fiction, except that there were a lot of them, and they seem to be the same people who constituted the readership of the papers. Lloyd does not hide how he operated, including a section on the back page of every issue of *Lloyd's Penny Weekly* which stories he will accept for future publication and which he will not. The 'Notice to Correspondents' usually begins with a statement explaining that 'All communications addressed (post paid) to the Editor, shall receive immediate attention', and then a list of 'accepted' and 'declined' stories. Accepted stories were accepted for any one of Lloyd's publications, such as the *Penny Sunday Times* or *Lloyd's Penny Atlas*. At one point Lloyd explains to a contributor that he had mislaid the contribution, but having found it, 'if the author will write a word as to which paper he would prefer its publication in, it shall be immediately attended to'.[140] Including 'notices to correspondents' was common in the periodicals in the 1840s, and can be found for example in a wide range of papers, from *Politics for the People* to *Reynolds's Weekly Newspaper*, Reynolds being Lloyd's main competitor.[141] The notices are remarkable ephemera in that they paint half a picture of how close Lloyd was to his readership, how 'writerly' the paper was. Addressing 'Nobody', who frequently writes in, Lloyd says only, 'Nobody. – They are';[142] to 'A Constant Reader' he says, 'We cannot say.'[143] We do not have, as far as I know, the initiating letters, but the conversational, immediate, public way of doing business cannot be lost. Lloyd is direct and often flip: to '"Titmouse." – We would advise you to learn to spell before you attempt to write a "Romance".'[144] Lloyd also conducted a wide variety of business with the 'correspondences', including, apparently, hiring: 'J. W. S. – We are not in want of a person in that capacity at present.'[145]

The shorter stories would also allow readers who could not afford to buy every weekly issue some satisfaction from a complete text in a single issue; the serialised stories are impossibly long and they often read as if to allow readers to skip an issue, but they are time-consuming in a way that the shorter stories are not. Short fiction was also very popular with the audience because it provided variety. In a 'correspondence', Lloyd tells one reader, 'With respect to the short quantity inserted each week, we can only say this, that we have had innumerable letters complaining of not having enough variety; and it is impossible to give variety if we fill our pages each week with the continuous tales.'[146] We might also glean that Lloyd was careful not to alienate his audience, telling one correspondent, 'We must beg to decline the contribution sent us by Charles, as we know not what young hands it might get into',[147] but the acceptance rate is high, suggesting that Lloyd was comfortable allowing the audience to determine the content of his papers.[148] Some of the strangest correspondences are replies to contributors trying to get unoriginal material published, strange because Lloyd apparently did not pay contributors (he tells 'G.A. – We do not pay for any contributions'),[149] but also because he would not publish the name of the writer even when provided (and because he initiated his career by publishing plagiarisms such as *Oliver Twiss* [1839]). For example, Lloyd tells one correspondent, 'We are surprised at Mr. T. PAGE sending such an old worn-out piece as "The country maid and her milk pail." If he had wished to impose upon our credulity at all, he might have picked out something not quite so well known.'[150] Lloyd repeatedly insists on original works, and it is a bit of a mystery why people would send in plagiarisms if they were not going to be acknowledged or paid: 'Does J. Wood take us for complete ignoramuses, that he sends us the celebrated poem of "Edwin and Angelina" under another title as original.'[151] If what appears to be a sort of game between Lloyd and his readers over the tenuous difference between the readership and writership has a point, it is for the audience to assert its influence, to shape the content, and to define working-class preferences.

But judging by both the longer and shorter entertainments in Lloyd's papers, there was a 'preference' for romance, murder, the supernatural, the moralistic, the lurid, the plain, the domestic, the epic, and nearly everything else. If the audience wanted 'variety' and if itself wrote variously, Lloyd accommodated. To reduce the political to just another preference, a convention, a mere style or commercialised enticement would undoubtedly detract from the radical cause, potentially making it more difficult to attract working people to the people's movement. But not necessarily so. To seduce with a spot of radical politics is also to promote radicalism, confirming that radicalism is an inseparable part of working-class identity, and that the political and the cultural cannot be separated. Enfranchisement was not the goal, nor were equal rights or 'working-class consciousness' and certainly not revolution. But the very indifference to democratic goals, the political ambivalence at a time when lines were being drawn, and the willingness to go in any direction and to side with the victors whoever they may be, were a sign that the people's movement belonged to the people after all.

Notes

1. See L. James. *Fiction for the Working Man, 1830–1850* (Harmondsworth: Penguin University Books, 1974), p. xvii. Discussing the rise of the Victorian middle classes, Rosalind Crone suggests that, 'Strongly influenced by several crucial intellectual shifts, such as evangelicalism, humanitarianism, politeness, sensibility and respectability, this new middle class was anxious to achieve social status and to distance itself from those below.' R. Crone, 'From Sawney Beane to Sweeney Todd', *Cultural and Social History*, 7:1 (2010), 63.
2. E. P. Thompson, *The Making of the English Working Class* (London: Penguin, 1980), p. 805.
3. J. Springhall, '"A life story for the people"? Edwin J. Brett and the London "low-life" penny dreadfuls of the 1860s', *Victorian Studies*, 33:2 (1990), 225.
4. Ibid.
5. J. Rose, *The Intellectual Life of the British Working Classes* (New Haven, CT and London: Yale University Press, 2002), p. 4.
6. Ibid. One has to admit that we only have, as Rosalind Crone puts it, 'Slivers of evidence relating to [the] actual reading experience' of working people. Crone goes on to say that what evidence we do have shows 'that penny bloods were eagerly devoured by the costermongers and their families in the New Cut, Lambeth, the casual inmates of the low-lodging houses and workhouses of the East End, city crossing-sweeps, and the rough boys of Spitalfields'. Crone, 'Sawney Beane', p. 64. But 'devoured' does not tell us how they were interpreted or what message was transmitted.
7. James, *Fiction for the Working Man*, p. 51.
8. S. Ledger, 'Chartist aesthetics in the mid nineteenth century: Ernest Jones, a novelist of the people', *Nineteenth-Century Literature*, 57:1 (2002), 32.
9. I. McCalman, *Radical Underworld: Prophets, Revolutionaries and Pornographers in London, 1795–1840* (Oxford: Clarendon Press, 2002), pp. 204–21.
10. M. Denning, *Mechanic Accents: Dime Novels and Working-Class Culture in America* (London: Verso, 1987), p. 3.

11 O. R. Ashton, 'Chartism and popular culture: an introduction to the radical culture in Cheltenham Spa, 1830–1847', *Journal of Popular Culture*, 20:4 (2004), 62.
12 R. D. Altick, *The English Common Reader: A Social History of the Mass Reading Public 1800–1900* (Columbus, OH: Ohio State University Press, 2nd edn, 1998), p. 344.
13 I. Haywood, *The Revolution in Popular Literature: Print, Politics, and the People, 1790–1860* (Cambridge: Cambridge University Press, 2004), p. 162.
14 S. Hackenberg, 'Vampires and resurrection men: the perils and pleasures of the embodied past in 1840s sensational fiction', *Victorian Studies*, 52:1 (2009), 69.
15 L. Creechan, '"Attend the tale of Sweeney Todd": adaptation, revival, and keeping the meat grinder turning', *Neo-Victorian Studies*, 9:1 (2016), 101.
16 D. Vincent, *Literacy and Popular Culture: England 1750–1914* (Cambridge: Cambridge University Press, 1993), p. 205.
17 James, *Fiction for the Working Man*, p. 20.
18 Vincent, *Literacy and Popular Culture*, p. 206.
19 Crone, 'Sawney Beane', p. 72.
20 In her hugely important contribution to the study of nineteenth-century popular entertainment, *Violent Victorians*, Crone mostly sees representations of violence as a 'form of cultural assertion', stating unequivocally that 'Violence did not, in any way, constitute a form of political protest' (p. 146), though she nonetheless provides evidence of how the representation of violence could be linked to 'the rhetoric of class war' (p. 145). R. Crone, *Violent Victorians: Popular Entertainment in Nineteenth-Century London* (Manchester: Manchester University Press, 2012), pp. 146 and 145. Rohan McWilliam's definition of what constitutes Victorian politics is helpful. He states, 'Any substantial engagement with popular culture in the mid-Victorian era reminds us that the political nation (in the sense of a polity shaped by participation in mass parties) was still very much in flux. We need to recognise that many people did not see themselves as part of the conventional political battle as they encountered it at the hustings during elections or as it was revealed to them in the mass press.' R. McWilliam, 'Liberalism lite?', *Victorian Studies*, 48:1 (2005), 105.
21 Crone, 'Sawney Beane', p. 78.
22 Suggesting that penny bloods were 'seen as even more dangerous than the Newgate novels' (p. 44), Troy Boone argues that penny fiction generated 'middle-class critical hostility' because it advocated

'a sustained agitation that refuses the regulatory fixing of the working-class body in space'. T. Boone, *Youth of Darkest England: Working-Class Children at the Heart of Victorian Empire* (New York and London: Routledge, 2015), p. 17.
23 Quoted in E. S. Turner, *Boys Will Be Boys: The Story of Sweeney Todd, Deadwood Dick, Sexton Blake, Billy Bunter, Dick Barton et al.* (London: Michael Joseph, 1975), p. 33.
24 E. Barton, 'Ida Walton; or, a tale of trials', in E. Lloyd (ed.), *The People's Periodical and Family Library* (7–14 April 1847), p. 446.
25 *Ibid.*, p. 447.
26 A random excerpt: 'For although borne down by the hand of affliction, doomed to dwell amid the haunts of vice and degradation, virtue and truth still maintained their supremacy over hearts willing to receive instruction from on High, and to be governed in their walks by the great principles of the Christian religion.' Anon., 'The history of a dime; or a peep into the world', *People's Periodical* (9 January 1847), p. 221.
27 T. Frost, *Forty Years' Recollections: Literary and Political* (London: Sampson Low, 1880), p. 93. Frost does not only arrive at his summations by examining the written words, he also considers audience response: 'We have only to watch the countenances, and listen to the whispered remarks, of the men and women of the lowest grades who crowd the gallery, eagerly gazing and listening, during the representation of a drama that excites their interest by exhibiting the trials of suffering virtue, to be convinced that the appreciation of moral loveliness is as keen, the feeling excited by the contemplation of injustice or cruelty as intense, among the poorest dwellers in Lambeth or Bethnal Green as among the most educated and refined of the residents of Belgravia. The sympathies of even the vicious are invariably enlisted on the side of virtue; and an outburst of honest indignation against the villain of the play, especially if he is a cowardly and treacherous villain, brings together every pair of rough hands to endorse it with applause.' *Ibid.*, pp. 93–4.
28 *Ibid.*, p. 94.
29 James, *Fiction for the Working Man*, p. 114.
30 Crone, *Violent Victorians*, p. 182.
31 Anon., 'The lesson: a tale of domestic life', *People's Periodical* (19 December 1847), p. 175.
32 Anon., 'Economy', *People's Periodical* (5 December 1846), p. 143.
33 James notes that in 1840, 'There were approximately eighty cheap periodicals circulating in London. Two thirds of this number cost

34 Ashton, 'Chartism and popular culture', p. 61.
35 I discuss two examples, *Howitt's Journal* and *Douglas Jerrold's Magazine*, in Chapter 5.
36 Ashton, 'Chartism and popular culture', pp. 70–1.
37 The *National*, an avowed moral-force Chartist paper, states, 'we believe in the all-sufficing power of the unenfranchised – *if united and earnest* – to achieve their own redemption. We have too much faith in their good sense and the healthfulness of their feelings, either to doubt the uncompromising and steady continuance of their aspirations for knowledge and freedom and equal happiness, or to fear that they can abuse their power.' Anon., 'Our political creed', *National* (12 January 1839), p. 28.
38 J. M. Rymer or T. P. Prest, *Sweeney Todd: The String of Pearls* (Mineola, NY: Dover, 2015), p. 58.
39 It is fair to say that many of Chartism's leaders would represent working people as ready for the franchise *and* in need of improvement and education. Thomas Cooper, for example, states in the first issue of *Cooper's Journal* that the 'great enterprise' is 'the enlightenment and enfranchisement of ALL ... the spread of intelligence with an united struggle for the franchise'. T. Cooper, 'To the young men of the working classes, letter I', *Cooper's Journal* (5 January 1850), p. 1.
40 In *Notes to the People*, Ernest Jones, for example, writes, 'MORAL force is physical force in the background'. E. Jones, 'Three to one; or, the strength of the working-classes', in *Notes to the People* (London: J. Pavey, 1851), I, p. 510. Earlier, in the *Operative*, Feargus O'Connor comments on the split between moral and physical force by saying, 'Most deeply do I regret that this division should ever have arisen.' F. O'Connor, 'Moral and physical force', *Operative* (23 December 1838), p. 115. John Walton describes physical and moral force as 'broad bands along a shifting continuum, rather than polar opposites'. J. Walton, *Chartism* (London and New York: Routledge, 1999), p. 59. Throughout the Chartist years, even moral-force Chartists held tightly to a belief in the right to bear arms and in the right to self-defence.
41 Walton, *Chartism*, p. 59.
42 *Ibid.*
43 James, *Fiction for the Working Man*, p. 116.

44 Vincent, *Literacy and Popular Culture*, pp. 205–6.
45 Altick, *The English Common Reader*, p. 289.
46 P. Joyce, *Visions of the People: Industrial England and the Question of Class, 1848–1914* (Cambridge: Cambridge University Press, 1991), p. 266.
47 Altick, *The English Common Reader*, p. 290.
48 Anon., 'Industry and integrity', *People's Periodical* (19 December 1846), p. 174.
49 Crone, 'Sawney Beane', p. 61.
50 *Ibid.*
51 R. McWilliam, 'Introduction', *Sweeney Todd: The String of Pearls* (Mineola, NY: Dover, 2015), p. vii.
52 See for example the semi-fictional 'Hard nuts to crack!' in the *English Chartist Circular* (n.d.), p. 41; Anon., 'The corn tax: a sketch', *Chartist Circular* (22 August 1840), pp. 196. Anon., 'The Corn-Law humbug', *National* (23 February 1839), pp. 110–11. In the *National*, W. J. Linton, the editor and likely author of the article, makes clear the strategy of advertising the Charter to address any or all social problems when he declares that 'we [are] the seekers of political power *for the sake of removing all evils*'. *Ibid.*, 110.
53 Rymer or Prest, *Sweeney Todd*, pp. 27–8.
54 *Ibid.*, p. 221.
55 *Ibid.*, p. 28.
56 *Ibid.*, p. 254.
57 *Ibid.*, p. 92.
58 *Ibid.*, pp. 142 and 143.
59 *Ibid.*, p. 147.
60 *Ibid.*, p. 1.
61 K. Hughes, *Victorians Undone: Tales of the Flesh in the Age of Decorum* (London: 4th Estate, 2017), p. 108.
62 Rymer or Prest, *Sweeney Todd*, p. 2.
63 *Ibid.*, p. 3.
64 *Ibid.*, p. 1.
65 *Ibid.*, p. 3.
66 *Ibid.*, p. 9.
67 *Ibid.*, p. 4.
68 *Ibid.*, pp. 244 and 245.
69 K. Marx, 'Preface to A Contribution to the Critique of Political Economy', in R. C. Tucker (ed.), *The Marx-Engels Reader* (New York: Norton, 2nd edn, 1978), p. 4.
70 Anon., 'Slaves', *Chartist Circular* (3 July 1841), p. 391.

71 Anon., 'White slaves', *Chartist Circular* (4 July 1840), p. 168. The attitude of Chartists towards American slaves arguably became more sympathetic as the movement matured. See B. Fladeland, '"Our cause being one and the same": abolitionists and Chartism', in J. Walvin (ed.), *Slavery and British Society 1776–1846* (London: Palgrave, 1982), pp. 69–99.
72 Rymer or Prest, *Sweeney Todd*, p. 32.
73 *Ibid.*, p. 33.
74 *Ibid.*, p. 157.
75 Sharon Aronofsky Weltman has documented how George Dibdin Pitt's dramatisation of the novel turned Hector the dog into Hector a Black boy and ex-slave set free by Thornhill (the dog's owner in the novel). She explains, 'Because the play (like the novel) is set in 1785, Thornhill's reply [to a question from the Colonial], that he "had no right to make a slave of him here or abroad" suggests that this 1847 melodrama continued to do the ideological work of abolition fourteen years after slavery was abolished in England (and, of course, in British Honduras). This dialogue indicates that Pitt expects the working-class audience at the Britannia to agree that Thornhill had no right to make a slave of Hector, not even when it was legal, as it would have been in the play's 18th-century setting.' S. A. Weltman, '1847: Sweeney Todd and abolition', *BRANCH: Britain, Representation and Nineteenth-Century History*, D. F. Felluga (ed.), Web (18 August 2018).
76 Rymer or Prest, *Sweeney Todd*, p. 245.
77 *Ibid.*, p. 248.
78 *Ibid.*, p. 22.
79 *Ibid.*, p. 96.
80 *Ibid.*
81 *Ibid.*, p. 180.
82 *Ibid.*, p. 92.
83 *Ibid.*, p. 91.
84 *Ibid.*
85 *Ibid.*, p. 175.
86 *Ibid.*, pp. 176 and 178.
87 *Ibid.*, p. 94.
88 *Ibid.*, p. 261.
89 *Ibid.*, p. 273.
90 *Ibid.*, p. 17.
91 *Ibid.*, p. 183.
92 James, *Fiction for the Working Man*, p. 37.

93 Dick Collins notes that the *London Gazette* reported Rymer as a bankrupt on 15 January 1847. D. Collins, in J. M. Rymer, *Varney, the Vampire; or, the Feast of Blood* (London: Wordsworth, 2010), p. 786.
 94 Rymer or Prest, *Sweeney Todd*, p. 175.
 95 *Ibid.*, p. 174.
 96 *Ibid.*, p. 108.
 97 *Ibid.*, pp. 163–4.
 98 *Ibid.*, p. 19.
 99 *Ibid.*, p. 152.
 100 When the chapter numbers are corrected, the first thirty-one chapters of the 1850 novel are essentially the same as the text in the *People's Periodical*, save that the paragraphing is very different. Perhaps a typesetting preference, the novel combines paragraphs to make them much longer. The illustrations are also different, though on occasion the novel uses an image from the journal. Up to Chapter 31, however, not much is changed; the 1850 novel even reproduces chapter-numbering errors from the original.
 101 Chapter 32 if correcting the chapter numbering.
 102 J. M. Rymer or T. P. Prest, *The String of Pearls; or, the Barber of Fleet Street* (London: E. Lloyd, 1850), p. 152.
 103 *Ibid.*, p. 334.
 104 *Ibid.*, p. 207.
 105 *Ibid.*, p. 326.
 106 *Ibid.*, p. 246.
 107 *Ibid.*, p. 495.
 108 *Ibid.*, p. 496.
 109 E. Jacobs, 'Edward Lloyd's Sunday newspapers and the cultural politics of crime news, *c.* 1840–43', *Victorian Periodicals Review*, 50:3 (2017), 620.
 110 Boone, *Youth of Darkest England*, p. 46.
 111 *Ibid.*, p. 56.
 112 Rymer, *Varney, the Vampire*, p. 385.
 113 *Ibid.*, p. 403.
 114 *Ibid.*, p. 404.
 115 *Ibid.*, p. 277.
 116 *Ibid.*, pp. 404 and 465.
 117 James, *Fiction for the Working Man*, p. 42.
 118 Rymer, *Varney, the Vampire*, pp. 196, 252, 254, 259, 262 and 292, 262, 273, 283, 297, and 273.
 119 *Ibid.*, p. 281.

120 As the 'rich man' is a colonel, it is likely that 'nabob' is used here in the sense of an individual returning from India with a fortune made through colonial exploitation.
121 Rymer, *Varney, the Vampire*, p. 755.
122 Springhall, '"A life story for the people"', p. 225.
123 James includes Sweeney Todd and Jack Sheppard in this category, saying 'Popular aspirations were expressed through figures opposed to the established order.' James, *Fiction for the Working Man*, p. 198.
124 McWilliam, 'Liberalism lite?', p. 105.
125 When *Ada* was coming to a conclusion, Lloyd accepted poetic verses from the reading public singing its praises. *Lloyd's Penny Weekly Miscellany of Romance and General Interest* (London: Edward Lloyd, 1843), pp. 816 and 828.
126 J. M. Rymer, *Ada, the Betrayed, or, The Murder at the Old Smithy*, *Lloyd's Penny Weekly Miscellany of Romance and General Interest* (London: Edward Lloyd, 1843), p. 784.
127 *Ibid.*, p. 489.
128 Frost, *Forty Years' Recollections*, pp. 87 and 94.
129 Anon., 'The old monastery; or, the deed of blood', *Penny Weekly*, pp. 549–51.
130 Anon., 'Janet; or, the persecuted', *Penny Weekly*, pp. 170–1.
131 Anon, 'The abduction', *Penny Weekly*, pp. 458–9.
132 Anon., 'Mary Evans; or, the maniac mother', *Penny Weekly*, pp. 619–20.
133 Rymer or Prest, *Sweeney Todd*, p. 228.
134 Anon., 'The highway robbery; or, the first crime', *Penny Weekly*, p. 267.
135 T. W. Allen, 'William and Mary Ann; or, the press gang', *Penny Weekly*, pp. 428–9.
136 E. Lloyd, 'Notice to correspondents', *Lloyd's Penny Weekly Miscellany of Romance and General Interest* (London: Edward Lloyd, 1843), p. 448.
137 Anon., 'The contrast: or, the gentleman and the itinerant', *Penny Weekly*, pp. 773–4.
138 Anon., 'The soldier and his wife', *Penny Weekly*, pp. 771–3.
139 Anon., 'The double murder', *Penny Weekly*, pp. 457–8.
140 Lloyd, 'Notice to correspondents', p. 624. The following suggests that the contributors would regularly indicate where they wanted their material to appear: 'W. M. P.—As our Correspondent did not inform us which of our papers he wished "The effects of tyranny" to appear

in we have it at present ready for insertion in the "Penny Sunday Times", and cannot alter our arrangements.' *Ibid.*, p. 688.
141 See A. Humpherys, 'Popular narrative and political discourse in *Reynolds's Weekly Newspaper*', in L. Brake, A. Jones, and L. Madden (eds), *Investigating Victorian Journalism* (Houndmills: Macmillan, 1990), pp. 33–47.
142 Lloyd, 'Notice to correspondents', p. 768.
143 *Ibid.*, p. 752.
144 *Ibid.*, p. 240.
145 *Ibid.*, p. 336.
146 *Ibid.*, p. 608.
147 *Ibid.*, p. 768.
148 Frost's well-known anecdote of Lloyd turning to 'a servant or a machine-boy' to help select the material to be published may also be recalled here. Frost, *Forty Years' Recollections*, p. 90.
149 Lloyd, 'Notice to correspondents', p. 640.
150 *Ibid.*, p. 784. Another example: 'We are surprised that F. R. S. should attempt to palm off a tale that has so often appeared in print, as original.' *Ibid.*, p. 384.
151 *Ibid.*, p. 828.

4

Mysteries and ambiguities: G. W. M. Reynolds and *The Mysteries of London*

Of all the remarkable scenes in *The Mysteries of London* – remarkable for *Mysteries* is after all a Victorian novel and one of the bestselling Victorian novels, if not the bestselling novel of the 1840s – the one that takes place just after the Resurrection Man and the Cracksman convince Henry Holford to break into and scope out Buckingham Palace, though the young man has his own, nobler motivations, might be the most remarkable. We are still in the relatively early stages of the novel, but have already experienced a bewildering number of plotlines and characters, some of which will become unrelenting; readers have already journeyed from 'low' scenes to 'high' and back again several times and encountered sundry forms of genre and address, direct and reformist, melodramatic and affective. Entering Buckingham Palace, Reynolds confirms he can bring readers anywhere, to the highest of the high, and make them party to the inner-chamber confidentialities of anyone, real or imaginary. This novel, like the novel project itself and the city lending its name to it, boasts that it is virtually limitless, boundless, unrestricted and defying restriction. As with *Oliver Twist*, *Mysteries* includes numerous images of enclosure and entrapment, and of the pressures of privatisation, but there's little that cannot be and will not be exposed, and with that ability to see into both the lowest and highest dens of corruption comes an emancipatory if not vengeful sense of mobility and empowerment.

So from a workhouse we arrive at an unapologetically voyeuristic scene where Henry spies on Victoria, peeresses, high-born dames, Melbourne, and other courtiers. Henry remains quiet, but the narrator describes and interprets what he sees:

At that time Victoria was yet a virgin-queen. If not strictly beautiful, her countenance was very pleasing. Her light brown hair was worn quite plain; her blue eyes were animated with intellect; and when she smiled, her lips revealed a set of teeth white as Oriental pearls. Her bust was magnificent, and her figure good, in spite of the lowness of her stature.[1]

That the young queen was not shy to display her bust is known, but to place a working-class boy so near to it, and to have a novelist feel so free as to comment on it, its magnificence, compared to 'the lowness of her stature', is to override all existing narratological (and social) protocols and announce that the representational gloves are off. More than the criticism of the Queen's total ignorance 'With regard to the condition of the humbler classes'[2] that immediately follows, having a working-class boy, and the working-class readers he seems to represent, check out the Queen's body is not simply to announce that this novel is going to be sensationally political, with a perspective from below (literally at points, as Henry hides beneath a couch), and to experiment with what happens when class politics come from below, but that it will dare do anything or write against anything.

After lengthy additional scenes where readers are privy to palace gossip, of which there is plenty to go around, and witness Albert and Victoria's courtship, they are ushered back to the 'Boozing Ken', to be introduced to a journeyman knacker telling his story of cutting up diseased horses, of diseases spreading, and in a strangely reformist diatribe, of how he would like to see the Lord Mayor 'appoint a proper veterinary surgeon as Inspector in Smithfield Market'[3] so as to regulate the selling of horse meat. Reminding readers of *Sweeney Todd*, the knacker explains that horse meat is sold to rich and poor, in the 'sassages' or as ox tongues that the wealthy might unwittingly buy, but which, he insists, are as good as what the people think they are purchasing; to workhouses; and to discount-hunters, as rotten pieces are covered up with suet to look and smell like fresh beef and sold at reduced prices at Saturday evening markets. Some of the lower quality meat is also taken by cat's-meat men, though that meat is also divided along class lines, the 'putrid and rotten' meat being 'taken up by the cat's-meat men in the poor neighbourhoods'.[4]

A number of observations might be made here regarding these two scenes that go beyond the juxtaposition of 'high' and 'low' and in fact subvert the simple division of high and low, or the hard division between 'Wealth. | Poverty.' that initiates the novel. First, that 'class' is both the novel's organising principle and interpreted to be London's organising principle, but that 'class' for Reynolds is not a simple matter of us versus them. Second, that unlike Salisbury Square fiction, *Mysteries* is preoccupied with topical and almost granular reformist agendas, set against its republicanism and audaciousness. Third, much like Pierce Egan's *Life in London*, that both the novel and the city are without a centre – we go everywhere and nowhere is privileged as the source of narrative – and that this centrelessness, another of the novel's peripatetic organising principles, exposes a dangerous, vengeful, dog-eat-dog hostility that proliferates in the absence of real justice or a sense of fairness. High and low spaces are also subject to infiltration by the low and high. Fourth, that despite its melodramatic sensationalism, the line separating fiction and reality in the novel is unbearably thin. And finally, that the politics of the novel are far from simple; again, it dares to write against any ideological or political position it might otherwise confirm.

In both its political and cultural confrontations, *The Mysteries of London* is a wildly ambiguous, elastic novel. As Rohan McWilliam says, 'Reynolds was like a sponge, absorbing the radical and romantic elements of his culture.'[5] Though in some sense the novel's politics conform to the conventions of the genres it employs, genre never hems the politics in. Genre theorists, as Kerri Andrews summarises, 'argue that some degree of modification, some degree of evolution, is both inevitable and inherent within systems of genre'.[6] Beside the outrageously romantic, gothic, and melodramatic is explicit political content. The 'penny blood' material does not simply make the politics 'more attractive', as Ernest Jones has it,[7] making the pill easier to swallow. The political content itself is presented as a selling feature, something 'attractive' and sensational in itself. One way of placing Reynolds in the turn towards the politicisation of fiction in the 1840s would be to say that while penny and Newgate fiction offer primarily cultural confrontations that are enhanced by political confrontations, exploiting the fact that audiences wanted both, and that thematically it makes sense to amplify a cultural contest by flirting with the political, Reynolds, on the other hand, gives us what is primarily a political confrontation in *The Mysteries of London*, enlarged by or developed through the stuff that makes for cultural confrontation. The fast-paced, ragbag narrative multiplications of the novel, Stephen James Carver and Anne Humpherys both contend, might have to do with contemporaneous urban upheavals, a 'response to the city itself'.[8] The efference of the narrative might also be a response to the indefinite politics of the 1840s, to rising movements, moral and physical forces of change, liberal and radical energies. Though I am not attempting to define Reynolds's work solely by its differences, both politically and narratologically it occupies a liminal space between Chartist writing and popular fiction, but also between popular fiction and middle-class fiction.

I have argued in previous chapters that the penny and Newgate fiction of the 1840s introduces tenets of radicalism, undeveloped inflections of republican propaganda often in the form of folk heroics or in the assertion of agency against both old and new forms of corruption, but that it does so from the ostensibly declaimed side of law and order or only to return to law and order. These narrative lines thus helped heighten an ongoing debate over the idea of freedom and its proper limitations – who should be licensed to act and when and who should be restricted from acting and why – that reappeared in the liberal social-problem novels of the 1840s and early 1850s, often introduced by female novelists such as Gaskell, Charlotte Brontë, and Eliot, who extended the debate to include and often focus on women. Penny and Newgate fiction are amenable to radicalism, offering up readings to radical ears, and maintaining full deniability as they dog-whistle to the crowd. They sneak in a more properly Chartist narrative that maintains the need for full, dominating working-class participation to make wrongs right. Reynolds's most significant novel, *The Mysteries of London*, by contrast wears its radicalism on his sleeve, but as numerous critics have complained of both then and now, something does not sit right. I do not argue that the novel's populism or popularity vitiates its radicalism or that its predominant critique of 'old corruption' and ostensive absence of a worthy poor or principled working class serve to lessen Reynolds's radical credentials: far from it. The novel is fantastically more radical than the Newgate novel or penny blood, but when exposing social ills and offering reformist solutions, it often gestures towards liberalism's solutions, moral versions of existing things, not unlike the way that penny and Newgate fiction, ostensibly non-political, gesture towards radicalism. *All* of Victoria is offered up to judgement, one might observe, but the way Albert and the true love between the royals is written jettisons away both the cultural and the political conflicts, and the novel's voyeuristic egalitarianism in one fell swoop:

> The queen and the prince seated themselves upon the sofa beneath which the pot-boy was concealed; and their conversation was plainly overheard by him. The noble and beauteous guests – the lords and the ladies of the court – withdrew to a distance; and the royal lovers – for such already were Victoria and Albert – enjoyed the pleasures of a *tête-à-tête*. We shall not record any portion of their discourse – animated, interesting, and tender though it were: suffice it to say, that for a short time they seemed to forget their high rank, and to throw aside the trammels of court etiquette, in order to give vent to those natural feelings which the sovereign has in common with the peasant.[9]

In this chapter, I argue that Reynolds wrote like a Chartist before he became one, but that he kept a door open to a reformist, liberal, cautionary, polite politics. I primarily focus on the first series of *The Mysteries of London* (1844–45) and not the second series (1846–48) that includes material from after Reynolds had taken the banner in 1848. It is in the first series that we see the best example of his republicanism shadowed by hesitation, somewhat enfeebled by his attempt to capture middle-class audiences in the same way that penny and Newgate fiction slip in radical material to attract the politicised working classes. Approaching *Mysteries* in this way, I do not mean to challenge the radical badge Reynolds wears so openly, but rather to place Reynolds as much as possible in the undetermined political atmosphere of the 1840s that made so many populists hedge their bets. 'Class' in Reynolds is frequently transformed into ethics, which Sonali Perera identifies as a way of thinking about 'social justice in the absence of guarantees': the language of ethics 'carr[ies] over the idealism of the revolutionary moment into the transformative task-oriented daily work that can only take place in the everyday'.[10] All the figures in this study attempted to appeal to as many readers as possible, including Reynolds. The dissonances between Chartist fiction and his own does not automatically set Reynolds happily among liberal reformers, even if they would have him. My argument has been that if commercial motivation turned the producers of popular fiction towards radicalism it nonetheless should not be dismissed or treated as an impure or inauthentic radicalism. Rather, we should see that it was offered up to the public, largely to working-class readers, to develop or pursue themselves: feeding a taste makes the beast stronger, wanting more of that taste. Reynolds's novel is predominantly a politically radical tract, but its appeals to the middle classes – direct at times – should not be read as a carpetbagging commercial venture, but as with the grotesque material said to appeal to the worst tastes of his primary market, the working classes, it can be read as softening the edges of radicalism to attract a larger market while potentially politicising that market. While Lloyd's productions and Newgate writing are mostly involved in democratising the literary marketplace, and the corollaries that come be what may, Reynolds is more firmly, more deliberately attempting the politicisation of the public, of all the readers he might attract.

A bad reputation

The standard way into a discussion of *The Mysteries of London* is through an examination of its place on what McWilliam nicely calls 'Radical Grub Street'.[11] Reynolds was disliked by the respectable Victorian classes and their voices in the literary and journalistic establishment, and he often continues to be ignored or confronted by critics today largely because of his popularity. His kind of popularity, I argue, stems from countercultural indecorum *and* radical politics, but with Reynolds, the indecorous raises questions about the putative authenticity of the latter because the politics are so pronounced. Louis James notes that, 'For the "respectable" Victorian reader, Reynolds was a writer who abandoned standards of taste and morality to exploit the lowest predilections of his readership.'[12] Reynolds came closer than anyone else in the period to symbolise the dangers of popular fiction because, as Berry Chevasco says, the hostile attitude towards the immodesty of his most famous novel 'was compounded by the enormous success of *Mysteries* among readers'.[13] But Reynolds was disliked not only because he was thought to be effectively exploiting and enlarging the public's bad taste; he was also thought to be exploiting the languages of radicalism. Dickens most famously questioned Reynolds's political objectives at the time, excluding him from the 'genuine working men who are Chartists' and mocking him as the 'draggled fringe on the Red Cap'.[14] Dickens had his own reasons – Reynolds's early plagiarisms of *Pickwick* – to paint Reynolds as a fraud. But the apparent pandering to the lowest common denominator, the commercial interest, is generally what makes critics even today deny the authenticity of the politics, and Reynolds is therefore seen as seeking profit over political or even moral change. The question of authenticity was something many of Chartism's leaders had to endure, from Ernest Jones to Feargus O'Connor, in no small part because they were so frequently accusing each other of charlatanism.

Looking at Reynolds unhidden commercial interests, Juliet John points out that there 'can be an assumption in today's post-Marxian theoretical climate that a political radicalism that purports to empower the working class should be anti-capitalist'.[15] This goes far to explain why middle-class writers – Dickens or the sensation novelists – tend not to be subject to the same criticism as a writer directly appealing to working-class readers with an ostensibly radical or revolutionary message. But the assumption that radicalism can only take place beyond the marketplace has to be examined for its inherent romanticism. The suspicion that Reynolds was spawning consumerism, not radicalism, or that his republicanism camouflaged commercial desire or was exploited to further commercial interests, is based on a static and purist image of 'the radical' that simply could not exist. Radicalism in the 1840s was complex and unfixed, mindful of and interacting with the evolving culture and politics of the period. At times educationalist, reformist, and gradualist, it could also be as populist as it might be republican and revolutionary. The expectation that radical or revolutionary work will be experimental, and in that way resist easy consumption, may have been given new blood by Raymond Williams, but it can never fully escape the echoing of a Coleridgian Mariner, the idea that the 'authentic' artist has to be an outsider. It also might be pointed out that the lingering aesthetic of disinterestedness in the standard critique of Reynolds is completely foreign to what Pierre Bourdieu would call the working-class culture of necessity, preferences that arise in adapting to scarcity, to absences, something pronounced in the novel. *Mysteries* is part of the world it represents. In *Mysteries*, the culture of necessity is modified, however, to include a working-class culture of vengeance and profiteering, something the novel examines intensely. To claim popularity is proof of an inauthentic radicalism is to unfairly (and ironically) privilege the aesthetic over the sociological in the same way that working-class writing has until recently almost exclusively been approached by privileging the sociological over the aesthetic. Finally, the idea that radical writing is required to defend its popularity also stems from the assumption that radical politics has to first elevate or educate the public. A good deal of *Mysteries* is instructive, morally and sociologically, complimenting Reynolds's official position that education must precede politicisation, but a good deal of it is not. Half-naked women and obscene violence might belie the devotion to a true educationalist agenda, and thus to Reynolds's attempt to politicise his readers, but only if the excess is held in isolation, essentially fetishised.

Commercial success, in any case, and the specific six goals of the Charter are not at odds. The degree to which a 'radical' needed to threaten the established order of things to be 'radical' is not something that can be easily or firmly established, so the political barometer might swing on whether an allegiance to the Charter or to republicanism is declared. But if radicalism means attempting to right social wrongs by getting to the root of the wrongs, as opposed to proposing a way to mitigate the wrong, there were clearly other and many forms of radicalism circulating in the nineteenth century. Even arguing for an equality of opportunity, which in some way defines Chartism and is no small part of Reynolds's massive project, is not in fact tantamount to rejecting society's values, as it rather amounts to giving society and its core political business a glowing stamp of approval by asking to be part of it. Chartism's dubious separation of moral and physical forces notwithstanding, the petitions themselves addressed only the means to change British society.[16]

That Chartism was both constitutionalist and revolutionary is part of its legacy. Reynolds's politics are similarly complex, radical, and provisional. As Humpherys importantly notes, 'Reynolds's political understanding was more complicated than he has been given credit for … Reynolds's politics as well as his editorial stance and the contents of his fiction reflected the inclusiveness of popular culture, his contradictions were the contradictions of the audience he was writing for.'[17] Ian Haywood argues along the same line when he documents how Reynolds 'aimed at a versatile reading audience with a variety of "high" and "low" desires and aspirations'.[18] Reynolds understood the various and contradictory desires of the reading public, which may at times be either revolutionary or reformist (or be amenable to reform or revolution). At other times, he recognised, his readers simply wanted 'entertainment', but also that the revolutionary and reformist in his work could be part of that entertainment without losing its political significance.

Lost in what is essentially the separation of cultural confrontations and political ones, the separation of the aesthetic and sociological, is not only the middle-class desire for sensation (which gets confirmed in the 1860s) but the lower-class desire to politicise the failings of its own culture, which *Mysteries* does to such a great extent that it so often reads like Mayhew unleashed.[19] The documenting of the basest moral corruption of the lower classes, of an unworthy poor, overwhelmingly dominates the representation of the underprivileged classes. Reynolds, it must be kept in mind, not only exploits the activities of the underclasses, the dangerous classes, he moralises against them as vehemently as he moralises against the aristocracy. To reduce his objective to an appeal to the lowest common denominator is to ignore the heavy judgement of those classes and the world that produces them, something that is not at all easy to do in *Mysteries*. To link the representation of widespread 'vice' to commercial interest is to ignore everything else that is said and done again in part, at least, for commercial interests. Gertrude Himmelfarb points out that to be popular he did not need to appeal to radical politics;[20] that he did either shows a genuine radicalism, that he conflated a politicised romanticism and a narratological one, or that he thought that adding a radical dimension would make the novel even more commercially successful.

Contemporary critics also tend to object to Reynolds because he seems in *Mysteries* to denounce 'old corruption' with the rusty weaponry of 'old radicalism' rather than employing a 'new radicalism' to challenge the 'new corruption' of capitalist reality. '"Old radicalism"', in the words of Juliet John, 'involved the idea of an opposition between "the people" and a powerful, corrupt aristocracy, whilst "new radicalism" involved a newer, class-based vision of inequality and politicised opposition.'[21] But despite Patrick Joyce positioning Reynolds as 'a crucially important bridge between the old radicalism and the new',[22] critics continue to be critical of the way Reynolds vilifies the aristocracy and not the always-rising middle classes. Rosalind Crone dismisses *Mysteries*, for example, as a 'throwback to old turn-of-the-century radicalism, in his demonisation of the upper classes as opposed to the newly emergent middle-class industrial magnates'.[23] Yet, keeping in mind the public's morphing desires, which include a generally conservative appreciation for familiar narratives, and Reynolds's argument in *Mysteries* that an undemocratic, unfair world produces its own systems of competitive, vengeful justice, *Mysteries* might be better seen as representing a complex form of class transmutations and transcendences, again despite what he says at the beginning of the novel, informing readers that there is only wealth and poverty. 'Class' in *Mysteries* is a shifting battlefield that the paradigm of old and new corruption cannot entirely contain. The aristocracy in *Mysteries* can be grotesquely decadent and vile, as in the death-bed scene of the Marquis of Holmesford drinking to the lees with his five kept 'ladies',[24] or it can be heroic, earning the loyalty of true servants, and offered as a sort of reward for selfless, generous heroism: Richard Markham, the novel's central hero, becomes a member of the aristocracy by earning his place in it and not only by marrying into it. The middle classes, in turn, can be heroic, as in the example of Richard, who is promoted to the nobility, maintaining the 'nobless oblige' that seems inherent to him, or it can be villainous, as in the case of Richard's brother Eugene, who cheats and swindles himself into becoming a member of a vile aristocracy.

The novel does not fully fit the paradigm of old and new corruption because it documents rampant corruption, corruption at all levels and in all places, in the absence of the mechanisms that can produce social fairness. To a greater extent than both contemporaneous middle-class or Chartist writers, Reynolds paints pictures of worthy and unworthy aristocracies, worthy and unworthy middle classes, and a worthy and unworthy poor, even though the unworthy poor vastly outnumber their counterparts. He also depicts the worthiness of class representatives in a constant state of motion. The sympathetic poor turn into the vilest men and women imaginable. Only about half of the aristocracy in the novel are genuine members of it. Others, like Chichester, lie and steal their way into it. The same members of the middle classes can sink or rise both in terms of their class positions and in terms of their morality. Class systems, or caste systems, exist within other class systems, seen, for example, in the elaborate society of the gypsies. Though the city and, by turn, *Mysteries* is presented as a place of 'fearful contrasts',[25] the novel disrupts the very binary it lays claim to. The fluidity of moral and class status exposes a new corruption in which the agents of old corruption continue to fight for dominance. In his representation of multiple microsystems that develop their own forms of justice – in the absence of the means to political, economic, or legal justice – Reynolds creates a world that demonstrates the need for something radically different. Until then, it can only be an arena for blind vengeance and pointless social ascendancy.

The post-industrial complaint that it is hypocritical for anti-establishment, radical rhetoric to seek out the mainstream – in this case the moustachioed, villainous aristocracy – was far from obvious in the 1840s. As Gregory Vargo makes clear, old corruption, blaming 'social ills on the depredations of a grasping elite', was a 'prominent current in radical thought', because in the radical imagination old corruption was 'rooted in fundamental patterns of social organisation',[26] as it is seen to be in *Mysteries*. It has to be kept in mind that for radical Victorians in the 1840s, old and new corruption needed to be rolled into one so as to establish a politically important and mobilising 'us versus them' narrative. Melodrama also demands the same simplified theatre of war. Chartist writers did not abide by the paradigmatic rules of old and new corruption either, frequently including aristocratic villains or, again like Reynolds, a scattering of benevolent, paternalistic aristocrats. Though too much can be made of Chartist fiction's ostensible drift into melodrama by the 1840s, certainly Ernest Jones and Thomas Frost freely mixed radical politics and romantic melodrama, and as melodrama polarises – right and wrong, rich and poor – the presence of the super wealthy might be expected. Finally, looking at Reynolds's representations of the aristocracy, which vary enormously in *Mysteries* from villain to hero, McWilliam explains that 'Until recently, historians often wrote off this kind of pronouncement as false consciousness or, at best, a form of romantic nostalgia because it did not take seriously the role of the bourgeoisie. However, given the current emphasis on the continuing importance of the aristocracy throughout the nineteenth century, Reynolds should perhaps be reclaimed as someone who was trying to define the real nature of the Victorian state.'[27]

Mysteries begins with stressing that society is simply divided into two economic categories, even though in a way it dismantles the motif almost as soon as it is introduced with the good brother/ bad brother narrative. Reynolds, nonetheless, repeatedly insists on this binary, opening his book and returning to the image of age-old Wealth | Poverty on several different occasions. Such a simplification is entirely undermined in the novel, as the poor victimise the poor and the wealthy war with the wealthy, or as Eugene's ascendancy is followed by his fall, for example, but the simplistic binary is kept in for its expression of political unity. Although the confrontational expression of 'us against them' is betrayed by intraclass divergence and class mobility, it simultaneously functions almost in a Marxian manner to polarise society and explain the rampant class resentment and desire for vengeance, as well as various kinds of corruption represented in the novel, dichotomising in order to insist on the inability of tinkling reforms or individual heroics to address society's flaws. Only *Mysteries* promotes so many tinkling reforms and relies on so much individual heroism to resolve its conflicts that it betrays the radicalism it otherwise manifests.

Mysteries and Chartist fiction

The Mysteries of London is not strictly speaking a Chartist novel, but it is about as close to a Chartist novel as a radical novel from the 1840s that fails to mention the Charter can be. McWilliam says it is 'a text that allowed the author to become a leading Chartist'.[28] Haywood confirms that 'Reynolds had espoused virulent republican politics since his days in France in the 1830s' and that 'Reynolds's entry into public politics was always ready to happen.'[29] Louis James says that 'Reynolds wrote as a Chartist and in *The Mysteries of London* we see the emergence in fiction of the radicalism of the Chartist press.'[30] When Reynolds is singled out as merely an entrepreneur exploiting the people's cause for personal gain, though a number of critics would have Ernest Jones keep him company, it might be because he is not sufficiently placed side by side with Chartist writers so as to see the narrative conventions he shared with them. Reynolds fits best into the Chartist fold, however, when it is remembered that Chartism was not a single, monolithic argument but was filled with contradictions and differences. Still, representing the seemingly irresolvable problem of class antagonism, or implying that the solution to this problem of a society divided so fundamentally between Wealth | Poverty lies in some extratextual act beyond the ability of the novel to represent, *Mysteries* firmly locates itself in the dominant conventions of Chartist fiction – except, of course, when it doesn't.

If Reynolds had an ambivalent relationship with Chartist fiction it might be in part because Chartist fiction does not simply do one thing. It might have dominant features, but they are not universally or evenly applied. Chartism itself was not an immovable ideology that refused variation. Commenting on Reynolds's politics in *Mysteries*, Michael H. Shirley argues that, 'The solution to centuries of stagnation was not, he believed, violent revolution to create a classless society, but a peaceful and yet constant agitation to bring about fundamental change.'[31] This not only mirrors Troy Boone's reading of *Varney, the Vampire*, it also echoes the voices behind moral-force Chartism. And yet when Richard fights for the revolutionary cause against a foreign dictator, who is represented as not wholly unlike the men of old British corruption, the *constitutionalist* victory of right against might is through direct violence. It was not unusual for Chartists to blur the distinction between moral and physical force either. Still, at one point in the novel Greenwood is suspicious of one of his servants because he reads the *Weekly Dispatch*.[32] The *Dispatch* had an enormous circulation, the highest of all newspapers between 1843 and 1845, and that in itself could cause Greenwood's anxiety, not unlike the anxiety that *Mysteries* caused among middle-class audiences. And again like Reynolds, the *Dispatch* courted working-class readers. Reynolds was the acting foreign editor of the paper when he was writing *Mysteries*. But the *Dispatch* was mostly a sensational paper and a sporting paper, though it was radical as well to some extent. It was not a Chartist paper, however, 'disapproving of the "physical force" Chartism of Feargus O'Connor's *Northern Star*'.[33] Reynolds can also demonstrate an ambiguous attitude towards Chartist fiction, but he at least seems to be interacting with it, influenced by it and not only influencing it by making it increasingly melodramatic.

Perhaps the greatest link between Chartist literature and Reynolds's *Mysteries* is in the way politics and melodrama interrelate in both, specifically the way the narrative is regularly suspended to include long, politically strident, nonfictional commentaries. McWilliam notes that, '*The Mysteries of London* is distinctive for the way in which Reynolds frequently breaks from the narrative and employs the novel as a platform or pulpit from which to lecture about the evils of the day.'[34] Himmelfarb also says, 'Where *The Mysteries of London* differed from the others in this genre was the occasional injection, sometimes suggested by the turn of the plot, sometimes entirely gratuitous, of social and political commentaries.'[35] But Chartist fiction also frequently interrupts the narrative and throws out the fourth wall to directly proselytise on the social issues that the story initiates. In fact, both Chartist fiction and *Mysteries* often read as if they introduce narrative plotlines only in order to get to a pressing social issue; though Reynolds's plotlines are especially elaborate, the direct address is not in fact gratuitous but at points the reason for the plot that surrounds it. At least it is sometimes difficult to establish whether the political editorialising or the narratives themselves are the intrusions. The novel begins as essay before getting to the dark and stormy night ('The night was dark and stormy').[36] Reynolds continues to begin many chapters with non-fictional address. The beginning of chapter XLIX is not untypical: ostensibly in order to introduce Greenwood's machinations, the narrator gives us a lengthy description of the deception and chicanery rampant in education, religion, and politics. The near rant is tenuously connected to the plot only by direct statement: 'London is filled with Mr. Greenwoods: they are to be found in numbers at the West End. Do not for one moment believe, reader, that our portrait of this character is exaggerated.'[37] Political editorialising begins Chapter CIV, documenting changes to Holywell Street,[38] ostensibly because Ellen, one of the novel's main characters, happens to be walking on it. Ellen, in this case, is merely an opportunity for the sociological topography that is Reynolds's interest. Not entirely breaking from the world of fiction, the reader is never allowed to fully escape into it, despite the lure of plot entanglements. Though a para-narrative, the detailed and lengthy descriptions of the workhouse, for example, complete with statistics and diagrams,[39] elides the border between journalism and fiction precisely in the way that Vargo describes the 'generic affiliations between fiction and journalism' in Chartist newspapers.[40]

In Chartist print culture, that is, fiction is not an all-together distinct category. Stories such as Ernest Jones's 'The London Doorstep' or Junius Senex's 'Field Lane' might be read as occasional pieces: they exist not for aesthetic consumption but to suspend it, to make a point about a social issue, and usually about the way that only electoral reform could bring about a resolution to the narrative problem. At one point in *Mysteries* we meet a group of prostitutes. Reynolds allows the women to tell their own sad stories, something that is done consistently in the novel. But an affective aesthetic is not to be divorced from a sociological investigation, so Reynolds supplements their stories of how they became prostitutes with footnotes.[41] Later, Chichester visits a pawnshop, and though Reynolds is building up intricate plotlines (Chichester is not the aristocrat he claims to be but the son of a pawnbroker), the short visit is largely an excuse to allow Reynolds to discuss the evils of pawnshops and the reforms that the government ought to pursue in order to improve the way people can borrow money.[42] Emerging out of the direct address, the narrator will say, 'But to continue',[43] which might be the novel's refrain. Comparing Chartist fiction and Reynolds, it is fair to say that narrative clearly dominates over the explicitly political in *Mysteries* in a way that is only seen in the late Chartist melodrama of Ernest Jones, such as in *The*

Lass and the Lady (1852), Reynolds and his success likely shaping Chartist fiction after *Mysteries* more than Chartist fiction provided a model and map for Reynolds. In addition, the Charter itself is not introduced as a way to resolve the issues *Mysteries* raises as is frequently the case in Chartist fiction. But the striking similarity in the approach to the function of fiction, beyond the use of affect that goes way and above Reynolds and Chartism, suggests that the alignment between the two was real and substantial, both learning from each others' successes.

This is not to say that there are no differences between Chartist fiction and Reynolds's work. Perhaps the greatest difference between them is that the Chartist author is much less likely to provide the comforting, satisfying resolution that *Mysteries* (and melodrama more generally) provides. *The Seamstress* (1850), which I discuss at further length later on in this chapter, conforms more precisely with what Chartists tend to do in their fiction. McWilliam says the novel 'was derived from Thomas Hood's "The Song of the Shirt" and Mayhew's descriptions of the plight of needlewomen',[44] which is likely, but there are more radical favourites as well that Reynolds could have soaked up, such as Douglas Jerrold's 'The Dress Maker', which includes a great deal of direct address as well, and the anonymous 'The Young Seamstress' (1847) that first appeared in Reynolds's own *Miscellany*. *The Seamstress* was written after he had become a Chartist. It ends with not only the death of the middle-class villain, and of the aristocracy that he was manipulating, but of the main, heroic, innocent figures as well, as if to argue that the happy ending is impossible given the social conditions that the novel explores. It ends, that is, on an impossibly sour note:

> With regard to the establishment of Messrs. Aaron and Sons, would to heaven we could announce that the earth had opened and swallowed it up, or that the red right arm of Jehovah had hurled the avenging thunder-bolt upon its roof! But it is not so. That establishment still exists, and the system whereon it is based flourishes more than ever; – and while poor Virginia, one of the countless victims of that diabolical system, sleeps in the silent grave, the toils of the WHITE SLAVES whom she has left behind her are still contributing to the colossal wealth accumulated within the walls of that PALACE OF INFAMY.[45]

This is more typical of Chartist fiction than the just desserts *Mysteries* offers; the ultimate vengeance seeking the ultimate justice has not yet happened. But even then, the interminability of the earlier novel functions in the same way as do the bleak endings of Chartist fiction. Reynolds proposes countless reforms in *Mysteries*, from ending capital punishment to Church reform. But this neverending list of social corrections, always stemming from the opening and returning contrast of Wealth | Poverty, at some level implies that reform is not enough, that something more is needed, that the very means to reform require reform. Furthermore, though *Mysteries* resolves its plotlines so that the good are 'rewarded' and the bad suffer and die, it is not as if the para-narrative problems raised intermittently throughout the novel are resolved. Rather, they constantly return to haunt future plotlines. Like the Resurrection Man disinterring bodies for inspection, Reynolds brings back social issue after social issue for study, the disease never being thoroughly addressed. In part this feeds into or feeds off the gothic aspects of the text, a political haunting of the past. Prison reform, workhouse reform, marriage reform and so forth all receive multiple lectures. We are especially reminded of returning social problems when Reynolds twice includes illustrations of gambling cheats. Certainly the size of Reynolds's project and the pressures of serialised writing would contribute to the repetitiveness, but the futility and subsequent repetitiveness of the narrator's angry outbursts undermine the comforting resolutions provided by the storylines.

Not unlike the frustration of narrative resolution, in both *The Seamstress* and *Mysteries* Reynolds frequently depicts the failure of charity. This is also a commonplace in Chartist fiction,[46] for if a private system of relief works there would not be the need for structural change; even gradualist reform is not as pressing if the wealthier classes are always ready to assist the worthy poor. Chartists literature frequently positions itself as 'writing back' against a cultural appropriation of working-class values by middle-class literature representing the ascendant class as generous. Reynolds may not give us much by way of a 'worthy poor', unlike in Chartist fiction, but to some extent this only acts to further the critique of sympathy and charity. As said, *Mysteries* depicts chaotic social wars where nearly everyone is seen plotting against everyone else, establishing ironically homogeneous conditions of existence. The novel's ethnographic ambivalence whereby vindictiveness and meanness cross class lines does not allow for much effective charity. In *Mysteries*, the very idea of charity undermines the central theme of the novel that society is organised around struggle and vengeance, defining nearly every character's ordinary relation to the world. Charity has no place here, which makes structural change an immediate necessity. Richard is a naturally generous person, as his brother is the opposite, but his charity frequently does not work. Ellen does everything possible to make money, but she sinks as low as to sleep with Greenwood, essentially prostituting herself, just as her father gets money from Richard. This is not simply the drama of bad timing, but rather an indication of the insufficiency of charity.[47] Reynolds also shows the poor abusing charity. Polly Bolter threatens to poke out the eyes of her own daughter Fanny so the child will make more money begging.[48] Volume Two begins with Richard being shown 'certain beggars that always turn out half-naked, on rainy days, or when the snow's on the ground; and people pity them so much on those occasions that the rogues get enough to keep them all through the fine weather'.[49] Reynolds's work contrasts much Chartist fiction in that *Mysteries* constantly gives us an unworthy poor. The point in representing a truly despicable class is not, however, to disqualify the actual working classes from full political entitlement and deny their political capacity, or even to inhibit charitable acts. Rather, Reynolds has in sight a heightening of a culture of vengeance spawned by the absence of justice in any form. Moreover, that Reynolds ignores the 'worthy poor' can be overstated. Virginia in *The Seamstress* is over-the-top worthy, and in *Mysteries* Miss Katherine, for example, has all the common attributes of the worthy poor, mostly moral but including abject powerlessness. Reynolds, however, is clearly more interested in victimisers than victims, or what has led to a world of cold-hearted victimisers, exposing the mechanisms of structural causality where deviations are few. Yet if charity is represented as a too-individualistic response to social problems, Richard nonetheless never ceases to be charitable, and though he has to learn how to discern between the worthy and unworthy as he progresses, he does so, making yet again for an alternative reading of charity, one that is more amenable to the wealthier, more socially empowered members of the reading public.

Louis James notes that Reynolds's great disagreement with the main Chartist movement was his view, expressed as early as in 1836 and never withdrawn, that 'Universal Suffrage in the hands of the people, before they are educated, is as dangerous as a razor in the hand of an infant.'[50] It should also be noted that this is not entirely a non-Chartist view, as one of the main pillars of Chartism, as discussed in the last chapter, was to advance working-class education; Chartists tend, however, to advocate for both education and the vote, suggesting that the franchise could only increase educational opportunities. That the reader's education and improvement are not an obvious priority in *Mysteries* is at the heart of many of the critiques it faces. Rather, one of Reynolds's projects, which he nonetheless can hold in sustained abeyance, is to eliminate claims to distinction among the classes, though this is not to deny that individuals are shaped by specific institutionalised trainings. But the social forces in the novel that cause all of London to revolve around vengeance suggest education and improvement must follow some prior structural change because the education that exists in the world of *Mysteries*, and the idea of improvement, teaches only the law of the talion: an eye for an eye.

Mysteries and the middle class

Reynolds's equivocal attitude towards enforcing a radical agenda might be a sign that he shared Chartism's sometimes conflicting messages, reform or revolution, or it might reflect the way that Reynolds wrote as a radical but with one eye on the middle class, attempting to please and expand his liberal audience, and the audience also of his fiercest competitor, Dickens. By placing Reynolds adjacent to middle-class writing I do not mean to caricaturise it as 'doing' only one thing. Rather, I follow Vargo's treatment of the 'radical canon' by arguing that Reynolds's writing is also 'syncretic', existing 'on a borderline between respectable forms of middle-class fiction and the sensational and prurient genres of melodrama and penny bloods'.[51] One of the most fascinating relationships in *Mysteries* is between

Richard and Morris Benstead, a good police officer. Richard first tries to enlist the police to help him capture the Resurrection Man, Anthony Tidkins, though they are reluctant to trust him because of Richard's ragged appearance. But Benstead recognises the decency of Richard, who in turn recognises that the police officer is efficient, honest, and has 'a good heart'.[52] The ever-benevolent Richard knows that Benstead cares for justice, rewarding him with a tip at one point, in the same way that he tips his devoted servants and friends, such as Morcar, the loyal gypsy. Before Dickens's Inspector Bucket, Reynolds's heroic Benstead assists the novel's hero in protecting the innocent (Katherine Wilmot) and capturing the guilty (Reginald Tracy, who had framed Kate for a murder he committed). The suggestion is that with the ascendancy of solid social leaders, such as Richard, and a benevolent, earned hierarchy, a degree of justice and order can be achieved. It is not typical of Chartist fiction to represent the inherent decency of the police. As with penny fiction, Reynolds demonstrates not just the need for the people to be institutionally governed by the law and its agents, but also that the law can do so effectively, though at other times he will undermine the right *and* the ability of the state to control and discipline its subjects, again like penny fiction. Reynolds temporises, telling his audience, 'the Law is vindictive, cowardly, mean, and ignorant. It is *vindictive* because its punishments are more severe than the offences, and because its officers descend to any dirtiness in order to obtain conviction.'[53] Later, when Reynolds is focused on one of his favourite topics, prostitution, its causes and hardships, the police are represented as corrupt, part of the problem, and pawns of a corrupt world: 'The moment she was accosted in the street by a gentleman, the officer would come up and order her brutally to move on; and perhaps he would add violence to harsh words.'[54] Reynolds continues to essay against the police, adding ominously that 'No one can conceive the amount of the wrongs inflicted by the police upon the most miserable class of women!'[55] The single officer is valued, not the police, which can be read as an appeal to middle-class preferences for individualistic solutions and an appeal to a working-class distrust of the police.

The attitudes toward the police are symptomatic: the novel constantly gives us good and wicked versions of what it represents, from class representatives to servants (Filippo and Marian, or Whittingham and Lafleur), to the inherent dichotomising of good and evil in narratives of brothers (Richard and Eugene) or sisters (Ellen and Kate or Mary-Anne and Isabella). In the Epilogue, we are told explicitly that Reynolds has endeavoured to demonstrate virtue rewarded and vice punished,[56] but no social group monopolises either virtue or vice. Good fallen women (Ellen) are juxtaposed to bad fallen men (Reginald); we even get good villains in Crankey Jem and Holford. Often the novel seems to be at war with itself over structure and agency, especially with the reciprocal 'Wrongs and crimes of the poor'.[57] The intercalated, first-person backstories go far to explain crime and vice. They can be read as ethnography, or in Humpherys' words, as an 'effort at totalisation through multiple tales'.[58] That the characters' tales are more likely to be voiced in good English, without the dialect or slang that usually marks the characters, as if they are returned to innocence when recollecting the past, itself suggests processes of internalisation, of forced changes in identity. Yet the vengeful anomie that results can be overturned through individual effort, as we see with the Rattlesnake or Crankey Jem. Moreover, the contrariness of Richard and Eugene cannot be explained by determinacy; as if they were in a Hogarthian sketch, one takes the good path and the other the path of vice, but why that happens is unclear. The defective binary structuring of the novel extends beyond structure and agency or between wealth and poverty or vice and virtue. *Mysteries* offers a series of hard dualities – between high and low, culture and politics, masculine and feminine – that are subsequently demolished as merely rhetorical means to organise what is essentially a fierce world that finds relief only in a liberal focus on the individual or a reformist focus on governance. Intersectional and interclass complications explode the conflicts of class antagonism that drive Chartist fiction.

Reynolds also gives us redemption and conversion narratives that confirm the ability to rise above environment. Smithers, the executioner, is transformed from the abusive father of Kate and Gibbet to a loving one; he is redeemed, and becomes decent and caring as a result of Richard and Benstead's efforts. Made corrupt by the system (he too gets a personal backstory), we see that personal reform is possible without any change to the larger systems of governance. The story of Eugene is also eventually a redemption story. Aspiring to the crimes of the aristocracy, and after attempting to rape Louisa as George Montague, he appears as 'Greenwood', a 'fashionable gentleman' with his valet Lafleur. He runs a steam-packet company and is a speculator, a 'capitalist';[59] he is a middle-class villain who ascends, unlike his brother, by cheating. When he becomes a parliamentarian, he fully turns his back on the poor. But by the novel's end, already humbled, he reforms; it turns out that all he needed was the love of a good woman. Reynolds does not often offer narrowly individualistic solutions to the vast social problems he addresses, and is not consistently part of the Victorian humanitarianism beginning to take hold of the public imagination in the 1840s, which is often accused of seeking a moralised version of the status quo to assure continued political and economic ascendancy. Through the representation of vengeance, as I will argue shortly, Reynolds accepts that without something radically different, the world can only be a struggle for agentic domination. But the novel nonetheless succumbs to the temptation to offer novelistic solutions to 'real' social problems, including the problems identified in its journalistic discourse.

As mentioned, *Mysteries* also offers schemes and practical ideas for all sorts of reform, from penal to marriage. Chartists would do so as well, but generally insisted that reforms would fall into place, a true liberalism could have its day, when the franchise was expanded. With proper representation, the issues that concern the masses would be dealt with in a way that would bring justice to the masses. Reynolds seems to argue that the people need to be reformed first through the reforming of society's institutions, fitting hand in glove with his general belief in the primacy of education and improvement. The cultural confrontation that *Mysteries* presents, however, the 'penny fiction' material the novel revolves around, suggests an alternative to middle-class ideas over the march of the intellect, even though other aspects of the work seem to be in search of common ground with middle-class reform fiction. The 'blood' (or the penny) made it virtually impossible for the middle classes to align themselves with Reynolds. In this way, Reynolds's cultural contest is more stridently oppositional than even some of the openly political commentary.

Remarkably, however, Reynolds appeals directly to his readers to reach out to potential middle-class audiences, asking his current readers to recommend his book to those above, to tell others who have heard bad things about the book that it is a very good book with very good morals. Reynolds's closing word to the 'Kind Reader', encouraging them to advertise and promote his book against the 'fugitive report that the mind will be shocked more than it can be improved', can be taken with a grain of salt. To insist that the book be promoted as a moral book, 'a book by means of which we have sought to convey many a useful moral and lash many a flagrant abuse' and that any other reading of it indicates a 'false fastidiousness' that would unfairly 'prejudge, from its own supposition or from misrepresentations made to it by others', is remarkably good marketing – 'kind reader, oppose that prejudice, and exclaim – "Peruse, ere you condemn!"'.[60] It is also an indication that Reynolds was willing to flip the meaning of a cultural confrontation, to tame it, to relinquish its purpose, and to offer it as cultural reconciliation. The book in some ways seeks harmony, a diminishing of cultural and political differences. The attempt to reach as wide an audience as possible through both aesthetic and political contortions, in the 1840s, necessarily detracts from the confrontational content.

Priced one penny

Yet Reynolds clearly knew that his book was at the centre of, and becoming a symbol of, a cultural contest. Humpherys documents 'the work's popularity among its working- and lower-class readers and the horror with which its middle-class readers rejected it'.[61] Carver points out that representing the underworld was in itself a cultural confrontation.[62] In this way at least the novel can be classified as penny fiction. Judith Flanders refers to *Mysteries* as 'The most successful penny blood';[63] Richard Altick refers to Reynolds as 'the most successful of all Salisbury Square romancers';[64] Sara Hackenberg calls it a 'penny blood';[65] and Carver calls it 'very much the successor of Edward Lloyd's penny bloods'.[66] But aside from sharing the 1d cost, as much separates Reynolds from Rymer or Prest as would group them together. *Mysteries* resembles the penny blood in that it represents a great deal of violence, but the latter does so as a guilt-free rejection of the moralist school, and in that way is a cultural confrontation. Reynolds's novel is a political novel that out-moralises, out-reforms the humanitarian fiction that is consistently seen to be directly in opposition to penny fiction (of which *Mysteries* is understood to be part and parcel of). As Himmelfarb says, 'What distinguishes this work from others of its kind is neither its sexuality nor its violence but its politics.'[67] Unlike Lloyd's authors, who add radical content to help sell copy, Reynolds might better be seen as a radical who adds in sensational content to deepen the political narrative.

Louis James also points out that 'Reynolds's radical attitudes do give him a point of reference amid all the scrambling diversity of the book, and they show a social conscious lacking in almost all other popular fiction at the time.'[68] *Mysteries* shares with penny fiction carnivalesque and gothic excess. It too confuses the beautiful with the good, the ethical and aesthetic, compounding the tendency to split characters along the lines of deserving and undeserving that we see in penny fiction, but also confirming the liberal division between characters who deserve more freedom and the ones who need more supervision. *Mysteries* especially has an attitude towards the public which it sees as in need of rules, but ruined by the rules that exist. Reynolds expands the penny genre by including so much explicitly political material and by refusing to separate the penny material from the political material. A treatise on cemetery reform begins chapter CVI, leading quickly to a critique of the class system: 'The poor, indeed! who ever thought of legislating for the poor. Legislate *against* them and all is well and good.'[69] Reynolds then gets immediately to the gruesome, 'penny blood' stuff of grave-digging, the digger throwing a skull with long hair left on it onto a fire so we can hear it hiss before 'the voracious flames licked up the thin coat of blackened flesh'.[70] Perhaps the middle-class reader would agree, 'Legislate *against* them', but that would miss the point. If the gruesome aesthetic is set up here as an explicit instrument of the political, a dramatisation of what the class system produces, then misreading the aesthetic as disposably grisly becomes a political act itself.

Vengeance is Reynolds's

Appealing to so many audiences with so many different discourses and styles, *Mysteries* nonetheless finds ways to connect its numerous plotlines. Shirley notes Reynolds's focus on an 'essential unfairness – the elevation of the undeserving and the degradation of the unfortunate' that 'gave birth to the republicanism that was at the heart of his discourse'.[71] Haywood argues that 'each of the fifty-plus plots of *The Mysteries of London* concerns the corrupting and often horrifically violent effects of a social system which exists to serve a profligate aristocracy'.[72] Plotlines also come together around the idea of class-based vengeance. It is through the concept of vengeance that Reynolds is at his most radical, documenting the effects of inequality – of a failed system of economic, social, and political justice – but also introducing a more liberal way out of the cycles of vengeful violence that otherwise dominate *Mysteries* and popular fiction more generally. In *Mysteries*, nearly everyone from the 'low' – who is allowed a backstory to explain how they became 'low' – is hell-bent on vengeance, their desire for vengeance coming about in the absence of the legitimately just society, and the reality of the brutally unjust societies they describe. The novel documents how this becomes cyclical: those abused by 'the system' make for an increasingly dangerous society. Reynolds's aesthetic of violence, the cultural confrontations, the outlandish revenge plots and gruesome viciousness, are also political. Cultural and political confrontations are not separable in a world that operates through class-based vengeance. Nearly all our villains, except the middle-class ones like Greenwood and Reginald, have been wronged, politically wronged, and that is why they go out to do wrongs themselves.

An almost teleological vengeance takes hold of many of the 'low' figures in the novel, with Tidkins, Cranky Jem, Holford, Lydia and others completely identifying their purpose in life to exact revenge. With these characters, Reynolds frequently drops the narrative thread to ensure that their desire for vengeance is read through the antagonisms class structures generate. Vengeance is not a new, experimental theme, and Reynolds's eye on the conventions of gothic, the past haunting the present, was sure to lead him to revenge plots. As Nico H. Frijda argues, the 'Desire for revenge itself is immoderate';[73] the law of the talion, an eye for an eye, a tooth for a tooth, demonstrates an attempt to regulate that immoderate desire. *Mysteries* and the gothic genre itself are immoderate, and Reynolds would likely be attracted to this motif for that reason alone. But the idea of vengeance or retaliation is easily made a social issue, and the personal desire for revenge is easily mixed up with a social counterpart. If 'curtailing personal vengeance is considered to be one of the major general sources of criminal law',[74] representing a world where personal vengeance is ubiquitous argues the failure of criminal law and the entire social apparatus that creates criminal law. Frijda goes on to say that, 'One may even assert that it [vengeance] is not a psychological experience at all, but a social one with a political or judicial motivation; or merely a mode of behaviour that follows from cultural example or norm.'[75] This is precisely what Reynolds seeks to demonstrate in *Mysteries*, and what Tidkins captures exactly when he explains that 'My law is that practised by all the world.'[76] The cruelty of the vengeful characters (which creates the culturally challenging material) is simply the product of the context (the polis). Reynolds in this way argues as best as possible within the trappings of melodramatic conventions that must produce some flawless heroes, that all who live by the market, die by the market. Frijda concludes that ultimately, 'Vengeance serves power equalisation. When individuals or groups endeavour to impose their will upon others, vengeance serves to correct them. Revenge is the social power regulator in a society without central justice.'[77] The Republican, a sort of *deus ex machina* figure kept in waiting, does not seek vengeance, in part because he has accepted that republicanism is an alternative and better social-power regulator. He tells Richard that he forgives George Montague 'From the bottom of my heart'[78] for betraying him to the government for his political beliefs, and subsequently robbing him. By the end of the second volume, Richard, who has fought for republicanism now himself, does the same, and of course George turns out to be his brother Eugene. If reconciliation between the two brothers and forgiveness work as symbols of social unity, an essential brotherhood of man, it should not be forgotten that the brothers come from the same social background, the same class to begin with. Forgiveness and reconciliation are not typically how the desire for vengeance concludes in *Mysteries* when class resentment is in play, the confusion of class roles being largely suspended for these plotlines.

The novel begins with a scene of random violence; in addition to the emphasis on vengeance, *Mysteries* includes a great deal of indiscriminate or accidental violence. Both random and vengeful violence imply anomie and insufficient or ineffective regulating forces. With vengeance, the emphasis is on an unfair justice system, an individualising of justice. With vengeance, Reynolds also rehearses a more standard argument for self-control, a very Victorian argument that might be shared equally by moral-force Chartists and liberals. George (aka Greenwood, Eugene) has no self-control, enters Louisa's room to rape her as she sleeps; she has a dagger under her pillow and sends him off. He spends a good deal of the rest of the novel plotting to revenge himself on her to feel the power of conquest, and though he is not a member of the 'low', he demonstrates 'lowly behaviour'. But the actual 'low' in the novel arguably have more self-control than he does insofar as their acts of vengeance are to create a balance of power. George seeks domination, but it is noteworthy that Reynolds sets his motivation, vengeance, in line with the truly wronged characters in the novel. It is the feeling of powerlessness that motivates the desire for revenge that we repeatedly see in the novel: 'abashed – humbled – beaten down to the very dust',[79] and lacking the goodness she has, George grows imperious, determined to bring Louisa *morally* down in the way that Tidkins wants to take Richard socially down.

Powerlessness also explains why 'low' characters often plot against members of their own rough circles. In *The Seamstress*, we begin by meeting the landlord, Mrs Drake, certainly not of the higher classes, taking a cut from Virginia's labour in a line of succession or stages of exchange that leaves Virginia almost uncompensated for her labour. The first drama of the novel is Virginia's attempt to 'learn if it be possible for the poor seamstress to obtain the real value of her labour'.[80] For Reynolds, the lower classes of society are simply carrying out their roles in 'a picture so made up with the vivid-colourings of poor woman's wrongs, the sombre hues of man's cold-bloodedness and cruelty, and the dark outlines of a vitiated society and a heartless world, that we wonder God's vengeance sleeps'.[81] Victoria, however, is all good, sympathetic, and worthy, at one point giving away everything that her lover had bought for her when she suspects his unfaithfulness. But Virginia, who chooses to be a victim of poverty rather than lower her standards, is the exception to the rule, rendering her a victim for standing above the fray. Her goodness is continually tested and she always passes, but when the narrator interrupts her story with a direct plea for reform, the voicelessness of Virginia, the uselessness of being conscious of the real value of her labour, her victimisation, makes it so the narrator, author, or reader has to vent anger on her behalf. As Lynn Alexander has argued, the seamstress was a figure used to generate feelings of reform or 'stir up compassion for the working classes',[82] precisely because she was not a threatening Chartist operative like the animated figures in *Punch*. In narrativising antipodes of the vengeful and victimised, Reynolds asserts that the only alternative to victimisation in his narrative worlds is personal vengeance and crime.

Mysteries also includes many victims, but unlike Chartist fiction or *The Seamstress* where the victim tends to become a martyred figure, victims in *Mysteries* are apt to seek revenge. Reynolds is preoccupied with vengeance, the victim who then victimises. Frijda argues that vengeance arises when an individual or a social group feels harmed by another individual or social group and responds, not to repair the harm or the relationship or even to win material gain from the source of the resentment, but simply to make the object of the vengeance suffer,[83] which makes violence a typical part of a revenge scheme. Vengeance in the novel thus acts only to destabilise the society further, not to create real justice; retribution does not provide the means for a better distribution of wealth. The gains made by successfully destroying another are always relative, never social. As Frijda says, 'All this is personal and emotional. It has nothing to do with a sense of justice. But the dolorous inequalities can be transformed onto an abstract and general plane and become formulated in a moral way, and so can the restoration of the balance of suffering. Then it indeed becomes a sense of justice. Those who cause pain should suffer in return, and, if possible, at least to an equal degree.'[84]

Reynolds ensures that the personal be read politically by commenting on the way personal vendettas have a social origin. For example, Lydia Hutchinson is bent on vengeance against Lady Ravensworth. Lydia's story is complicated but fascinating in the way it gives us a failed working-class Bildungsroman, a working-class version of *Jane Eyre*. We first meet Lydia destitute and desperate on the street, passers-by ignoring her until Viola, herself a hapless victim, offers aid. As is typical in *Mysteries*, we then get her history, which includes an abusive boarding school, a stint as a teacher, and then harassment as a governess. The story details what Brontë only implies; as a governess she suffers her employer's sexual advances. The main part of this Bildungsroman happens when Lydia is led by Adeline Enfield into the company of a libertine, leading to a seduction plot then a fallen woman and kept woman plot. Adeline gets pregnant, but claims the hidden lifeless child is Lydia's. Lydia is ostracised and eventually becomes a prostitute in a brothel before we catch up to her destitute in the street where she was first introduced. Adeline, however, lives the fashionable life and becomes Lady Ravensworth. In true gothic fashion, Lydia returns as the Lady's servant to torment and blackmail her, having the ability to expose Adeline. This is all very personal and melodramatic, but Reynolds breaks into the narrative, as it were, to draw a lesson on class-oriented vengeance:

> The aristocracy conceives that it may insult the democracy with impunity. The high-born and the wealthy never stop to consider, when they put an affront upon the lowly and the poor, whether a day of retribution may not sooner or later come. The peer cannot see the necessity of conciliating the peasant: the daughter of the nobility knows not the use of making a friend of the daughter of the people.
>
> But the meanest thing that crawls upon the earth may some day be in a position to avenge the injuries it has received from a powerful oppressor; and the mightiest lord or the noblest lady may be placed in that situation when even the friendship of the humblest son or the most obscure daughter of industry would be welcome as the drop of water to the lost wanderer of the desert.
>
> Yes! Most solemnly do I proclaim to you, O suffering millions of these islands, that ye shall not always languish beneath the yoke of

your oppressors! Individually ye shall each see the day when your tyrant shall crouch at your feet; and as a mass ye shall triumph over that proud oligarchy which now grinds you to the dust!

That day – that great day cannot be far distant; and then shall ye rise – not to wreak a savage vengeance on those who have so long coerced you, but to prove to them that ye know how to exercise a mercy which they never manifested towards you; – ye shall rise, not to convulse the State with a disastrous civil war, nor to hurry the nation on to the deplorable catastrophe of social anarchy, confusion, and bloodshed; – but ye shall rise to vindicate usurped rights, and to recover delegated and misused power, that ye may triumphantly assert the aristocracy of mind, and the aristocracy of virtue![85]

I quote the Shelleyan passage at length because the leap that Reynolds makes from the mimetic to the diegetic, from Lydia's story to the plea for a moral revolution where the people rise above their desires for 'savage vengeance', at first seems so enormous that the passage comes off as nothing more than a badly veiled threat. In *Mysteries*, without the Republican's calm assistance, vengeance is savage, bringing about a 'deplorable catastrophe of social anarchy, confusion, and bloodshed' but on a smaller scale. Reynolds's direct presentation of how the desire for vengeance escalates, especially because it does not seem to be in proportion to the narrative, runs counter to what works of art are supposed to do, insofar as art is said to operate, according to Diarmuid Costello, 'in ways that provoke "more thought" than a direct conceptual elaboration of the idea itself could facilitate'.[86] But not in Reynolds and not generally in Chartist fiction either. Lydia may desire to restore something like an equality of misery with Adeline, but to bring the object of vengeance down carries no promise to raise the vengeful. Vengeance also begets vengeance, in theory and in the novel, and is part of an endless repetitive cycle, even if it takes years to enact. Lydia eventually gets revenge on Lord Dunstable, her seducer, but when Adeline can take no more of Lydia's taunting, she has the Resurrection Man murder Lydia. Tidkins then has power over Adeline. When the buried body of Lydia is discovered, Tidkins threatens to turn in Adeline, but she falls dead after seeing the corpse; panicked, Tidkins knocks over a candle as he runs away and the aristocratic hall is burnt down. The violent end to the aristocracy – Adeline is from below and has only schemed her way into the aristocracy – does not have to be, but will be if the 'suffering millions of these islands' have no peaceful alternative to justice.

An equally interesting story about revenge is Holford's. The Holford narrative documents a working-class feeling of exclusion, pathetic as it might be. After the initial scene in Buckingham Palace, Holford returns to the palace on several occasions. He takes in a good deal of gossip (that Reynolds evaluates in long footnotes), and allows the narrator to critique the luxuries of palace living compared to 'bitter poverty',[87] as well as to delve into Victoria's relationship with Albert and the difficulty of having a wife in a superior position to a husband. Before Albert catches Henry and removes him from the palace, the narrator's essayistic discourse details the way the royals avoid reality, rampant poverty, and misery. Holford's only role here – unnecessary in the narratological design – is to give the audience access to the palace and therefore to the narrator's criticism of the sovereign's ostentatious lifestyle. But Holford, made angry by being turfed out of the palace, reads about assassination attempts on monarchs (actual ones) and, wanting to be a 'martyr',[88] attempts to kill Victoria (and/or Albert), though Crankey Jem spoils his plans. Reynolds seems to have the 10 June 1840 Edward Oxford attempt in mind, as Oxford was declared mad and Holford ends up in Bedlam, but by the time he was writing *Mysteries* there had been three assassination attempts on the monarchs and Reynolds was likely conflating the Oxford attempt with the 30 May 1842, John Francis attempt, at least. Again, Holford's personalised story of trying to 'avenge my expulsion from the palace! – now to make my name a subject for history'[89] is politicised, generalised. Reynolds interjects to comment on the way the poor will be driven to revenge, even though Holford is hardly a politically conscious figure – despite his reading of history's martyrs – motivated by unbalanced wealth distribution:

> Enough has been said in the more serious and reasoning parts of this work to prove that society is in a vitiated – a false – and an artificial condition. The poor are too poor, and the rich too rich: the obscure are too low, and the exalted too high. The upper classes alone have

opportunities of signalising themselves: the industrious millions have no chance of rising in the State.[90]

At this point in the narrative, however, Crankey Jem had just been shown as rising through his industry, making room for himself between the too low and too high and giving to Holford an opportunity to follow him on the straight and narrow.[91] Still, Reynolds continues: 'Now, such being the case, – with a dominant aristocracy on one hand, and the oppressed millions on the other, – is it not evident that every now and then some member of the latter class will brood upon the vast, the astounding contrast until feelings of a deplorably morbid nature become excited in his mind?'[92] Reynolds insists that this is a 'deplorable' state of affairs and that the use of violence is never appropriate to vindicate 'just rights', but only that vengeance is inevitable in these conditions:

> But if these instances of outbreaking revenge – if these ebullitions of indomitable resentment do now and then occur, no small portion of the blame must be charged against that aristocracy which maintains itself on an eminence so immeasurably above the depths in which the masses are compelled to languish. And when the poor creature who is goaded to desperation, does strike – can we wonder if, in the madness of his rage, he deals his blows indiscriminately, or against an innocent person? He may even aim at royalty itself – although, in every really constitutional country, the sovereign is little more than a mere puppet, the Prime Minister of the day being the virtual ruler of the nation.[93]

Aside from what appears to be a threat or warning to the Prime Minister, a reminder that Robert Peel would be the better target, in the narrative proper, Reynolds insists that the retribution and power equality promised by revenge is elusive or not meaningful. Holford's desire for retribution is inseparable from his adolescence, not his politics. Reynolds's direct commentary redirects readers to understand that Holford's consuming passion is born from feelings of estrangement that not only have a political counterpart but also a political origin. It functions as a way to draw political conclusions from the 'cultural confrontations' in the plot. The many diatribes on legal and penal reform demonstrate that the law is also vindictive,[94] establishing a cycle or revenge which is social but manifests personally. The gypsies live outside of society's rules, but they have adopted equally harsh laws of vengeance. It should be noted that the representation of the gypsies in *Mysteries* is remarkably progressive in many ways. Morcar, son of Zingary, the king of the gypsies, follows Richard to Castelcicala and fights honourably with him. But their system of justice is harsh and unforgiving, which we see when the Rattlesnake is found guilty of aiding Tidkins and sentenced to death; Crankey Jem is sent away, thus beginning his obsessive desire to revenge himself on Tidkins. The way the novel pretends to be passive, helplessly and inexorably drawn from one scene to the next – the near refrain of 'We must now transport our readers back to ...'[95] – creates the sense that life in London is so overdetermined that even the narrative trajectory is determined. The melodramatic plotting itself is determined by the extratextual context, though it exists independently from context as well (as with Holford's story). The idea of vengeance is treated in the same way, as something that invariably manifests when no trust can be placed in existing systems of justice – legal, social, economic, political – and what they have produced.

With the Resurrection Man, Anthony Tidkins, we get the heightened 'aesthetics of *making* monstrous, of demonstrative magnification and amplification'[96] common to gothic storytelling. Tidkins's monomaniacal pursuit of Richard is as unreasonable as Holford's desire to kill the monarchs because they had the audacity to boot him out of their own home. Tidkins is angry at Richard because Richard foiled his attempt to rob him. But as Sara Hackenberg explains, his motivation goes deeper: 'The Resurrection Man ... emerges as both an uncanny double for the serial's hero and a shadow image of republican energy. ... like the Republican, Richard has been imprisoned in part for tenaciously sticking to his values and ideals; but also, and thus like the Resurrection Man, his imprisonment is the result of being in the wrong place at the wrong time.'[97] The relationship between Tidkins and Richard resembles the relationship between Uriah Heep and David Copperfield, or between Orlick and Pip, 'disrupting any easy categorisation of virtue and vice'.[98] The use of the double in Dickens's work, as Alex Woloch has shown, often implies the hero's sheer circumstantial luck in becoming the hero, the minor double figure reduced to the role of 'the proletariat of the novel'.[99] Tidkins, Hackenberg shows, swears to revenge himself on Richard because he knows that he was denied the advantages that Richard takes for granted. In this way the novel challenges the concept of Nietzschean *ressentiment*. Nietzsche sees slave morality as bitterly reactive, angry at everything that is different from it. Master morality, on the other hand, is not concerned with anything outside of itself, such as the feelings of the slave. Nietzsche argues that *ressentiment* distorts slave mentality so as to construct the master class as badly as possible, essentially to feel better about itself. But Reynolds shows that the desire for vengeance that is inevitable among the lower classes breeds clever, scheming villains, such as the Resurrection Man. Tidkins might be a slave to feelings of inferiority, but hardly figures himself as 'good' and Richard as 'evil' per Nietzsche's *ressentiment*. Tidkins, rather, accepts that he is 'evil' because Reynolds's focus is not on mentalities, but ultimately on material or circumstantial realities.

Tidkins's constant brooding and obsessive pursuit of Richard is pathological, but again Reynolds insists that personal pathologies have a social counterpart. Tidkins defends himself by saying he follows a 'universal practice', *'the oppression of the weak by the strong'*.[100] Near the end of his sad backstory, where he explains how he was 'hardened' by the penal treadmill, he speaks of desire for vengeance in political terms, saying 'I owed him [the magistrate] a recompense for my month on the treadmill; and I thought I might as well add *Incendiary* to my other titles of *Rogue* and *Vagabond*.'[101] The easy slippage from rogue to incendiary, as we saw with the Newgate calendar from the Chartist period, is significant insofar as it demonstrates that the political is never that far away from the personal or cultural. Tidkins concludes his backstory with a song he composed on the occasion of collapsing casual and political crime together, called 'The incendiary's song'. A song of vengeance by a Jack Sheppard would normally work only to lend the character the quality of the folk hero, but Reynolds takes the occasion to move a personal experience to a class-based one, to the language of us and them:

> The Lucifer-match! the Lucifer-match!
>   'Tis the weapon for us to wield.

> How bonnily burns up rick and thatch.
>   And the crop just housed from the field!
> The proud may oppress and the rich distress,
>   And drive us from their door; –
> But they cannot snatch the Lucifer-match
>   From the hand of the desperate poor!
>
> The purse proud squire and the tyrant peer
>   May keep their Game Laws still;
> And the very glance of the overseer
>   May continue to freeze and kill.
> The wealthy and great, and the chiefs of the state,
>   May tyrannise more and more; –
> But they cannot snatch the Lucifer-match
>   From the hand of the desperate poor!
>
> '*Oh! give us bread!*' is the piteous wail
>   That is murmured far and wide;
> And echo takes up and repeats the tale –
>   But the rich man turns aside.
> The Justice of Peace may send his Police
>   To scour the country o'er;
> But they cannot snatch the Lucifer-match
>   From the hand of the desperate poor!
>
> Then, hurrah! hurrah! for the Lucifer-match;
>   'Tis the weapon of despair. –
> How bonnily blaze up barn and thatch –
>   The poor man's revenge is there!
> For the *worm* will turn on the feet that spurn-
>   And surely a *man* is more? –
> Oh! none can e'er snatch the Lucifer match
>   From the hand of the desperate poor![102]

Vengeance is never isolated as a strictly personal vendetta in *Mysteries*. The political world makes the personal world, leading to ubiquitous forms of violence. In this way, Reynolds maintains that changes to the political are part of what is needed to restore the individual's world to some level of tolerable decency, as the ostensibly random violence of the Resurrection Man, the man who always returns, turns out to be a political return of the oppressed. Despite the individualistic heroism of Richard, individualised or moral solutions to social problems are rendered inadequate when the personal and political are so inevitably linked. Reynolds consistently politicises the vengeance that initiates so much of the sensational storytelling. Tidkins also promises revenge on Crankey Jem, but Crankey Jem, possibly another double for Richard, accomplishes what Richard desires but fails to do – disempower (blinding him), isolate (burying him alive), and kill him. It is hardly a triumphal scene, despite the savage satisfaction offered in seeing the Resurrection Man finally put down for good. Rather, if the complicated cycles of violence evoked in *Mysteries* are inherently political, they do not come to an end with the end of a single villain.

However, and finally, the novel does not generally show, despite's Tidkins's song, individual characters seeking political vengeance. The narrator is needed to bridge those gaps; only the Resurrection Man voices political discontent, and that is mostly contained in his backstory. *Mysteries* depicts London in the 1840s as bent on irrational vengeance, the 'low' not knowing the true source of their anger. This is far from Carlyle's claim that Chartism was reducible to 'Bellowings, inarticulate cries as of a dumb creature in rage and pain; to the ear of wisdom they are inarticulate prayers: "Guide me, govern me! I am mad, and miserable, and cannot guide myself!"' ('Chartism' 157).[103] Yet Reynolds does to some extent represent the false consciousness of an unguided people. Representing displaced desires for vengeance would not disqualify the actual working classes from full citizenship or deny the value of their agitational practices. But by reducing the class struggle to a 'thousand games of' retaliation,[104] all of them futile, and obscuring the antinomies that Reynolds knows are necessary to initiate his class arguments in the first place, Reynolds is in fact not that far from the nineteenth-century liberalist slight of hand that addresses class conflicts through personal, resolvable ones. The social problems explored in the novel demand radical answers, but reform is proposed. Charity is represented as futile, but Richard's charitableness is rewarded. Class is the source of conflict, but class boundaries are vague and the newly elevated class is a source of harmony. Vengeance is misplaced but has no place. Reynolds writes as a radical, but keeping an eye on the possibility that it would be small, liberal steps that led to radicalism's heights, he writes in other ways as well.

Notes

1. G. W. M. Reynolds, *The Mysteries of London* (Kansas City, MO: Valancourt Books, 2013), I, p. 505.
2. *Ibid.*
3. *Ibid.*, p. 525.
4. *Ibid.*, p. 526.
5. R. McWilliam, 'The mysteries of G. W. M. Reynolds: radicalism and melodrama in Victorian Britain', in M. Chase and I. Dyck (eds), *Living and Learning: Essays in Honour of J. F. C. Harrison* (Aldershot: Scolar Press, 1996), p. 184.
6. K. Andrews, 'Neither mute nor inglorious: Anne Yearsley and elegy', in J. Goodridge and B. Keegan (eds), *A History of British Working Class Literature* (Cambridge: Cambridge University Press, 2017), p. 86.
7. Jones justifies the combination of politics and romance in his own work by saying, 'I do not see why Truth should always be dressed in a stern and repulsive garb. The more attractive you can make her, the more easily she will progress.' E. Jones, 'Preface to *De Brassier*', in *Notes to the People* (London: J. Pavey, 1851), I, p. 20.
8. S. J. Carver, 'The wrongs and crimes of the poor: the urban underworld of *The Mysteries of London* in context', in A. Humpherys and L. James (eds), *G. W. M. Reynolds: Nineteenth-Century Fiction, Politics, and the Press* (Aldershot: Ashgate, 2008), p. 162.
9. Reynolds, *The Mysteries of London*, I, pp. 515–16.
10. S. Perera, *No Country: Working-Class Writing in the Age of Globalization* (New York: Columbia University Press, 2014), p. 20.
11. R. McWilliam, 'The French connection: G. W. M. Reynolds and the outlaw Robert Macaire', in Humpherys and James (eds), *G. W. M. Reynolds*, p. 35.
12. L. James, 'Time, politics and the symbolic imagination in Reynolds's social melodrama', in Humpherys and James (eds), *G. W. M. Reynolds*, p. 181.
13. B. Chevasco, 'Lost in translation: the relationship between Eugène Sue's *Les Mystères de Paris* and Reynolds's *The Mysteries of London*', in Humpherys and James (eds), *G. W. M. Reynolds*, p. 139.

14 Quoted in Carver, 'The wrongs and crimes of the poor', p. 159. See also J. John, 'Reynolds's *Mysteries* and popular culture', in Humpherys and James (eds), *G. W. M. Reynolds*, p. 164.
15 John, 'Reynolds's *Mysteries* and popular culture', p. 175.
16 As Engels said, 'Chartism is essentially a social movement. The middle-class Radicals had regarded the "Six Points" of the Charter as the be-all and end-all of the movement, but the working classes consider that the "Six Points" and any further constitutional reforms to which they might give rise, are only a means to an end. Nowadays the rallying cry of the Chartists is: "Political power brings social happiness".' F. Engels, *The Condition of the Working Classes in England*, trans. W. O. Henderson and W. H. Chaloner (Oxford: Basil Blackwell, 1971), p. 267.
17 A. Humpherys, 'G. W. M. Reynolds: popular literature and popular politics', *Victorian Periodicals Review*, 16:3 (1983), 87–8.
18 I. Haywood, *The Revolution in Popular Literature: Print, Politics, and the People, 1790–1860* (Cambridge: Cambridge University Press, 2004), p. 140.
19 Humpherys points out that *Mysteries* is 'coterminous with the rise of sociological investigation'. A. Humpherys, 'An introduction to G. W. M. Reynolds's "Encyclopedia of Tales"', in Humpherys and James (eds), *G. W. M. Reynolds*, p. 133.
20 G. Himmelfarb, *The Idea of Poverty: England in the Early Industrial Age* (New York: Alfred A. Knopf, 1984), p. 450.
21 John, 'Reynolds's *Mysteries* and popular culture', p. 169.
22 P. Joyce, *Visions of the People: Industrial England and the Question of Class, 1848–1914* (Cambridge: Cambridge University Press, 1991), p. 66.
23 R. Crone, *Violent Victorians: Popular Entertainment in Nineteenth-Century London* (Manchester: Manchester University Press, 2012), p. 178.
24 Reynolds, *The Mysteries of London*, II, pp. 1062–76.
25 *Ibid.*, I, p. 3.
26 G. Vargo, *An Underground History of Early Victorian Fiction: Chartism, Radical Print Culture, and the Social Problem Novel* (Cambridge: Cambridge University Press, 2018), p. 9.
27 McWilliam, 'The mysteries of G. W. M. Reynolds', p. 192.
28 McWilliam, 'The French connection', p. 35.
29 Haywood, *The Revolution in Popular Literature*, pp. 171 and 172.
30 L. James, *Fiction for the Working Man, 1830–1850* (Harmondsworth: Penguin University Books, 1974), p. 194.

31 M. H. Shirley, 'G. W. M. Reynolds, *Reynolds's Newspaper* and popular politics', in Humpherys and James (eds), *G. W. M. Reynolds*, p. 87.
32 Reynolds, *The Mysteries of London*, II, p. 389.
33 L. Brake and M. Demoor (eds), 'Weekly dispatch', in *Dictionary of Nineteenth-Century Journalism* (Gent and London: Academia Press, 2009), p. 668.
34 McWilliam, 'The French connection', p. 41.
35 Himmelfarb, *The Idea of Poverty*, p. 438.
36 Reynolds, *The Mysteries of London*, I, p. 4.
37 *Ibid.*, p. 409.
38 *Ibid.*, pp. 891–3.
39 *Ibid.*, pp. 497–9.
40 Vargo, *An Underground History of Early Victorian Fiction*, p. 11.
41 Reynolds, *The Mysteries of London*, I, pp. 568–9.
42 *Ibid.*, pp. 680–2.
43 *Ibid.*, II, p. 12.
44 McWilliam, 'The mysteries of G. W. M. Reynolds', p. 187.
45 G. W. M. Reynolds, *The Seamstress; or, the White Slave of England* (London: John Dicks, 1853), p. 134.
46 Bronterre O'Brien, for example, argued that 'Charity to those, to whom justice is denied, is only a bribe to make them submit to tyranny and injustice.' B. O'Brien, *Bronterre's National Reformer* (7 January 1837), p. 8. In *Chartism* (1840), William Lovett says, 'If men, too, were generally imbued with that independent feeling which springs from the cultivation of intellect, they would never permit their children to wear the badge and livery of charity.' W. Lovett and J. Collins, *Chartism: A New Organization of the People* (New York: Leicester University Press, 1969), p. 59.
47 Reynolds, *The Mysteries of London*, I, pp. 492–5.
48 *Ibid.*, pp. 135–6.
49 *Ibid.*, II, p. 7. Reynolds's *Drunkard's Progress* (1840–41) also has a long scene where beggars celebrate their rich spoils in a drunk den laughing at the people who gave them alms.
50 Quoted in James, 'Time, politics, and the symbolic imagination', p. 189.
51 Vargo, *An Underground History of Early Victorian Fiction*, p. 10.
52 Reynolds, *The Mysteries of London*, II, p. 20.
53 *Ibid.*, I, p. 275.
54 *Ibid.*, II, p. 354.
55 *Ibid.*
56 *Ibid.*, p. 1132.

57 *Ibid.*, I, p. 561.
58 Humpherys, 'An introduction to G. W. M. Reynolds's', p. 126.
59 Reynolds, *The Mysteries of London*, I, p. 449.
60 *Ibid.*, II, p. 1133.
61 Humpherys, 'An introduction to G. W. M. Reynolds's', p. 133.
62 Carver, 'The wrongs and crimes of the poor', p. 149.
63 J. Flanders, *The Invention of Murder: How the Victorians Revelled in Death and Detection and Created Modern Crime* (Hammersmith: Harper Press, 2011), p. 59.
64 R. D. Altick, *The English Common Reader: A Social History of the Mass Reading Public 1800–1900* (Columbus, OH: Ohio State University Press, 2nd edn, 1998), p. 290.
65 S. Hackenberg, 'Vampires and resurrection men: the perils and pleasures of the embodied past in 1840s sensational fiction', *Victorian Studies*, 52:1 (2009), 63.
66 Carver, 'The wrongs and crimes of the poor', p. 152.
67 Himmelfarb, *The Idea of Poverty*, p. 442.
68 James, *Fiction for the Working Man*, p. 197.
69 Reynolds, *The Mysteries of London*, I, p. 906.
70 *Ibid.*, p. 908.
71 Shirley, 'G. W. M. Reynolds', p. 87.
72 Haywood, *The Revolution in Popular Literature*, p. 179.
73 N. H. Frijda, 'The lex talonis: on vengeance', in S. H. M. van Goozen *et al.* (eds), *Emotions: Essays on Emotion Theory* (Hillsdale, NJ: Lawrence Erlbaum Associates, 1994), p. 264.
74 *Ibid.*
75 *Ibid.*, p. 265.
76 Reynolds, *The Mysteries of London*, I, p. 312.
77 Frijda, 'The lex talonis', p. 270.
78 Reynolds, *The Mysteries of London*, I, p. 193.
79 *Ibid.*, p. 150.
80 Reynolds, *The Seamstress*, p. 19.
81 *Ibid.*, p. 85.
82 L. Alexander, 'Creating a symbol: the seamstress in Victorian literature', *Tulsa Studies in Women's Literature*, 18:1 (1999), 29.
83 Frijda, 'The lex talonis', p. 266.
84 *Ibid.*, pp. 274–5.
85 Reynolds, *The Mysteries of London*, II, pp. 635–6.
86 D. Costello, 'Greenberg's Kant and the fate of aesthetics in contemporary art theory', *The Journal of Aesthetics and Art Criticism*, 65:2 (2007), 225.

87 Reynolds, *The Mysteries of London*, II, p. 527.
88 *Ibid.*, p. 657.
89 *Ibid.*, p. 669.
90 *Ibid.*, p. 662.
91 *Ibid.*, p. 471.
92 *Ibid.*, p. 662.
93 *Ibid.*, pp. 662–3.
94 *Ibid.*, I, p. 275.
95 *Ibid.*, II, p. 298.
96 R. Chow, *Ethics after Idealism: Theory, Culture, Ethnicity, Reading* (Basingstoke: Palgrave Macmillan, 1998), p. 16.
97 Hackenberg, 'Vampires and resurrection men', p. 71.
98 *Ibid.*, p. 73.
99 A. Woloch, *The One vs. the Many* (Princeton, NJ: Princeton University Press, 2003), p. 27.
100 Reynolds, *The Mysteries of London*, I, p. 312.
101 *Ibid.*, p. 545.
102 *Ibid.*, pp. 546–7.
103 T. Carlyle, 'Chartism', in *The Works of Thomas Carlyle in Thirty Volumes* (New York: Charles Scribner and Sons, 1904), XXIX, p. 157.
104 Jacques Rancière identifies 'thousand games of social mobility' as that which complicates the polarising of oppositional practices and tastes among the classes. J. Rancière, *The Philosopher and His Poor* (Durham, NC: Duke University Press, 2004), p. 194.

5

Distant friends of the people: *Howitt's Journal* and *Douglas Jerrold's Shilling Magazine*

The popular press was not alone in addressing itself to an imagined audience of politicised working people. I have been focusing on the way the penny press read the reader – rough but sentimental, mired in the quotidian but politically excitable – aiming to satisfy a desire for rousing entertainment in part by establishing ties to what it considered to be working-class political ambitions and grievances, but there were many other presses claiming to know how working-class politics and culture intersect or should intersect, and trying to capture working-class audiences by offering up congenial political content. None of these could speak about the reforms that working people or the poor needed, or wanted, as if Chartism did not exist, even if some of them seemed to want to do exactly that. *Howitt's Journal* (1847–48) and *Douglas Jerrold's Shilling Magazine* (*DJSM*) (1845–48), the two papers I am discussing in this chapter, are not representative of middle-class periodicals claiming to support the interests of the working classes because representativeness would be very difficult to establish in this field. The sheer number of interventionist, reformist, and usually family-friendly papers emerging in the late stages of Chartism, or just after its understood demise, from John Cassell's anti-Chartist *Working Man's Friend, and Family Instructor* (1851–53) to the pro-Chartist *Eliza Cook's Journal* (1849–54), underscores not only the imprint left by the Chartist press but by the penny presses as well. Huge discrepancies characterise the kind and amount of sympathy, antipathy, or just attention offered Chartism or other forms of radicalism in, for example, John Saunders's *People's Journal* (1846–47) or *Politics for the People* (1848–49), briefly discussed at the beginning of this book,[1] but they universally throw scorn on the popular press. Individual contributors to these periodicals also had some license to bend the editors' or proprietors' will, meaning that the papers are not ideologically consistent. However, the way these papers respond to the linking of class politics and culture illustrates the extent to which the yoking of Chartism and the popular press – even though the combination was largely denied by both – affected the conversation around reform.

With the exception of *Politics for the People*, reform journals were arguably more expressly favourable to Chartism than to the popular press, though they tend to imply a connection between physical-force Chartism and the materials produced by the popular press. Chartist papers share with reform journals the high, utilitarian seriousness that so often accompanies writing about 'justice', and too often leads to the idea that romances are politically empty. Brian Maidment, speaking on 'The distinction between the journals of popular progress and the popular penny fiction-based weeklies like *The London Journal* or *Reynolds's Miscellany*', which is enormous, suggests that 'the closest comparison' for the journals of popular progress, such as *Howitt's*, 'is with the Chartist and radical journals'.[2] *Howitt's Journal* and *DJSM* are themselves very different from each other, the former much more willing to countenance Chartism than the latter. But both papers are focused on the grievances of the poor in ways not always unlike Chartist literature; they both include material by well-known Chartists; and they both separate out 'the poor' and 'the working classes' in a way that recognises the political determination of the latter. Though only *Howitt's* admits, inconsistently and with shifting degrees of reservation, the Chartist narrative – that social amelioration cannot happen without participation from working people, without acceptance of the working classes as decision makers – both attempt to inculcate some understanding of the rise of Chartism to middle-class readers, showing some sympathy for democratic reform. But they insist that for reform to happen, the connection between class politics and class culture established in the penny press must first be entirely undone.

If there is a link between reform and penny literature, insofar as they both reach out to the politically conscious or politically active working person, a probable Chartist reader, the connection ends there, before it barely begins. With their wide-ranging representations of confrontation, penny journals were the polar opposite of improvement or progress journals. In an article citing and enumerating the successes of improvement papers and temperance societies, William Howitt exclaims, 'that dreadful trash that is weekly devoured with the avidity of opium, that literature of murder, of crime, and of wildest extravagance be the end at which we aimed at educating people. We answer – No.'[3] *Howitt's Journal* and *DJSM*, unlike both Chartist and popular publications, are above all else desperately non-confrontational. Instead of conflict they offer images of, or the means to, cultural reconciliation and interclass dialogue, assuming that a form of political reconciliation would coincide. The way that these papers attempt to elide class and class division makes clear that the use of class hostility in the popular press had a political counterpart. Finally, they differ from both Chartist and popular papers insofar as in their campaign for class reconciliation they aggressively promote a hard division between moral and physical force, associating moral force with a preferred image of the working classes desiring self-improvement and physical force with stock phantasmagorias of working-class 'roughs' from the popular press. Submitted as a humanitarian gesture, the need to rise above party politics is repeatedly specified, but only physical-force Chartism is categorised as a partisan enterprise. Reinforcing the division between moral and physical agitation that most Chartists, or at least 'physical-force Chartists', downplayed – and a division between moral and physical acts that the popular press effectively disallowed – was the condition under which Chartism could be brought into the conversation.

In this chapter I look at the way images of cultural cooperation and progress were constructed so as to defuse or erase political tensions: the way progress, improvement, or reform journals set out to oppose and overturn the grouping of cultural and political differences in the popular press. I relate middle-class attitudes towards the Chartist narrative, always diverging and conflicting, to the appropriation of it by the popular press, where cultural and political confrontations are linked in the image of a unified 'lower class'. The Howitts and Jerrold, on the other hand, insist on a divided *people*, the 'poor' and the 'working class', and link cultural maturity to political potential. However, although *Howitt's Journal* begins by confirming progress and insisting on positivity, the programme soon unravels: as the political environment intensified leading up to the Chartist meeting at Kennington Common on 10 April 1848, *Howitt's Journal* adopts a qualified but increasingly stark version of the Chartist narrative, and the more it comes to terms with the idea of political anger the more it accepts essential class differences. *DJSM*, which also concluded its run shortly after the 'monster meeting' at Kennington Common, is consistently anti-Chartist, but the way it struggles with representing poverty as a social and not a political crisis, so as to mediate Chartist concerns, suggests a deeper struggle with the Chartist or democratic narrative. However, I mostly discuss *DJSM* to underline the way reform journals treated cultural and political confrontation as one and the same, illustrating what was at stake when *Howitt's Journal* began to express dissatisfaction with the platitudes of social progress and harmony. The journals of social reform could not or did not simply reject or ignore Chartism, and though there are clear signs that they would have preferred to advocate on behalf of the poor without the Chartist spectre above them, the turn to acknowledging Chartism's argument suggests an awareness of its popularity, recognition of its ability to speak for *its* audience, the same audience these journals at least ostensibly sought. It also suggests that in 'moral-force Chartism' they thought they found an antidote to the penny radicals' promise of political confrontation in cultural difference.

Bordering Chartism, proceeding with one eye on it, this strain of 'popular literature' was anything but incendiary or agitational. Instead of capitalising on the prospect of revolution, progress journals aim at redirecting energies towards education and culture, not entirely unlike their more direct and obvious progenitor, Charles Knight's *Penny Magazine* (1832–45). If reform journals attempted to ease social tensions through encouraging a refinement of taste, their alter ego, the penny press, was there to reignite them. This is not to deny the sincerity of the reformist agenda of both the Howitts and Jerrold and their deep investment in addressing working-class grievances. Again, if the penny blood, Newgate calendars and novels, and crime fiction from the period play coy with inciting revolution, allowing themselves to be used or understood as part of a movement but only indirectly, *Howitt's* and *DJSM* lend themselves more directly to Chartist goals: it is the method of achieving the goals that concerns the papers and leads to a preoccupation with shaping working-class culture so as to look the opposite of how it looks in the penny press. Accepting selected tenets of Chartism, or the cause of the Chartist complaint, and eventually the Chartist narrative, this form of middle-class conciliation literature insists, as said, on the division between moral and physical force. Involved in such a strategy is the furtive slippage of 'moral-force Chartism' into moral or personal reform: 'moral force' is not simply the attempt to bring in the Charter peacefully, but primarily the means to force working-class advocates to confess that personal reform or improvement – a refinement of working-class culture on a larger scale – is a precondition for the franchise.[4] Looking at Chartist poetry and the poems reproduced in Chartist papers, Mike Sanders is correct to point out that Chartism's strategy to demonstrate vote worthiness through giving evidence of aesthetic maturity or 'the argument from culture' was 'made with increasing frequency and confidence'[5] in the second half of the 1840s. It is also the case, however, that Chartist *fiction* by and large refuses this posturing, arguably moving towards more and more popular forms just as the poetry was becoming more and more refined.

The deep ambiguity Chartism demonstrates around individual reform – especially as a precondition to the Charter – is absent from reform journals. Eliza Meteyard, for example, who wrote for both papers (and was given her pseudonym 'Silverpen' by Jerrold), as well as Chartist papers, argues in *Howitt's Journal* that to demonstrate *'temperance, self-education, and moral conduct'*[6] is to demonstrate vote-readiness (public demonstration itself is a sign of non-vote-readiness). Seeing evidence in 'the Chartist demonstrations throughout the kingdom, and the threatened resort to physical force' that Chartism was in danger of eschewing 'constitutional and legitimate methods' of change, she links moral-force Chartism directly to self-improvement.[7] It might be speculated here that the image of a morally perfect Richard Markham in Reynolds's *Mysteries of London*, violently engaged in the fight for constitutionalist reform, would be anathema to her. Eyeing the Kennington

Common meeting as a show of physical force, Meteyard asks, 'is this the Chartism of William Lovett, of the latter opinions of Thomas Cooper? No! They have emphatically told us, that besides widening the basis of representation, other contingent reforms are necessary, reforms of ourselves.'[8] Meteyard insists on a hard division between 'sorts' of Chartism, the kinds that seek self-reform and the kinds that seek the 'destruction of what sort soever, pulling down parliament houses, sacking a city, or burning acts of parliament'.[9] Warning against the 'sort of oratory' that might inflame the people, she embraces a conditional Chartism by hardening the distinction between its 'forms': 'this sort of Chartism is the offspring of popular ignorance; and had the governing class taught instead of quibbling over religious dogma, every man that now in most deplorable ignorance, shouts "destruction" would have said, we need two reforms, and will have them, constitutional reform, and personal reform'.[10] The linking of constitutional and personal reform, and the insistence on knowing what the working man 'would' say, reveals the limits of the paper's liberalism, or more generally the limits Victorian liberalism would place on freedom, market, and otherwise. *Howitt's Journal* and, to a lesser extent, *DJSM* were vested in empowering working people to achieve full citizenship as long as the middling classes were somehow involved in mediating the process of empowerment and maintaining cultural conditions for democratic reform.[11]

Howitt's Journal

Mary and William Howitt's *Howitt's Journal* was a sixteen-page weekly that began in 1847 as a continuation of the *People's Journal*. Linda Hughes pegs the audience at '25,000–30,000 artisan and middle-class readers'.[12] That it had deep, meaningful connections to Chartism and Chartist leaders was not a kept secret: it was 'published (for the proprietor) by William Lovett'. Works by Thomas Cooper, Ernest Jones, Goodwyn Barmby, John Mitchell, Silverpen (Meteyard), William Thom, W. J. Linton, Ebenezer Elliott, Richard Cobden, and Samuel Bamford are available in both *Howitt's Journal* and Chartist papers. Discussing William Howitt, Donald Ulin says, 'his credentials as a radical reformer and advocate of working-class causes are remarkably strong. He was an open and unapologetic advocate of universal adult suffrage, abolition of the death penalty and the Corn Laws, and the disestablishment of the church.'[13] The paper was also pro-free trade, anti-game law, and pro-temperance. Topics circulating from issue to issue include poverty in Ireland, contingent differences between rich and poor, and histories from France and Italy; it regularly carried poems (especially from poets of 'the people'), literary reviews, memoirs, children's stories, and columns on 'Remarkable Places'. A separately paginated 'Weekly Record', usually by William Howitt, engaged in topical matters such as reports from sanitary commissions. Not carrying 'news', it set out to create 'a periodical to the entertainment, the good, and the advancement of the public'.[14]

The 'public' to be advanced is clearly not the middle class. Referring to *Howitt's* appeals to both the middle and working classes, Maidment says, 'The double address of these journals is immediately obvious to a reasonably attentive reader.'[15] The address to the 'public' might also be further split between an imagined apolitical general reader, the 'millions', and a politically conscious reader, a member of the 'working class', though they are at points rhetorically conflated. In their opening address, the Howitts say:

> Amid the million there lies enormous need of aid, of comfort, of advocacy, and of enlightenment; and amongst the million, therefore, shall we labour, with hand and heart, with intellect and affection. To promote their education, and especially their self-education – a process full of the noblest self-respect and independence – to advocate their just rights, to explain their genuine duties, to support the generous efforts of those many wise, good, and devoted men and women who are now every where labouring for their better being and comfort: these will be the dearest employments of our lives, the truest pleasures that we can experience.[16]

To say that the journal exists for the promotion of 'their self-education' – autodidacticism being a staple of Chartist philosophy – to value their 'independence', and to support their political efforts while explaining the need to 'educate' them and 'advocate' for them, 'explain' to them 'their genuine duties', might not be the careful obfuscation it appears, but rather an attempt at saying that the liberalised middle class is available to a politicised working class for a cooperative effort to improve and politicise the general millions, a more helpless cohort. The Howitts's multiplication of audience is not only evidenced in their use of pronouns. If they desire the attention of a politicised working class, they also desire to have some impact – cultural and political – on a wider population, ensuring that the 'millions' are not politicised by way of strictly oppositional cultural choices. Veering between celebrating and fearing working-class agency, the Howitts declare, 'We shall say to the people, inform your minds on your rights; combine to maintain them; be industrious and get money; be temperate and save it; be prudent and invest it to the best advantage; but learn at the same time to respect the rights of your fellow-men. Look around, and be at once firm and patient.'[17] The journal identifies with a politicised working class but insists on running some interference between it and 'the people', countering the assumptions of the popular press that intermittently naturalise a conflation of political and cultural tastes.

Orchestrating reciprocal homilies, at least at the outset of the journal, William Howitt first needs to insist on inclusion, on soliciting 'the opinions of others of all classes'.[18] Looking at the attempt to reconcile the middle classes and what he calls artisanal voices, Maidment says, 'One key way in which such class reconciliation was to take place, and one strongly, if implicitly, defended by the journals of popular progress, was through deliberately giving a voice to artisan writers.'[19] Linda Hughes applauds 'the diverse political orientations, class positions' of the contributors, including Chartist writers.[20] But Maidment and Hughes also note that processes of combination or incorporation awkwardly run up against material if even remotely discordant. *Howitt's* wanted to establish or foster ties between the middle and artisanal classes, but it demonstrates 'unease' when staging political material written by radicals or members of the working classes, especially if they were to use confrontational language.[21] Hughes also identifies the journal's attempt to mediate the more directly political content, first suggesting that 'Opening *Howitt's Journal's* pages to known

Chartist leaders and workerpoets signalled sympathy with activist politics and an openness to radical ideas', but then quickly pointing out that by some arrangement the contributions from radicals were generally less radical than what one might expect to find in a radical journal by the same writer: 'radicals and workers often contributed apolitical lyrics that might elevate readers' thoughts but did not call on them to act'.[22] In other words, at least when the journal started up, the integration of potentially confrontational politics was heavily refereed, shaped so as to minimise both cultural and political differences, elide anger, and conflate the politicised working class with the liberalised middle class over mutual concerns for the poor.

At first, the Howitts allow themselves to be read as either excluding Chartism or accommodating it. They state in their introduction:

> To all the onward and sound movements of the time – a great and glorious time! – to the cause of Peace, of Temperance, of Sanatory reform, of Schools for every class – to all the efforts of Free Trade, free opinion; to abolition of obstructive Monopolies, and the recognition of those great rights which belong to every individual of the great British people – our most cordial support shall be lent.[23]

Does this throw support behind Chartism – even a clearly demarcated moral-force Chartism – or does it avoid listing the movement in order to help erase it? At stake, of course, is attracting working-class readers without alienating middle-class ones. The Howitts are conspicuously careful early on to always signal that the redistribution of power would not be a reduction of power for the middle classes: 'But not the less do we regard the rights and enjoyments of every other class. They who would advocate the claims of one section of the community at the expense of those of the others, or of any other, would, so far from advancing the happiness of the section they appeared to patronise, inflict the severest blow on its progress.'[24] Mixed messages that might attract a variety of audiences abound: at points the paper sounds truly conservative, insisting that England's lost innocence can be recovered, though rural nostalgia might also have been an appeal to, and appealed to the working classes. At other points, promising that reform will usher in more harmony and reconciliation, and that harmony and reconciliation would lead to more reform, its liberalism is mostly pronounced. Looking specifically at *Howitt's Journal*, Maidment argues that it is necessary 'to challenge the widely held notion that the journals of popular progress represent a fully developed, static, confident middle-class propagandist endeavour'.[25] The ambivalences of the magazine were largely, I argue, the result of the inevitable failure of its positivity in the face of working-class confrontations.

Howitt's Journal begins with an almost comic faith in optimism and progress, its fiction as positive as Chartist fiction is depressing. Instead of the class-imbued threat of violent vengeance in popular fiction comes a fantasy of the good mood. The paper partakes in a form of utopian enactment, a performance of utopia where the perfect future is represented 'as if' breaking through in the present. Without doubt, the Howitts know the reality, know their middle-class audience lives under a threat of violence, and their working-class audience suffers not just the threat of misery but misery itself. Yet they ask, 'Where are the insurrections, the massacres, the bloody and barbarous deeds of men and multitudes? They are not in our time; they lie behind us, in the years of ignorance and despotism.'[26] Looking at transformative, non-violent histories, Stellan Vinthagen describes utopian enactment as

> *focused on the individual's relationship to the other*, the opponent, and it attempts to counter prevailing images, emotional predispositions and attitudes towards the activists by acting in a way that is the *opposite* of the expected behaviour. At the same time, it embodies an attractive, *shared* possibility of living together in respect and mutuality, in the hopes of opening up new relationships with the other.[27]

Almost forcing a relationship between 'others', Howitt creates an image of pervasive harmony. He says, for example:

> See what a different tone has manifested itself in government and in the press. How the old dogmas of a stereotyped condition slide away into oblivion; how the popular rights are acknowledged; and what men and women, too, of rank, and wealth, and intellect, are zealous to put a shoulder to the wheel of peaceful progression. Every omen of evil has been falsified – knowledge and discussion are found not to promote riot or discontent, but a firm assurance of all necessary reforms, which is the root of peace and harmony.[28]

Howitt's opening argument would obviate the pleas for charity and education cutting across the rest of the journal and make the censuring of the penny press redundant. A mantra of unbridled optimism and cheery progress seems to be the rubric the paper's many and varied authors adopted; Hughes, mentioned above, hints that the working-class authors writing in the journal fell in line with this de-combative perspective, but it was most pronounced by Howitt's middle-class contributors. Following Howitt's opening address, Southwood Smith writes specifically to 'the working classes', continuing the difficult argument of denying class divides that are also obvious to the author: 'No class is higher or better than another in the sense of having more or different sentient, intellectual, moral, and religious faculties.'[29] Smith's primary concern is with sanitation, but the strain caused by being unremittingly certain of good while also preaching the desperate need for reform underlines the work that moral or personal reform through education and cultural refinement was to do. The overwhelming positivity of the paper underwrites an attempt to reshape the relationship between politics and culture so as to eliminate the possibility that conflict in one category could seep into the other.

Though including messages of hope, Chartists tend to represent the poor as naturally good, family-oriented, attempting to be morally and physically clean but unable to keep up their values in the world that is.[30] The Howitts are not blind to the effects of poverty – 'The masses cannot satisfy their hunger, their only hope is to benumb it'[31] – but the amelioration script generally insists that poverty is not able to corrupt the poor, that they are good, unsoiled, and that what the media reports (and the penny press exploits) about murders, riots, gin palaces, and wife abuse is unfounded.[32] Even Chartist stories such as 'The Outcast'[33] or 'Field Lane. Criminal Manufactories'[34] do not go this far to promote the potential respectability of the poor. The first work of fiction in *Howitt's Journal* begins on cue, as if to validate the opening argument of the journal. Meteyard begins 'Life's contrasts; or, New-Year's Eve' by stating, 'Happily for man, in accordance with the laws of nature, every step trod by the giant Time brings hope and amelioration to the many sorrowed generations of the earth.'[35] But the genre she is writing in, a form of the condition-of-England narrative, insists on hard, stark descriptions of social differences, and Meteyard corroborates here as well, depicting misery for some and riches for others: 'Upon this New-Year's Eve, misery, and want, and squalor; ignorance, degradation, and crime, might surely and rightly question the happiness, the plenty, and the revelry that come within their famished gaze, and ring so lustily in their chill and tremulous ear.'[36] Readers might be asked here to question the opening, positive argument. It is a difficult balancing act: to end the misery, 'Pity' is needed and 'bright hope', education and reform are implied as necessary, but mostly what is needed is just 'Time' or 'ameliorating Time'.[37] Meteyard's forced need to hit a triumphal note reveals a fear that representing unrelenting 'misery, and want, and squalor' would outpace the positivity and argue for urgency, action, or desperate anger.

Mary Howitt's first story in the *Journal* is also overwhelmingly positive, as if *Howitt's* had banned negativity. 'The Beginning and end of Mrs. Muggeridge's wedding-dinner'[38] describes Mrs Muggeridge as a perfect wife to her perfect gardener husband, who works for a wealthy man and comes home only one day a week. They have two lovely children. Their only complaint stems from an earlier unrepresented episode where Mrs Muggeridge had lent family money to a relation and it was never paid back. Now they are unable to buy a hare for a meal that she would love to cook for her husband because she knows how much he likes it. Though their condition is not dire, money is a problem for the family: the husband wants his wife to do some needlework to earn extra money – she is nonetheless represented as hardworking and clean – and she wants him to raise flowers that could win them a financial prize. One day, she goes to the butcher, but discovers hares are not for her economic class, which Howitt represents as a terrible injustice. Back home, a boy approaches Mrs Muggeridge to sell her a hare for a price she can afford. She buys it and cooks it for their anniversary. At the table, the husband agrees that it is good, but not better than the simpler food they usually have, and the kids prefer the stuffing. Later, Mrs Muggeridge is arrested for buying from an unlicensed seller. She puts up an aggressive defence, saying she should have the right to eat hare as much as rich people and it is not her fault that she was approached by someone selling hares – it is not her duty, she contends, to check for his licence. Though her arguments seem reasonable, and the magistrates seem like uncaring, cruel elites, she raises her voice, and therein lies her error. She has to pay five pounds or go to jail, and so she sells the beloved family furniture. Her husband comes home and she promises to do needlework and he promises to grow prize flowers. Fifteen years later they are still happy. The moral that working people can always work harder, or should be content with what they have, or need to be more prudent, was not uncommon at the time. More interesting is the insistence that working people must not raise their voice to complain, even if the system, Howitt agrees, is unfair, even if authority or the 'world-as-is' is unjust. Howitt sympathises with Mrs Muggeridge's complaint, but not her confrontational manner and not her lapse of a positive, affirmative attitude.

The story of Mrs Muggeridge is straightforward in part because it does not represent poverty per se, but only a degree of financial hardship: mixing cheery positivity with gloomy poverty presents added complications. In early issues of the paper, the Howitts avoid graphic representations of poverty common in both Chartist and penny papers. William Howitt's first monthly address begins by celebrating the power of sentiment and nostalgia, reminding readers of how winters used to be so much colder, bringing more snow than in recent years. But the cold and snow, he predicts, are coming back in all their force this year, which brings him to his objective: to argue the need for charity. So with the pleasant idea of 'our old-fashioned winter' returning, 'we must open our hearts to an old-fashioned hospitality, and sympathy with the suffering'.[39] Evoking the politics behind Cobbettian rural living or critiquing the Malthusian meanness behind the Poor Laws may be the implicit moral here, but the rhetoric focuses on equating a benign cycle of poverty and charity to the return of winter fun while young, 'sliding, skating, shooting, and snow-balling'.[40] Tying charity and gentle reform to natural processes, and insisting that alleviating poverty would be a simple pleasure, underwrites not only an effort to eliminate any threat to reform, to depoliticise it, but also to avoid discussing the means to initiate reforms. Reform is yoked with comforting reminiscence, with cultural synchronisation, with rural life and sport: with an image of class interaction or classlessness that pleasantly denies the urban chaos of the penny press.

The denial of oppositional cultures works in concert with a denial of confrontational or class politics. On 9 January 1947, a correspondent reports on a meeting of the Co-operative League, which George Holyoake describes in *Sixty Years of an Agitator's Life* (1892) as 'a body bent more on social reform than political agitation'.[41] Holyoake seems to get some things wrong – like Howitt not being associated with the League – but the description of the meeting in the paper matches the non-political roots of the organisation, emphasising the 'mutual congratulations and expressions of pleasure' that marked the interactions between middle- and working-class reformers.[42] It is interesting, however, that Holyoake reports that these meetings were attended by government spies and that the papers generally reported them to be promoting Chartist agitation.[43] Howitt's attempt to defuse tensions by representing easy social coherence authorises a world free of conflict, remaking the image of the working classes for all his audiences by countering media hungry to report conflict.

The first full-length story in the journal by R. H. Horne also promotes a defiant belief in harmony and social progress, even if 'Peter Winch: The man who always had a penny' might also pass as a story by Harriet Martineau. It is a story of the fallen artisan, a subgenre that also appears frequently in Chartist papers throughout the 1830s and 1840s. Winch is a hard-working labourer who has never had to borrow or seek relief because he is prudent, always keeping a penny in his pocket for when things go badly. But he falls in love and has a family with his equally hard-working wife. No matter how hard they work, too many children means too many bills for medicine and so forth, and so age catches up with Winch and he can no longer work as he did, meaning poverty sets in, his wife needs to seek relief, and the workhouse looms. Winch dies, leaving his family bereft. In a Chartist story, the death of the protagonist to forces beyond their control argues the need to wrest control through the Charter. Here the moral first conforms to the journal's elevation of education. It turns out that the problem was that Winch had been overworked his entire life and therefore had no time for learning or religion: 'All his vitality had been exclusively devoted to gravel-pits and roads, and every other kind of hard work that fell in his way; and he had no time for the chance of his mind's fair growth.'⁴⁴ The moral of the story directly conveyed on Winch's tombstone disagrees, however, arguing rather that Winch's life, despite his death and his wife and family now heading to the workhouse – presented strangely as a sort of happy ending – is a model for all working people:

> He was a Labourer, whose constant hard work, from Boyhood to the end of his life, enabled him to support himself and family throughout various periods of domestic trouble, without once asking for parochial relief; to act uniformly as an honest, upright man, and a Christian, and always to have money in his purse. His whole life is an example for all working men.⁴⁵

The difficulty the story has in finding a suitable message to satisfy its various programmes and audiences generates this forced combination of a Martineau-like message of prudence, given the 'condition of England' setting, with faith in work, education, Christianity, positivity, and progress. William Howitt's 'Weekly Record' might help to straighten out the story's meanings insofar as it argues that 'our age … is the age of progression' *because* 'majesty consists in the patience of the people under suffering' and progress can be seen 'in the industry of the people in educating themselves',⁴⁶ though apparently not the people's representative in the story.

This is the difficulty the paper has as a whole at this incipient stage in its development: trying to ignore and deny confrontation as an element of both working-class politics and culture while desperately trying to improve not just 'the people' but the world which confronts 'the people'. The paper goes out of its way to say things are progressing splendidly even though it is also dedicated to demonstrating the need for social reform. It represents working people as patient and content, satisfied by middle-class efforts to improve the conditions of their lives: 'all they who mix privately with, and address publicly the people, know how instantly, how cordially, nay, how rapturously, they respond and cooperate'.⁴⁷ The working classes are said to be participating in the effort to reform the nation. Reform is progressing, lives are getting better, but Winch is dead. Mentions of Chartism at this point are absent in the paper likely because Chartism was an indication of working-class dissatisfaction with piecemeal reform, patience, or the ideology of progress and improvement. Listing the issues of the day, William Howitt produces an enormous list of objectives, but does not include electoral reform or the instruments needed to bring about reform:

> Peace, Temperance; the Extension of Schools and Libraries; the Early Closing of Shops; the Abolition of Slavery; the Elevation of Women in the scale of intelligence and comfort; the opening of Athenaeums, and Literary Institutions, where the industrious classes can find, in their few leisure hours, at once relaxation and mental growth; the defence, and reform, and rescue of the unhappy victims of seduction ...[48]

The list goes on for some time. The absence of Chartism is all the more conspicuous because Howitt has declared that 'So far as our space allows we shall, in short, endeavour to notice every new step in the universal progress, whoever makes it.'[49] To then fail to mention 'Chartism' is not a simple oversight but essentially a statement on working-class participation in reform, reducing it to moral reform, self-improvement. The rejection of popular literature, which itself is understood to be the explicit rejection of self-improvement, in this way coincides with the rejection of a politics deemed at risk of being confrontational.

But this is only how *Howitt's Journal* starts out. After the first few issues, the Howitts show palpable frustration with reform, backtracking from their initial anti-agitational optimism, insistence on happy mutualism, and promise of improvement. From attempting the pursuit of cultural sameness – introduced as a way to shut down political confrontations – *Howitt's Journal* shifts towards pushing its own boundaries, subverting its own cautious politics. Read in the context of the 'Chartist menace', it might be seen as rebranding Chartism to allow its passage into polite society, but this seems only to lead to its own rebranding. In no way do the Howitts show an openness to social unrest, to accepting the binaries of rich and poor, or to representing enfranchised and unenfranchised as having non-reconcilably divergent, competing political and cultural interests. The radical energies that slip into its design are as intermittent as the radical energies in the popular press. But the paper does eventually move towards the kind of conclusions it initially attempted to avoid or subvert in its earliest issues, recognising that in its attempt to appeal to the same audience that attracted

Chartists readers, it needed to relinquish its chirpy affirmativeness for the bleaker Chartist narrative. Hughes confirms the change of direction in the paper, noting that Mary 'Howitt's social protest poetry sharpened in 1848 … when the last volume of *Howitt's Journal* was unfolding against a backdrop of intensified Chartist and revolutionary ferment at home and on the Continent.'[50] Though Mary Howitt was always worried about what Hughes calls 'the impact of pessimism',[51] as the Kennington Common meeting approached the image of inactive, patient working classes largely slipped away. Over its run, its insistence on a cultural mutualism in which education and improvement are represented as universal goals is increasingly displaced by the Chartist narrative, where democracy becomes a precondition to reform, where patience leads nowhere, and where misery continues and anger ferments for those without political agency.

The overwhelming positivity of the journal could not and did not sustain itself. That political and class reconciliation was possible through cultural reconciliation became an implied critique of the paper itself. Attempting to appease working-class taste by offering up what was considered amenable political content equally palpable to its middle-class audience made changes inevitable. Images of cooperation and mutuality do not disappear, but narratives more familiar to the Chartist argument which imply activist and agitational measures find more voices in the weeks that follow the opening address. More and more emphasis, for example, is placed on the way that the government ignores the interests of working people, creating anger among working people and their middle-class adherents – the contributors themselves. Still relatively early on in its run, W. J. Fox, though focused on education and creating cultural accord through museums, states that 'Our rulers do not know the people. They only regard the masses as a half-washed swinish multitude. They fear to trust them, and so do very much that tends to make them not trust-worthy.'[52] Instead of the message of charity, E. Youl follows a rather tame poem by Thomas Cooper with 'The verdict of the poor' in which he argues, 'Heav'n hath daughters – daughters three, / And one's name is Charity; She is fair, / but more I prize / Her sister of the bandaged eyes.'[53] Youl continues to lampoon charity a few issues later in a short story called 'Bob

Rackett's search for shoes'.[54] A poor boy, Bob, gets some donations so he can survive, but no shoes, because there is no shoe charity. He gets fired from a job he finds because he is shoeless. Charity doesn't work; Bob needs the means to get his own shoes. Chartists make the same point repeatedly, except it is the franchise that is needed for self-sustainment. In the story, a rich uncle appears out of nowhere to give the family a fortune. The happy-ever-after contrasts the image of helplessness common in Chartist literature, but the subversion of charity, not entirely undone by the *deus ex machina* (the uncle is a family member, not an outsider), of the value of piecemeal reform (a new shoe charity), is a strategy common in Chartist papers. On the one hand, the editors of the paper, the Howitts, insist on the value of charity, as seen in William Howitt's naturalising of charity discussed above. On the other hand, the proprietor of the paper, Lovett, insists *'that justice is about to be withheld, and wrong perpetuated towards the millions ... UNLESS THE VOICE OF ENGLAND SHALL UNITE WITH THAT OF IRELAND IN A DEMAND FOR JUSTICE, AND NOT CHARITY'.*[55]

Cracks in the edifice of optimism gradually appear in the journal. A story called 'A labourer's home' by Mary Gillies[56] seems to be made for the Chartist press. A working-class family travels to London for the father's work. The mother, Sally, tries to adjust to their new home, but simply cannot get the house clean because there is no clean water, filth pouring in from outside. Disgusted, the father starts going to the gin palace instead of the filthy home; the children start dying, then Sally dies. Chartist in structure, the story ends miserably. The post-narrative commentary, however, is not one that might be expected from a Chartist, even though post-narrative commentaries were very common in Chartist fiction. Gillies says, 'Let us arouse from our apathy, and demand from our legislature that it shall be so no longer.'[57] Though Gillies claims that 'All this suffering might be averted',[58] her story seems as if freed from a mandate of positivity and progress and at least more amenable to the desperation of the Chartist narrative. That *Howitt's Journal* inches towards dismantling its early optimism suggests its blind sanguinity was less and less thought to be reconcilable with representing poverty realistically and advocating to alter the conditions under which poverty grows, but it also suggests a familiarity with the images to which working-class readers of the paper were more accustomed. If this is still merely a recognition of the emotional power of a story like *A Christmas Carol*,[59] a cautious approval of condition-of-England messaging, it develops into an affiliation with the Chartist narrative at the same time that 'Chartism' is acknowledged by the paper.

Not only does the journal begin to dismantle its own message of progress but it begins a kind of flirtation with narratives of confrontation. The 6 March 1847 issue includes a poem called 'Just instinct and brute reason' by 'A Manchester Operative'.[60] Maidment says of the poem, 'The metaphor is complex, but brilliantly worked out, and the poem succeeds very well in sustaining social indignation, complex metaphor, and social threat within a simple lyric framework.'[61] The poem does not promote violence, but comparing the violence of a hawk to the way 'Man, the souled, should piecemeal murder' in the industrial system, locates violence at the heart of the industrial or class system. The 'Operative' is also unmistakably angry. The Howitts are clearly troubled by the poem, making a distinction between the goal of the paper and the author's severity: 'Our Operative is severe, but perhaps his sufferings are, and for misery we must make ample allowance. At all events, he is a poet, and poets "learn in suffering".' Maidment is clearly correct to argue that 'their editorial gloss shows all too clearly the limitations they placed on working-class self-expression' and that 'the Howitts felt the necessity of mediating the poem's indignation into middle-class awareness by attempting to strip it of its menace'.[62] The Howitts' *use* of the Operative's sufferings, however, is indicative of their scepticism over the programme of positivity that initiates the journal and suggests an amenability to a strategy more radical than what was supposed to define the journals of popular progress. It is possible to read the journal as attempting to contain working-class anger; the poem itself insists on the 'souled' rising above violent instincts. But even the dialogism evoked by the editorial gloss – the admission that working people and their middle-class supporters do not always see eye to eye – points to a struggle emerging in the paper over the role of naked confidence.

Weeks later in the journal is a strikingly positive review of the *Labourer*, Ernest Jones and Feargus O'Connor's Chartist magazine.

The Howitts do their best to characterise the *Labourer* as a vehicle for 'moral force' – weakly commenting that the fact it is called the 'Labourer' and not the 'Fighter' is an auspicious sign of the times – insisting that the magazine will 'show that we are every day growing more alike in opinion, spite of our names and badges of party'.[63] They claim that 'in labour, in co-operation, and in the purchase of land' *Howitt's Journal* and the *Labourer* are on the same page. But they also single out 'Insurrections of the people' and Jones's tale of insurgency, *The Romance of a People*, as especially valuable (as well as Jones's poetic skills more generally). Interestingly, 'Insurrections' is mistitled, its title in the *Labourer* being 'The insurrections of the working classes', suggesting that the Howitts were not entirely ready to either explicitly exclude themselves from or endorse the more radical elements of the paper. However, even if diminishing the value of working-class political action – if it was not a simple typo or slip – the Howitts are nonetheless promoting a long historical series that rather obviously hints at the way insurrection has been a progressive historical force. On the one hand, this advertisement for the *Labourer* might be seen as co-opting a Chartist programme, of reconciling the land plan with William Howitt's nostalgia for rural life. The cooperation the *Labourer* promotes is between and among working people, as the magazine has the explicit function of advocating for the land plan. On the other hand, it is an advertisement for the *Labourer*. A second and equally favourable review of the *Labourer* reproduces from it a 'melancholy scene' to ask if the land plan goes far enough, though it agrees that 'Chartists are trying its [a cooperative movement's] power on the most spirited and extensive scale.'[64] Reaching out to Jones, publishing a poem of his weeks later called 'Life'[65] – albeit a nostalgic and non-political poem – and approving of his and O'Connor's magazine, is significant. Exchanges between the Howitts, Jerrold, and 'moral-force' or anti-O'Connor Chartists were common. Jerrold and Southwood Smith (mentioned above) wrote for Linton's paper, the *National*, and Linton wrote for the Howitts. Thomas Cooper is represented in both *Howitt's Journal* and *DJSM*. Stephen Roberts notes that in August 1846, Cooper was 'branded a traitor by O'Connor' for his 'repudiation of physical force' and Cooper had then sought an 'alliance of middle-class and working-class radicals'.[66] Though the Howitts may have been attempting a kind of assimilationist deradicalisation by welcoming Jones and O'Connor into the fold – just as Jones and O'Connor may have been attempting a kind of assimilationist radicalisation by including works by the Howitts, Jerrold, and many other middle-class writers in their papers, or by praising their works in reviews[67] – these exchanges manifest not just cat-and-mouse games but experiments in developing new boundaries.

In the issues of the journal immediately following the first review of the *Labourer*, numerous stories turn to promoting schemes for working-class cooperatives similar to the land plan, showing great interest in the question of land reform. Mary Gillies's essay/story 'Associated homes' begins by stating, 'The advantages of combination have already been proved in many ways by working men.'[68] She then argues for 'the establishment of Associated Homes'[69] where working people would work together to build and maintain their own homes. While good domestic economy might have been considered fair territory for a woman writer, Gillies also offers a tacit approval of the land plan and an image of working-class independence. The story that follows is set in the future, 1857: everything is clean, no gin shops, no poverty and misery, and everyone happy. The working classes are still working classes and live contently without the presence of the middle class. There is still a class system, but with combined living arrangements, working people have created their own comforts and culture. Domestic arrangements reinforce conservative patterns – 'No married women nor widows with children went out to work, but they might if they pleased take offices within the household, compatible with their duties as wives and mothers'[70] – but this also is to be found in the Chartist story and is too easy to dismiss as a middle-class ideal imposed on working people. Simple living based on associated living, together with temperance and tight-knit family values, in many ways reproduce 'The Charter and the land', a story in the *Labourer*: both convey the power of combination without (or at least after) middle-class mediation.

I am not arguing that *Howitt's Journal* entirely dropped its initial discourse of positivity and working-class endurance, only that divergent messaging complicated the character of the paper.

A story by Mrs Hodgson called 'Have Patience'[71] introduces a boy named Stephen who is beaten by his master, his mother telling him to have patience. Years go by with him being abused. Finally, he has the nerve to delicately tell his master how poor he and his mother are, that she has to take up mangling to make ends meet. The employer, angry at being confronted with this negative image, immediately rips up the indenture papers and sends Stephen on his way. As Stephen is telling his tearful mother that they are destitute (though he plans to look for more work), a letter comes from the employer with ten pounds and an offer for Stephen to have his old job back. He takes it and will eventually become the proprietor. The title of the story reinforces its basic meaning: being an honest, humble, hard worker will eventually reap awards. But even here there is some ambiguity insofar as the employer, who is described as 'eccentric', responds positively to a working-class complaint after initially responding negatively to it, coming to terms with misery when confronted by it. Some of the paper continues to be unambiguously optimistic, such as Valentine Bartholomew's poem 'Be patient, poor ones of our land!' This, however, sits beside a tribute to William Lovett by Dr Smiles which conveys the value of agitation, not patience. Though Lovett, proprietor of and contributor to *Howitt's Journal*, was decidedly moral-force, his role in 'that great and absorbing movement of the working classes of England and Scotland, known as the Chartist agitation'[72] is described without distinction between moral and physical force.

Mary Howitt's stories in the journal were frequently written for children, but 'The Deserter in London' is written as if to attract an adult Chartist audience. The severity of her critique of the military is not unlike 'The soldier: a story illustrative of the flogging system' in the *English Chartist Circular*.[73] Howitt is sympathetic to the deserter, saying military law is not God's law and that the deserter may be better off being executed than the soldiers leading him away, who will be shot on the battlefield. Howitt promises compensation in the afterlife, which is not how the typical Chartist story about the cruelty of military life proceeds, and there is little mention of class, but the bleakness of the story replicates the Chartist narrative wherein the absence of the means for reformation leads inevitably to suffering. In writing about reforming the military, the journal is often more radical than when writing about the means to bring about reform. But what is most interesting is the way that the paper forgoes its positivity and adopts the bleak imagery of the Chartist narrative. Late in its run, *Howitt's Journal* includes stories such as Henry C. Wright's 'Dick Crowninshield the assassin, and Zachary Taylor the soldier; the difference between them' which argues that there is no difference between an assassin and a soldier, except one would be hanged if caught and the other celebrated. The story pulls on heartstrings, describing scenes where the soldier kills with imagery so graphic that it is Mary Howitt's or Hans Christian Andersen's contributions to the 'Child's Corner' that begin to seem out of place: 'Look at that nursery! See the mother watching her four little ones, lovingly at play in one corner. Zachary discharges a gun loaded with grape-shot at them and the mother sits amid their mangled remains. In another nursery is an infant sleeping in a cradle: the mother sits by it rocking, and singing its lullaby. Zachary hurls a cannon ball at that mother and infant, and tears them in pieces.'[74]

Howitt's Journal becomes increasingly sympathetic to Chartism, and further into 1847 and 1848 most contributors seem only to be struggling with the exclusivity of the people's movement, wanting to open it up to reformers such as themselves, and in that way blur the lines between Chartism and reformism. A poem called 'The slave of the oven' by John Hurrey reproduces the 'white slavery' in England narrative common to the Chartist press.[75] Hurrey argues that industrialised work is as dehumanising as slavery, that it leads to nothing but death, hardly suggesting progress or the benefits of reform, especially as abolition was one of the stated reforms that the paper had made a priority. William Howitt still speaks about improvement papers and temperance societies successfully generating an elevated working class, but now he argues that the elevation leads to politicisation, celebrating 'those who have taken a political turn as George Thompson, Henry Vincent, William Lovett and the like'.[76] The Howitts publish a remarkable letter dated the very day of the Kennington Common demonstration – though interestingly not published for two months after – criticising Chartism for not going far enough in that it had abandoned women: 'I address myself in these remarks to those who admit the claim which is being made by the male members of the working classes for complete suffrage, and I think the onus lies with these persons to show why the same claim may not be put forward on behalf of women.'[77] Howitt also begins to recognise and confirm the power of Chartism, even a Chartism that includes 'physical force':

> While we blame the Chartists for violence and extravagance, they are the only portion of the community who show the true degree of zeal and union. What they want they demand fearlessly, and combine that they may make themselves heard. In that they set a great example. We must unite and insist, or we are nothing. We are either mere sticks that any child can break, or the bundle of sticks which nobody can break.[78]

Though the image of an unbreakable bundle of sticks is not definitively violent, it certainly can be read as authorising activist energy. Howitt is not clear here who he means when he calls on 'we' to 'unite and insist', but his repeated use of the word and image of 'combination' suggests that he had more than come to terms with the idea of a distinct, independent, and agentic working class. He continues to say, 'The people must combine, if they are to live. They must determine that their weight shall be felt, not on the pauper roll of the parish, but in the councils of the nation, as the largest portion of it.' Stating 'Combine, then, perishing men, and you that would not have men perish. Combine! combine! combine! for those National Reforms which must introduce social ones',[79] he delegates a diminishing role for would-be liberal reformers. While the Howitts continue to imply that the movement is available to middle-class reformers, using the concept of 'General progress' – 'We call, therefore, on all to pledge themselves with renewed zeal to the work of general progress'[80] – to insinuate reformers into the conversation, the threat of working-class violence has not only put an end to the unrelenting positivity, it is written as if a catalyst to reform.

To be clear, *Howitt's* does not tolerate the image or prospect of violence, but as Kennington Common approached and just after the demonstration, the paper no longer pretends that working people feel the same way it does about confrontation. The messaging of the paper becomes closer to desperation than confidence. William Howitt now argues that without measurable and immediate reform, revolution is inevitable. The people want violence and 'it rests with the middle classes, with the property and educated classes to determine whether this tableau of horrors and devastation shall present itself or not'.[81] Continental violence, an increasingly strident Chartist press, an evident lack of 'progress', and (likely) internal publishing difficulties push the Howitts off their initial campaign of progress and positivity, forcing them to admit the realities of a classed world. The paper at this point largely abandons the notion of a working-class audience or that it was enabling a process of incorporation, almost admitting that the culture the journal proselytises fails to correspond with working-class culture. Reconciliation is a bust, cooperation a broken dream, cross-class dialogue silenced; whatever cultural 'improvement' can be boasted, it has not led to political harmony, to the same political tastes.

Though George Dawson[82] appears to return to the tenors of prescriptive positivity that dominate the early agenda of the paper just two weeks after Kennington Common – 'In these times, what is England to do? Are we to have a Revolution? In the usual sense of that term, No! Barricades are exotics here, not likely to be naturalised. Englishmen love not scenes in the market-place. Physical force we will not have, we need it not, we love it not' – he cannot but return to the spectre of revolution to motivate for reform: 'How shall we prevent Revolution and violence? By the only sure plan – Reform. Is Europe to be reconstructed and England remain still?'[83] Dawson's difficulty in denying a working-class will to violence, a culture comfortable with confrontation, leads to an appeal to the middle classes, the only assumed audience at this point, to alter their approach to reform, to conform to Chartism in the same way that earlier working-class audiences were being asked to conform to reform: 'Many of the working men look for their political salvation in the Charter. They hope too much from it – you fear too much. But many of the middle classes never read the Charter. Is it right to oppose that of which we are ignorant?'[84] Before listing the reforms he would like to see, including secret ballots, an expanded franchise, shorter parliaments, and reform to electoral districts – but also freer trade, religious equality, and other matters that were not so pronounced by Chartists or that Chartists tended to be against, such as free trade – Dawson says:

> The Charter, I know, goes too far for some, for some too fast. Many recognise it as an ideal to be worked up to, rather than as a plan for immediate realisation. My present purpose is neither to advocate nor oppose it, but to ask the middle classes, what, at this crisis, they mean to do? If you like not the 'People's Charter', produce your own. Say what you want, and how far you will go. Will you take the points in detail? Draw out your list of Reforms, give the nation your points. Anything but inaction and timidity. On you it depends whether we advance peacefully but quickly in the path of progress, or whether we must succumb to injustice on the one side, or anarchy on the other. Remember, Reform delayed is Revolution begun. A true Reform Bill would soon become to the demagogue, the brawler and the physical-force man, a fool's cap in which he would be hissed off the political stage. Show you are in earnest and men will wait. Organise in every locality – petition (if you will) – 'pronounce'. If you do not go for the Charter, say so, but say for what you do. Inspect the following list, mark off in what you agree; let those who want little, band for that little, those who ask much, for much, those who want all, for all.[85]

'The brawler and the physical-force man' are still the cultural and political enemy, but Dawson at least recognises that working-class 'reformers' are not a friendly mirror to the middle-class reader. The paper has abandoned prescribing middle-class habits to working people. Though Dawson implies that middle-class intervention can still prevent violence, he accepts that confrontation is the way of the people. Howitt in his 'Weekly Record' also addresses the need for reform because the working-classes are angry and violent, though he emphasises the reciprocity created by the violence of the state:

> Distress increases every day amongst the working class; the government attempts to crush their complaints instead of relieving their sufferings. They cry for freedom, and the government presents them with the muzzles of cannon. They complain of their treatment in public meetings, and they are treated with a gagging bill! We are as much convinced of the fact as Carlyle himself – that 'where there is smoke there is fire'.[86]

The positivity of the paper is gone. Poverty, hardship, oppression lead to violence. Howitt claims that 'we are surprised to hear people who are well off themselves still asserting that there is no real distress',[87] though earlier issues of his own paper might be said to minimise the effects of distress. Now the 'people' no longer welcome 'self-improvement' or value middle-class political or cultural interventions. Accepting that working people were different, miserable, angry, and confrontational is not to admit the value of the Chartist or penny press, but it demonstrates that *Howitt's Journal* grew to accept or was forced to accept that merely voicing political and cultural sameness, or aspirations to that sameness, did not make it so. The image of a working class primed for political violence may reflect historical reality and may have been confirmed by Chartist oratory and literature, but it was also readied and popularised by a penny press, a penny culture that improvement literature was failing to overcome.

Douglas Jerrold's Shilling Magazine

The degree to which *Howitt's Journal* countenanced the legitimacy of a paradigmatic, frontline working-class presence where political and cultural instincts are blurred is thrown into stark relief when comparing its appropriation of the Chartist narrative to the difficulty *Douglas Jerrold's Shilling Magazine* (*DJSM*) had with accepting that the terms of political address could be set by – as distinct from 'set for' – a working-class cohort aware of its own identity and self-interests. Jerrold's attitude towards the working-class ally was in some way more complicated than the Howitts because he never pretended that the working class was the mirror image of the middle class in waiting. Like *Howitt's*, *DJSM* includes works by Chartist writers or writers who appeared frequently in the Chartist press, such as Thomas Cooper and Goodwyn Barmby; William Howitt himself is a regular contributor to *DJSM*. Jerrold's 'The Factory Child' was repeatedly reproduced in Chartist papers such as the *National* (13 April 1839), *Northern Star* (same day, 13 April 1839), *English Chartist Circular*, *Charter* (3 March 1839), and *Cleave's Gazette of Variety* (16 March 1839). Both *Howitt's* and

DJSM promote the ideas of class reconciliation, of improvement, and of reform. Surveying periodicals that advertised themselves for working people, Monica Fryckstedt argues, 'In moral outlook, it is perhaps the Howitts among the editors that come closest to Jerrold, for, like him they favoured everything that would increase "mental cultivation" and which gave "to labour, its due reward" and would "furnish to every rational creature his due share of God's gift".'[88] However, the differences between the two go beyond the stylistic, the avuncular sincerity of the Howitts' paper and the sardonic, biting commentary of Jerrold's. Both are liberal reformist, but whereas the Howitts struggle with how to accept a political culture from below, Jerrold can only reject the idea of a self-decided working-class politics, of a working-class political consciousness. *DJSM* insists on separating out the political working classes from 'the masses', the poor who deserve the benefits that middle-class reform can bring, in a way that *Howitt's* cannot sustain. The Howitts move from celebrating a patient, congenial working-class politics to at least accepting the image of a confrontational working class. Jerrold rejects that image, and when forced to consider it he cannot tolerate it. Importantly, Jerrold also directly maligns the penny press in a way that is not seen in *Howitt's Journal*, as if he were fearfully aware of a relationship between cultural and political dissonance. It should not be a surprise that a paper promoting education and improvement would vilify popular writing, crime stories and the like. But that the vilification of popular writing is so much more pronounced in Jerrold's paper than the Howitts's, and that Jerrold's paper was so much less amenable to the idea of a working-class politics, and especially of a working-class confrontational politics, suggests that the popular press was understood as expressing political content, that it was somehow against the interests of *DJSM*'s political leanings.

Another central difference between the papers is that Jerrold's clearly did not have an imagined working-class reader in mind in the same way that the Howitts did. If *DJSM* imagined a dual audience, the one from below was frequently kept in the shadows. The magazine mostly speaks *about* individual members of the working classes as if to explain the hardship they had to endure to a middle-class audience. Still, it was important for the image of class reconciliation that Jerrold promoted to make the magazine as if available to working people, as if sharing the working person's point of view, even his or her idiom. Jerrold promised that it 'shall appeal to the hearts of the Masses of England'.[89] Though this was likely part of a strategy to convince the middle-class audience that individual working people were not a threat, were worthy of sympathy, the magazine was unquestionably 'devoted to a consideration of the social wants and rightful claims of the People'.[90] *DJSM* was adamantly and urgently reformist and issue oriented, sardonically undermining capital punishment, the clergy, the monarchy, and even addressing local issues such as the window tax. It was also ostensibly an improvement paper, claiming a 'large and hitherto unoccupied sphere of instruction, amusement, and utility',[91] though once again it is very thin on what might have been considered 'instruction' for working people compared to the wide variety of periodicals from the time that expressly offered cultural instruction. *DJSM* promotes goodwill and charity, as well as individualised decency and, much like its antagonists in the popular press, vehemently rejects partisan politics. Yet unlike what is found in the popular press, the end goal of reform is explicitly stated to be class reconciliation, to resolve 'the present social contest', in part by rejecting party politics: 'Whig and Tory – Conservative and Radical – will be no more to us than the names of extinct genera.'[92] Jerrold, rather, explains that his only interest in politics is 'in their social relation, as operating for the good or evil of the community'.[93] Its anchoring to the cause of the oppressed poor is most consistently pronounced in its insistence in both its fiction and editorials that crime is the result of poverty. Though mostly arguing the case for the worthy poor, or demonstrating an underlining worthiness that the middle classes could foster, *DJSM* reveals sympathy for individual working people, drawing the line, however, at what was widely considered the dominant political and cultural expressions of working people in the Chartist and popular press.

F. David Roberts groups Jerrold with the 'Bohemiani Londonienses', journalists interested in 'exposing the plight of the poor' with scornful wit and Swiftian humanitarianism rather than the high seriousness of both Chartist and popular progress papers. Speaking on Jerrold's contributions to *Punch* as 'Q', Roberts points out that Jerrold was known as 'the king of wit', combining 'a flair for satire with a waspish anger at the high and mighty and a warm feeling for the low and humble'.[94] Written 'for the Proprietors of PUNCH, at the PUNCH Office', *DJSM* shared the free-floating irreverence towards 'humbug' that made *Punch* such a popular source of material in such a wide variety of periodicals – excerpts from *Punch* are to be found in all types of conservative, liberal, radical, and popular magazines from the era. In a way, *DJSM* combines the high reformism of *Howitt's* with the gleeful style of Pierce Egan in *Life in London*: its continuous observations about class, about the contrasts in a London divided by workhouses, beggars, and jails on the one hand and the fashionable clubs that housed 'the indifference of the nouveau riche and old aristocracy'[95] on the other, make entertainment out of class division. Noting its 'compassion and irreverence', Roberts states that *DJSM* 'knew of no promising remedies' for the social conflicts it identifies, save reform.[96] It denounces both old and new corruption, but frequently turns to linguistic calisthenics as a way to avoid reaching conclusions about the poverty and misery that it exposes. In an article called 'The Coming Reformation', for example, 'Vivian' (George Henry Lewes) calls radicalism – defined as 'Chartism, Socialism, Fourierism' – as 'anarchical' and 'an exponent of Progress with Destructive tendencies',[97] but is equally as critical of Tories as of Whigs, calling for the advent of a 'New Party' but not defining its objective, save to be better than the other parties.

The paper might be at its most consistent when representing a misunderstood, unthreatening poor, incapable of and uninterested in political activity, and worthy of charity. Coinciding with the (morally) sanitised image of the poor is the rejection of penny literature, especially crime literature. Jerrold might not have the popular presses immediately in mind when at the outset of the paper he insists that its 'chief object' is to make all the content 'breathe with a purpose',[98] but 'improvement' periodicals were unlikely to corroborate the image of the lower classes in popular fiction. The Chartist press, likewise, with its own programme of improvement and education, was similarly reluctant to admit that the people preferred crime fiction: on the surface, the preference does not make the argument for a serious, vote-ready working man. Unlike the Chartist press, however, Jerrold's rejection of crime fiction corresponds with a rejection of a politically active working class. In 'The morbidness of literature' by 'An Optimist', we read that 'It is a characteristic of the present day to charge this or that literary production with morbidness, and the charge is in many cases correct. What is this morbidness? Does it mark progress or decline? We shall find the readiest answer to the first question by first answering its opposite, "What is healthiness in literature?"'[99] Healthy literature is essentially determined by the honesty or integrity of the approach. The definition of 'morbid' literature eventually returns readers to Thackeray's rejection of Newgate storytelling – to the blurring of good and evil, right and wrong, protagonist and antagonist[100] – but literature is specifically 'morbid' or unhealthy because the fascination with crime makes for the wrong kind of political thought, be it conservative or radical: 'The thoroughly morbid man feels dissatisfaction only – he may fly to the chivalry of the past, or he may build an imaginary Socialism in the future, provided he escapes the present.'[101] The charge of escapism corresponds with a vague 'dissatisfaction' that inhibits reform and ushers in thoughts of romantic quests. The Optimist states, 'the healthy man of the better order reveres the present with all its failings and imperfections as the necessary step towards a brighter future'.[102] The 'Optimist' does not claim that the morbid man is apolitical, just the opposite: he simply prohibits reform by adopting a grander political outlook. The connection drawn between 'morbid' literature, dissatisfaction, and an escapism that leads to 'an imaginary Socialism' suggests that the Optimist understood that the cultural confrontations of penny fiction had political counterparts. Recognising the cultivation of dissatisfaction in crime fiction, the 'Optimist' sees a political corollary that would undermine the political project of the magazine. Roberts points out, however, that Jerrold and *DJSM* were not above creating 'romantic tales to enable the poor to escape the misery that poverty caused':[103] far from it. Setting *DJSM* as an alternative to penny, non-improving fiction was largely a matter of disallowing or discarding the political corollary. To this end, the paper constructs a worthy, complaisant, ingratiating poor suitable for charity and sharing the same conciliatory cultural and political preferences as *DJSM*.

The History of St. Giles and St. James, Jerrold's serialised novel that was in many ways his flagship contribution to the magazine, takes a slightly different approach, denying a connection between 'morbid' literature and the political, though it itself is stuffed with reprobate rascals and gallows humour. It begins by pointing out that 'It was a time when the very poor, barred from the commonest things of earth, take strange counsel with themselves, and in the deep humility of destitution, believe they are the burden and the offal of the world.'[104] This was likely comforting to middle-class audiences; representations of devastating poverty in some way ensure that whatever might be meant by reconciliation is not a threat. The problem does not turn out to be that the poor fail to exert their rights, but that support from above is frustrated by selfishness. The novel is largely about creating class relations that would enable charity:

> It was a time, when the easy, comfortable man, touched with finest sense of human suffering, gives from his abundance; and, whilst bestowing, feels almost a shame that with such wide-spread misery circled round him, he has all things fitting; all things grateful. The smitten spirit asks wherefore he is not of the multitude of wretchedness; demands to know for what especial excellence he is promoted above the thousand, thousand starving creatures: in his very tenderness for misery, tests his privilege of exemption from a woe that withers manhood in man, bowing him downward to the brute. And so questioned, this man gives in modesty of spirit – in very thankfulness of soul. His alms are not cold, formal charities; but reverent sacrifices to his suffering brother.[105]

The novel revolves around opposites and, not unlike *Mysteries of London*, opposites exist within classes, though the division in society between rich and poor is paramount. Against the charitable middle classes are the selfish middle classes: 'It was a time when selfishness hugs itself in its own warmth ... all made pleasanter, sweeter, by the desolation around. ... A time when such a man sees in the misery of his fellow-beings nothing save his own victory of fortune – his own successes in a suffering world. To such a man the poor are but the tattered slaves that grace his triumph.'[106] Antagonism between the classes is expressed here, but it is personal, psychotically aberrant, and only from the top down. The disgruntled poor, the working-class or political poor, are mostly absent, and the cautious alliance in *Howitt's* between political groups never has an opportunity to manifest.

The novel contrasts the poor Giles and the wealthy James, purporting to illustrate that circumstance leads to crime and that human connections between rich and poor stabilise society. Despite the egalitarianism implied by exposing how privilege works, the novel can be unstomachably racist for the sake of a laugh and, as with a lot of the magazine itself, snobbish. Thackerayan humour is far from the 'coarse' pleasures of penny literature, despite the unintentional appeal of *Catherine*. But while denigrating the 'coarse' reader, Jerrold's novel seems to ask what to do when common readers will not give up their 'coarse' tastes. Most noteworthy is that of all the influences corrupting Giles, of which poverty was supposed to dominate, Jerrold insists that he is damned by reading Newgate calendars and fiction:

> He had listened to tales of felon fortitude, of gallows heroism; and ambition stirred within him. He had heard of the Tyburn humourist, who, with his miserable jest in the jaws of death, cast his shoes from the cart, to thwart an oft-told prophecy that he would die shod. All these stories St. Giles had listened to, and took to his heart as precious recollections. While other children had conned their books – and written maxim copies – and learned their catechism, – St. Giles had learned this one thing – to be 'game.' ... The foot-pad, the pickpocket, the burglar, had been his teachers: they had set him copies, and he had written them in his brain for life-long wisdom. Other little boys had been taught to 'love their neighbour as themselves.' Now, the prime ruling lesson set to young St. Giles was 'honour among thieves.'[107]

Eventually, 'our hero of the gutter'[108] becomes a hardened thief. Jerrold condemns the literature of non-improvement and cultural confrontation, simultaneously dismissing that it has a political counterpart. Giles does not complain about the unfairness of being James's social opposite, that is done on his behalf. When in Newgate, and soon to be sent to Botany Bay after being rescued from the scaffold by James, the Ordinary attempts to read to Giles some Christian improving material, but Giles says, 'It's no use your reading that stuff to me ... I don't under stand nothin' of it; and it's too late to learn. But I say, can't you tell us somethin' of Turpin and Jack Sheppard, eh? Some thing prime, to give us pluck?'[109] Jerrold accuses the kind of crime literature that makes a hero of the rogue as culturally or psychologically stunting the growth of the poor; maturity for Giles, moral growth, means becoming worthy of James's goodwill and sympathy. The rejection of penny literature stimulates humility, social harmony, and political oblivion.

DJSM repeatedly investigates the causes of crime to demonstrate the relationship between an individual's moral failure and overwhelming social hardship. Its explanationism theoretically offers a challenge to 'moralists', so the paper needs to stay clear of representing an unworthy poor that has some fun with its unworthiness or would translate cultural confrontations into social or political dissatisfactions. Unlike *Howitt's Journal*, *DJSM* is hardly 'polite' itself, but it avoids representing cultural confrontations in the same way it confronts cultural differences or a lack of understanding between rich and poor. It also demonstrates some need to stay clear of representing 'working classes', as the characterisation of working classes, as distinct from an individualised poor, was a political grouping. *DJSM* consistently demonstrates the social causes of crime, representing individuals who turn to crime as a result of their poverty. 'My temptations, by a poor man' typifies *DJSM* approach to crime.[110] The 'Poor Man' states:

> There are those who (themselves altogether above want) wonder at the 'shocking depravity' of the poor, feel a thrill of pious horror at the idea of a man who pleads poverty as an excuse for dishonesty, and who would not hesitate to affirm, that they would die of starvation before they could commit so great a sin as to appropriate to themselves anything which they might not call their own. Ah! how little can they imagine the feelings of one who has nothing which he can call his own, save the loved ones who are perishing with him! Let such stern moralists (lolling back in their arm-chairs over their wine after dinner) read my simple story.[111]

Neither the politically conscious working class nor the irreverent rogue can exist. In *St. Giles and St. James*, Giles is arrested for being a troublemaker, but he learns to improve with the aid of the wealthy James. Jerrold is at his best when arguing that society mistakenly treats poverty as a crime: 'Nothing was proved against St. Giles but want; which, being high treason against the majesty of property, that large offence might be reasonably supposed to contain every other.'[112] But sympathy for the poor is conditional on the individual not transforming into the working class, on rejecting cultural and political conflict. In the popular press, the unworthy poor and the working class are one and the same.

DJSM, that is, consistently demonstrates sympathy for the poor but 'disgust' for the working classes: the biggest difference between the two is that the poor are represented by individuals and the working class is always a group, making it political. The 'disgust' for the 'People', for working or 'industrial' classes, or 'lower orders' who have grouped together to demand change is especially striking given that *DJSM* savagely critiques the 'disgust' that the wealthy have for the individualised poor. *DJSM* saw the extension of the franchise as a worthy ideal, but one that the 'People' were not ready for. In an article called 'The Lower Orders' by Geraldine Jewsbury, who had achieved success two years earlier with *Zoe: the History of Two Lives* (1845) with the help of the Carlyles, and was at the time composing *The Half Sisters* (1848), we read:

> Let the People, the newly-developed order in humanity, rejoice in their strength, in their savage powers, and *unblasé* faculties. The recognition of their rights, their entrance on their own heritage, so long withheld, makes a grand, a divine epoch in the world's life. ... But when we descend from the Mount of Vision to the actual and practical working of the thing, and stumble amid the coarse material details, enthusiasm is well nigh stifled with disgust; and, except to those gifted with the most keen and loving insight, the Divine Idea, which at first seemed so glorious, is effaced on nearer contemplation of the irreverent ignorance, the presumption, the intense vulgarity, the coarse and clumsy attempt to meddle with high things, the utter absence of all modest misgivings, the absolute want of preception for taste and refinement, which characterises these new barbarians.[113]

The relationship between the cultural and political is never as clear in the magazine as it is here. Grappling with the licensing of political power, the attitude towards the very members of the working classes who might otherwise be categorised as 'poor' changes dramatically. The dichotomising of the working classes and the poor appears in the Chartist press as well, but not generally in popular fiction. The link between political activity – 'the coarse and clumsy attempt to meddle with high things' – and a lack of 'taste and refinement' is not new, but that 'bad taste is a sin always symptomatic of something more deeply seated'[114] not only points to the way that popular fiction was read, it points to the way it should continue to be read.

Jewsbury goes on to describe working-class and likely Chartist agitation – though the word 'Chartism' is avoided – as 'this unlovely chaos', but she nonetheless recognises that working-class consciousness is growing, perhaps inevitably, and needs to be contained and controlled from above:

> in them a spark of Deity lies smouldering, which may yet break up this unlovely chaos, and transform it into shapes of beauty and life. But the Mass have not yet realised this hope; they are, as yet, only beginning to stir with blind, uneasy motion, and a dim consciousness of uncertain strength.
>
> The tone of flattery assumed towards the 'People', in all the books, poems, lectures, and talk that goes on about them at the present time – the endeavour to create sympathy with them at the expense of the higher classes – the fashion it has grown to exploiter the Lower Orders, – is not precisely the wisest method to form the race, which will in all likelihood form the main element in the next generation of society. Nothing is so demoralising as making a fashion of a principle. Mass needs civilising, and nothing can be more vulgar than the tone in which they are addressed.[115]

It is tempting to imagine that Jewsbury specifically had *Howitt's Journal* in mind when saying 'The gross flattery which is addressed to the imperfect, undeveloped, Industrial Class, is enough to check their growth for ever',[116] especially as the Howitts had more and more began to accept the validity of the Chartist argument. Remarkably, she also comes out against mechanics' institutes, suggesting she subscribed to the idea that without the processes of cultural incorporation that vulgar, morbid literature frustrated, political instability was inevitable.

It would be unfair not to point out that Jerrold allows a deviating point of view that admits value in intermittent airings of cultural and political dissent, though not to the same extent that the Howitts trialled. 'Democracy in 1847' details the 'honest spirit of self-assertion ... to do away with class legislation'.[117] The article seems to be entirely in favour of democracy and its adherents: 'There is a mighty spirit at work throughout the land, that calls for the destruction of the ulcers which disfigure the British constitution: give heed to the just askings of this giant spirit, for it has right on its side and will not be hushed.'[118] 'A Vision' is a poem about injustice and the futility of fighting injustice[119] that sounds as if written by Ernest Jones. *DJSM*'s review of Thomas Cooper's *Purgatory of Suicides* (1845) begins by stating that contemporary Chartists have much more respectability than they did just a few years back. Though mostly favourable, the review does not dwell on the politics of the poem but on poetics. Jerrold's clear appreciation for Cooper,[120] as with the Howitts' admiration for him, signals a willingness to recognise moral or anti-O'Connor Chartism, though Jerrold and his contributors do not say so as clearly as do the Howitts and theirs.[121] But as with *Howitt's Journal*, *DJSM* is willing to accept some political common ground with Chartism as long as it is made palatable through gestures of cultural benignity.

'The Revolutionary Firebrand' might be the most remarkable departure in the magazine from its staunch rejection of confrontational idioms, though again it does not touch on cultural rows. The erasure of cultural differences is hugely important for it turns out that the 'Revolutionary Firebrand' must not be working class. The article begins by taking account of the 'fearful pestilence stalking abroad ... a Firebrand flashing in the air ... on the eve of being hurled into the powder magazine of the State'.[122] The anxiety, predictably, is that it will be exported home, but it turns out that the firebrand is either mischaracterised or justified: 'Know, then, that it has been discovered, aye and demonstrated, that the great Revolutionary Firebrand, which is to make our "Glorious constitution" an inglorious heap of blackened ruins, is no less a thing than this: the earnest Protest against Wrong!'[123] At this point, the anonymous author[124] might as well be writing for a Chartist paper. Even though the article complains that reformists are falsely labelled firebrands or revolutionaries so as to marginalise arguments for the reforms they demanded, it in fact provides a defence of political organisation, or protest, potentially opening up the legitimacy of political confrontation to all classes:

> Think what you please, but beware how you utter it, unless you belong to the 'right thinking and enlightened class'. Sicken, if you

will, but dare not to protest. Dare not to tamper with the edifice which Time and the misery of millions has sanctified; dare not to remove even a withered branch from that Tree, under whose branching shade our forefathers grew up, lest, in removing the blighted branch, you peril the stability of the whole. The Tree is a noble tree, with all its tortuous misgrowths, with all its paralysed limbs. You must respect it for what it has been. It has its defects. It has also its great qualities. The defects are inseparable from its greatness, and therefore ought not to be removed. Attempt to remove them, and you light the Firebrand.[125]

There is something deeply, uncontrollably confrontational here. Though the author's claim that liberal reformists have generated the people's protest dangerously appropriates the Chartist cause, the language of confrontation is not avoided. But the author, then, has to backtrack and make it explicit that the 'millions' are not themselves to do the confronting, are not themselves to play with fire:

You will be told that there is wrong in the world, there always has been, always will be. Our life is a 'mingled yarn' – the evil is inseparably woven in with the good. What, then, is the use of raising seditious cries about particular wrongs? If you protest, you endanger 'vested interests.' If you endanger these you endanger the welfare of the State, and, as the State is composed of all classes, including the millions, it follows, by a very beautiful deduction, that your protest is a dangerous Firebrand, which, if listened to, will destroy even the millions in whose favour it is made, since their welfare is, of course, bound up with that of the State![126]

The author clearly maintains that the middle classes must articulate grievances on behalf of working people – 'to utter the thought which is struggling for utterance in the dumb millions'[127] – but he does not shy from suggesting that privileged classes will characterise honest endeavours at social amelioration as 'raising seditious cries'. Accepting only fragments of the Chartist narrative, *DJSM* can never be cleared of a charge of co-opting reform in order to ensure the erasure of confrontation as a means of change. Jerrold's biographer, Michael Slater, says 'that Jerrold was far from being a Chartist' but that he 'shows sympathy and understanding towards'[128] the movement insofar as he understood – like Dickens, Carlyle, and Gaskell – why the movement existed. But Slater also argues that by aiding and supporting the poor, demonstrating the middle-class support for causes of the poor, and vilifying the wealthy, Jerrold thought that society would 'hear less of Chartism'.[129]

The attitude the article has towards political confrontation is not wholly unlike the magazine's attitude towards cultural confrontation: despite claiming to carry only 'wholesome' material, *DJSM*, and especially Jerrold's contributions to it, can be wickedly countercultural, impolite, defiantly mocking 'the lovers of social order'[130] in a way that might make Jack Sheppard raise a glass. But Jack himself is not to show up. Situating the reformer as having the only role in or the sole prerogative to reform – to define and execute it – *DJSM* would erase the threat of both penny literature and Chartist politics, deny the popularity of them both, even while absorbing elements from both. Whether *DJSM* understood penny literature and Chartism as converging around companionate poles promising violence and expressing working-class self-determination, the potential power of the 'millions', it did, like other interveners trying to throw water on fire, but not too much of it, ironically help confirm the bond between them. Though Jerrold and the Howitts were vested stakeholders vying for something like administrative status, to be the managerial class, and to take control away from the people they would manage, as managers do, they should not be understood as cynically attempting to hold on to their political power for its own sake. Rather, they saw in the conflation of penny violence – working-class preferences – and Chartist politics the real possibility of class-based violence, and they were likely correct to do so.

Given that the Howitts and Jerrold, for example, wrote stories for the Chartist press, or were reproduced by it, the politics of incorporation or systems of assimilation built into editorial selection must have been thorny and complex. Understanding them can only be a matter of interpretation, and if taking into account markets, political anticipations, formal and informal pressures of reciprocity, the hedging of bets, the forming of alliances, ideologies and conscience, the need to fill white space on the page or the need to make decisions day-to-day, and whatever else, then much work lies ahead. The Chartist 'drift' to melodramatic forms late in its history might also speak to more than just the need to grab market share; it might signal an appreciation of the prospective radical energies latent in penny fiction, from the motivational value inherent in images of defiance and working-class agency to the tactical value of showcasing a physical threat behind moral acts – the way penny fiction almost casually points out that social chaos and public violence are virtually guaranteed when the working classes get riled. Just as Thomas Cooper and Ernest Jones were included in reform journals – selected material – Chartists papers reproduced material from non-Chartists, but mostly when that material was compatible with the Chartist narrative or Chartist politics. If the strategies of incorporation from either side betray an attempt at something closer to dominance, influence, redirection, recuperation, or even obliteration, it does not follow that all the players had a strategy.

It is likely safe to say that the producers of popular periodical fiction for the entertainment of a general public were less concerned with attaining generic consistency, matching form and content, creating nuanced social messaging, or influencing readers one way or another than most other literatures from the period. The scene was more than triangulated – conservative papers, trade magazines, women's journals, and so much more – but the relationship between popular, radical, and reformist was marked, again suggesting the political role the popular was thought to have. Just as reform journals from the 1840s wrote under the shadow of Chartism, so did its other distractor. Freeloading or freeriding, even fellow-travelling, the producers of the popular were not exactly interlopers, for the literature also did some heavy lifting, just not much uplifting. But by creating images of an underclass resisting polite containment and allowing reckless crowds to be read as a real menace, if not the Chartist menace per se, while insisting on class divisions to a degree that even the Chartist press might reject, the cheap entertainments of the 1830s and 1840s did more than counter the new seriousness and dull respectability of the age. They also reminded the nation that it was and would be a place of conflict, political and otherwise, making, for better or worse, the folding of radicalism into liberalism, the other two parties, seem as unnatural as it was.

Notes

1. Charles Kingsley infamously says in *Politics for the People*, 'My only quarrel with the Charter is, that it does not go far enough', but then immediately rejects Chartism, saying, 'I want to see you free; but I do not see how what you ask for, will give you want you want.' C. Kingsley, 'Letters to the Chartists, No. I', *Politics for the People* (13 May 1848), p. 28. He goes on to vilify Chartism, something that is done regularly in *Politics for the People*.
2. B. Maidment, 'Magazines of popular progress & the artisans', *Victorian Periodicals Review*, 17:3 (1984), 83.
3. W. Howitt, 'Visit to a working man', *Howitt's Journal* (16 October 1847), II, p. 242.
4. Moral-force Chartists such as John Collins and William Lovett also promote the need for, and the value of, working-class education, but so too did 'physical-force Chartists'. The difference between moral and physical force, pronounced mostly in the early years of the Chartist movement or before 'physical-force Chartism' came into ascendancy to victoriously call itself just 'Chartism', was based primarily on accepting the place violence – verbal or physical – should potentially have in bringing about the Charter. By 1845 or 1847, when *DJSM* and *Howitt's Journal* began to publish, very few Chartists were still debating 'moral' versus 'physical' force. For Chartism's rejection of moral and physical force as legitimate categories, see M. Chase, *Chartism: A New History* (Manchester: Manchester University Press, 2007), pp. 46–7, 51 and 54; and J. Walton, *Chartism* (London and New York: Routledge, 1999), pp. 52–3.
5. M. Sanders, *The Poetry of Chartism: Aesthetics, Politics, History* (Cambridge: Cambridge University Press, 2009), p. 77.
6. E. Meteyard, 'Weekly record', *Howitt's Journal* (24 June 1848), III, p. 413.
7. *Ibid.*
8. *Ibid.*
9. *Ibid.*
10. *Ibid.*
11. After the Reform Bill of 1832, Chartists frequently expressed doubts and suspicions over middle-class reformism. Edward Royle quotes Bronterre O'Brien from 1837: 'The man who would not give you the franchise, though he were to offer you everything else, ought not to be trusted. Without the franchise, you can do nothing, and those

who give to-day, may choose to *take away* tomorrow. Knaves will tell you, that it is because you have no property you are unrepresented. I tell you, on the contrary, it is because you are unrepresented that you have no property.' Quoted in E. Royle, *Chartism* (London: Longman, 3rd edn, 1996), pp. 92–3. Royle adds that 'A generation of working people, overworked or unemployed, badly housed, de-skilled, exploited and suffering from what were seen as the effects of the Whig "class" legislation of the 1830s, believed this argument.' *Ibid.*, p. 93.
12 L. K. Hughes, 'Mary Howitt and the business of poetry', *Victorian Periodicals Review*, 50:2 (2017), 275.
13 D. Ulin, 'Reforming Wordsworth: William Howitt and the "great Republican Conservative"', *European Romantic Review*, 20:3 (2009), 311–12.
14 W. Howitt, 'Weekly record', *Howitt's Journal* (2 January 1847), I, p. 1.
15 Maidment, 'Magazines of popular progress & the artisans', p. 88.
16 W. and M. Howitt, 'William and Mary Howitt's address', *Howitt's Journal* (2 January 1847), I, p. 1.
17 *Ibid.*, p. 2.
18 Howitt, 'Weekly record', I, p. 1.
19 Maidment, 'Magazines of popular progress & the artisans', p. 89.
20 Hughes, 'Mary Howitt and the business of poetry', p. 275.
21 Maidment, 'Magazines of popular progress & the artisans', pp. 90–1.
22 Hughes, 'Mary Howitt and the business of poetry', pp. 277–8.
23 Howitts, 'William and Mary Howitt's address', I, pp. 1–2.
24 *Ibid.*, p. 2.
25 Maidment, 'Magazines of popular progress & the artisans', p. 86.
26 Howitts, 'William and Mary Howitt's address', I, p. 2.
27 S. Vinthagen, *A Theory of Nonviolent Action: How Civil Resistance Works* (London: Zed Books, 2015), p. 209.
28 Howitts, 'William and Mary Howitt's address', I, p. 2.
29 S. Smith, 'An address', *Howitt's Journal* (2 January 1847), I, p. 3.
30 See for example, Anon., 'Dates and violets', *Northern Star* (23 December 1848), p. 3; J. Senex, 'The Bridge of Westminster', *National Instructor* (14 September 1850), pp. 268–72; or E. Jones, 'The London door-step', *Labourer*, 3 (n.d.), pp. 228–32.
31 W. Howitt, 'Interior of a gin-palace', *Howitt's Journal* (8 January 1848), III, p. 19.
32 Howitt, 'Visit to a working man', II, p. 242.
33 Anon. ('A hardwareman'), 'The outcast', *National* (9 March 1839), pp. 129–32.

34 J. Senex, *National Instructor* (12 October 1850), pp. 333–6.
35 E. Meteyard, 'Life's contrasts; or, New-Year's Eve', *Howitt's Journal* (2 January 1847), I, p. 4.
36 *Ibid.*
37 *Ibid.*
38 M. Howitt, 'The beginning and end of Mrs. Muggeridge's wedding-dinner', *Howitt's Journal* (9 January 1847), I, pp. 25–8.
39 W. Howitt, 'The month in prospect – January', *Howitt's Journal* (2 January 1847), I, p. 9.
40 *Ibid.*, p. 10.
41 G. J. Holyoake, *Sixty Years of an Agitator's Life* (London: T. Fisher Unwin, 1893), II, p. 310.
42 Anon., 'Weekly record', *Howitt's Journal* (9 January 1847), I, p. 3.
43 Holyoake, *Sixty Years of an Agitator's Life*, pp. 309–10.
44 R. H. Horne, 'Peter Winch: the man who always had a penny', *Howitt's Journal* (2 January 1847), I, p. 11.
45 *Ibid.*, p. 12.
46 Howitt, 'Weekly record', I, p. 1.
47 *Ibid.*
48 *Ibid.*
49 *Ibid.*
50 Hughes, 'Mary Howitt and the business of poetry', p. 276.
51 *Ibid.*
52 W. J. Fox, 'The British museum closed', *Howitt's Journal* (16 January 1847), I, p. 30.
53 E. Youl, 'The verdict of the poor', *Howitt's Journal* (16 January 1847), I, p. 42.
54 E. Youl, 'Bob Rackett's search for shoes', *Howitt's Journal* (13 February 1847), I, pp. 91–3.
55 W. Lovett, 'To the people of the United Kingdom, on the state and condition of Ireland', *Howitt's Journal* (17 April 1847), I, p. 220.
56 M. Gillies, 'A labourer's home', *Howitt's Journal* (30 January 1847), I, pp. 61–4.
57 *Ibid.*, p. 64.
58 *Ibid.*
59 Arguably the most important 'condition-of-England' novelist, Elizabeth Gaskell, wrote three stories for *Howitt's Journal*.
60 Anon., 'Just instinct and brute reason', *Howitt's Journal* (6 March 1847), I, p. 132.
61 Maidment, 'Magazines of popular progress & the artisans', p. 90.
62 *Ibid.*, p. 91.

63 Anon., 'Literary notices', *Howitt's Journal* (20 March 1847), I, p. 166.
64 Anon., 'Literary notices', *Howitt's Journal* (2 October 1847), II, p. 222.
65 E. Jones, 'Life', *Howitt's Journal* (30 October 1847), II, p. 276.
66 S. Roberts, 'The later radical career of Thomas Cooper *c.* 1845–1855', *Transactions of the Leicestershire Archaeological and Historical Society*, 64 (1990), pp. 65 and 67.
67 See G. Vargo, *An Underground History of Early Victorian Fiction: Chartism, Radical Print Culture, and the Social Problem Novel* (Cambridge: Cambridge University Press, 2018), pp. 19–28.
68 M. Gillies, 'Associated homes', *Howitt's Journal* (27 March 1847), I, p. 171.
69 Ibid.
70 Ibid. p. 172.
71 Hodgson, 'Have patience', *Howitt's Journal* (10 April 1847), I, pp. 203–5.
72 Anon., 'William Lovett', *Howitt's Journal* (8 May 1847), I, p. 257.
73 M. Howitt, 'The deserter in London', *Howitt's Journal* (11 September 1847), II, p. 162; Anon., 'The soldier: a story illustrative of the flogging system', *English Chartist Circular*, II, pp. 142–3.
74 H. C. Wright, 'Dick Crowninshield the assassin, and Zachary Taylor the soldier; the difference between them', *Howitt's Journal* (17 June 1848), III, p. 396.
75 J. Hurrey, 'The slave of the oven', *Howitt's Journal* (10 July 1847), II, p. 32. See K. J. Mays, 'Slaves in heaven, laborers in hell: Chartist poets' ambivalent identification with the (black) slave', *Victorian Poetry*, 39:2 (2001), 137–63.
76 Howitt, 'Visit to a working man', II, p. 242.
77 Anon. ('C'), 'Rights of women', *Howitt's Journal* (17 June 1848), III, p. 398.
78 Howitt, 'Interior of a gin-palace', III, p. 19.
79 Ibid.
80 W. and M. Howitt, 'The editors' address to their friends and readers', *Howitt's Journal* (1 January 1848), III, p. 16.
81 W. Howitt, 'Weekly record', *Howitt's Journal* (18 March 1848), III, p. 191.
82 Lecturer, reformer, and nonconformist preacher, Dawson founded the Unitarian Church of the Saviour. He is credited for originating the 'Civic Gospel', 'an organised attempt to use the powers of a local authority to implement the social implications of Christianity'.

A. Vail, 'Birmingham's protestant nonconformity in the late nineteenth and early twentieth centuries: the theological context for the "Civic Gospel"', in I. Cawood *et al.* (eds), *Joseph Chamberlain* (London: Palgrave Macmillan, 2016), p. 212.
83 G. Dawson, 'George Dawson on the present crisis', *Howitt's Journal* (22 April 1848), III, p. 272.
84 *Ibid.*
85 *Ibid.*
86 W. Howitt, 'Weekly record', *Howitt's Journal* (29 April 1848), III, p. 287.
87 *Ibid.*
88 M. Fryckstedt, 'Douglas Jerrold's Shilling Magazine', *Victorian Periodicals Review*, 19:1 (1986), 16.
89 D. Jerrold, untitled prospectus, *Douglas Jerrold's Shilling Magazine* (*DJSM*), I, p. iii. Volumes of *DJSM* correspond with these dates: Volume I, January to June, 1845; Volume II, July to December, 1845; Volume III, January to June, 1846; Volume IV, July to December, 1846; Volume V, January to June, 1847; Volume VI, July to December, 1847; and Volume VII, January to June 1848.
90 Jerrold, untitled prospectus, I, p. iii.
91 *Ibid.*
92 *Ibid.*
93 *Ibid.*
94 F. D. Roberts, 'More early Victorian newspaper editors', *Victorian Periodicals Newsletter*, 16 (1972), 19.
95 *Ibid.*, p. 20.
96 *Ibid.*, p. 21.
97 'Vivian', 'The coming reformation, part 3', *DJSM*, VI, p. 35.
98 Jerrold, untitled prospectus, I, p. iii.
99 Anon. ('An Optimist'), 'The morbidness of literature', *DJSM*, I, p. 489.
100 The Optimist's criticism of crime literature sounds as if penned by Thackeray: 'instead of being "the man's a rascal and there's the end of it", it became "the man's a rascal, but that's only the beginning of an inquiry". The contented, healthy, abhorrence of vice, that fancied itself so perfectly undefiled, and that so complacently shut the door against the erring portion of humanity, began to give way. A disagreeable relationship with the parias was discovered. There were no longer those distinct contrasts of black and white, but a sort of dusky colour manifested itself, that rendered it a hard matter to tell where the black begun and the white left off.' *Ibid.*, p. 490.

101 Ibid., p. 492.
102 Ibid.
103 Roberts, 'More early Victorian newspaper editors', p. 22.
104 D. Jerrold, *The History of St. Giles and St. James*, DJSM, I, p. 3.
105 Ibid.
106 Ibid.
107 Ibid., p. 190.
108 Ibid., p. 285.
109 Ibid., p. 399.
110 Another interesting example of the paper's devotion to the individualised hardships of the poor is an article on a 'man of good character, and perfectly sober', Edward Laws. Laws, an engine driver, 'negligently caused a collision between the engine he was driving and that of the mail-train'. But the article asks for sympathy, for a reduced sentence, saying that 'humble' men like Laws deserve recognition for their contribution to the nation. The sentiment is genuine and remarkably personalised: Laws was not advocating for himself. Anon., 'Serving the people', DJSM, II, p. 313.
111 Anon., 'My temptations, by a poor man', DJSM, II, p. 55.
112 Jerrold, *The History of St. Giles and St. James*, II, pp. 97–8.
113 G. Jewsbury, 'The lower orders', DJSM, V, p. 364.
114 Ibid., p. 365.
115 Ibid.
116 Ibid., p. 367.
117 Anon., 'Democracy in 1847', DJSM, VI, p. 211.
118 Ibid., p. 216.
119 Anon., 'A vision', DJSM, III, p. 58.
120 The appreciation was reciprocated. Cooper dedicates *Wise Saws and Modern Instances* (1845) to Jerrold, who had helped him find a publisher for *Wise Saws* and *Purgatory*. In the later months of 1846, Cooper became a correspondent for Jerrold's *Douglas Jerrold's Weekly Newspaper*.
121 DJSM would also review 'The baron's yule feast' (1846) (III, p. 180) and later Cooper has a poem, 'The poor man's coat' (III, pp. 397–9), and a short story, 'Crickum Crankum' (IV, pp. 75–82), in the paper.
122 Anon., 'The revolutionary firebrand', DJSM, V, p. 327.
123 Ibid.
124 Fryckstedt suggests that it was likely written by Jerrold. Fryckstedt, 'Douglas Jerrold's Shilling Magazine', p. 9.
125 Anon., 'The revolutionary firebrand', V, p. 328.
126 Ibid.

127 *Ibid.*, p. 329.
128 M. Slater, *Douglas Jerrold: 1803–1857* (London: Duckworth, 2002), p. 123.
129 *Ibid.*, p. 143.
130 Anon., 'The revolutionary firebrand', V, p. 329.

Select bibliography

Ainsworth, W. H. *Jack Sheppard* (London: Penguin, 2010).
Ainsworth, W. H. (ed.) *New Monthly Magazine*: *Part the First* (London: Chapman and Hall, 1847).
Alexander, L. 'Creating a symbol: the seamstress in Victorian literature', *Tulsa Studies in Women's Literature*, 18:1 (1999), 29–38.
Altick, R. D. *The English Common Reader: A Social History of the Mass Reading Public 1800–1900* (Columbus, OH: Ohio State University Press, 2nd edn, 1998).
Andrews, K. 'Neither mute nor inglorious: Anne Yearsley and elegy', in J. Goodridge and B. Keegan (eds), *A History of British Working Class Literature* (Cambridge: Cambridge University Press, 2017).
Ashton, O. R. 'Chartism and popular culture: an introduction to the radical culture in Cheltenham Spa, 1830–1847', *Journal of Popular Culture*, 20:4 (2004), 61–81.
Bender, J. *Imagining the Penitentiary: Fiction and the Architecture of Mind in Eighteenth-Century England* (Chicago: University of Chicago Press, 1987).
Bennett, T. 'Popular culture: history and theory', *Popular Culture: Themes and Issues* (block 1, unit 3, Milton Keynes: Open University Press, 1981).
Boone, T. *Youth of Darkest England: Working-Class Children at the Heart of Victorian Empire* (New York and London: Routledge, 2015).
Borrow, G. *Celebrated Trials, and Remarkable Cases of Criminal Jurisprudence from the Earliest Records to the Year 1825* (6 vols, London: Smackell and Arrowsmith, 1825).
Brake, L. and M. Demoor (eds) 'Weekly dispatch', in *Dictionary of Nineteenth-Century Journalism* (Gent and London: Academia Press, 2009).
Breton, R. 'Crime reporting in Chartist newspapers', *Media History*, 19:3 (2013), 1–13.
Buckley, M. 'Sensations of celebrity: *Jack Sheppard* and the mass audience', *Victorian Studies*, 44:3 (2002), 423–63.

Campion, W., R. Hassell, and T. R. Perry (eds) *The Newgate Monthly Magazine* (London: R. Carlile, 1825).

Carlyle, T. 'Chartism', in *The Works of Thomas Carlyle in Thirty Volumes* (New York: Charles Scribner and Sons, 1904), XXIX, 118–204.

Carver, S. J. *The Life and Works of the Lancashire Novelist William Harrison Ainsworth, 1805–1882* (Lewiston, NY: Edwin Mellen Press, 2003).

Carver, S. J. 'The wrongs and crimes of the poor: the urban underworld of *The Mysteries of London* in context', in A. Humpherys and L. James (eds), *G. W. M. Reynolds: Nineteenth-Century Fiction, Politics, and the Press* (Aldershot: Ashgate, 2008).

Chalmers, T. *The Christian and Civic Economy of Large Towns* (3 vols, Glasgow: Chalmers and Collins, I, 1821).

Chase, M. *Chartism: A New History* (Manchester: Manchester University Press, 2007).

Chevasco, B. 'Lost in translation: the relationship between Eugène Sue's *Les Mystères de Paris* and Reynolds's *The Mysteries of London*', in A. Humpherys and L. James (eds), *G. W. M. Reynolds: Nineteenth-Century Fiction, Politics, and the Press* (Aldershot: Ashgate, 2008).

Chow, R. *Ethics after Idealism: Theory, Culture, Ethnicity, Reading* (Basingstoke: Palgrave Macmillan, 1998).

Collins, W. *The Woman in White* (Oxford: Oxford University Press, 1998).

Costello, D. 'Greenberg's Kant and the fate of aesthetics in contemporary art theory', *The Journal of Aesthetics and Art Criticism*, 65:2 (2007), 217–28.

Creechan, L. '"Attend the tale of Sweeney Todd": adaptation, revival, and keeping the meat grinder turning', *Neo-Victorian Studies*, 9:1 (2016), 98–122.

Crone, R. 'From Sawney Beane to Sweeney Todd', *Cultural and Social History*, 7:1 (2010), 59–85.

Crone, R. *Violent Victorians: Popular Entertainment in Nineteenth-Century London* (Manchester: Manchester University Press, 2012).

Denning, M. *Mechanic Accents: Dime Novels and Working-Class Culture in America* (London: Verso, 1987).

Devereux, S. 'Chartism and popular fiction', in J. Lucas (ed.), *Writing and Radicalism* (London: Longman, 1996).

Dickens, C. *Barnaby Rudge* (Harmondsworth: Penguin, 1977).

Dickens, C. *Oliver Twist* (Oxford: Oxford University Press, 2008).

Dulcken, H. W. *Epochs and Episodes of History: A Book of Memorable Days and Notable Events* (London: Ward, Lock, and Co., 1882).

Egan, P. *Life in London* (Cambridge: Cambridge University Press, 2011).

Engels, F. *The Condition of the Working Classes in England*, trans. W. O. Henderson and W. H. Chaloner (Oxford: Basil Blackwell, 1971).

Falke, C. 'On the morality of immoral fiction: reading Newgate novels, 1830–1848', *Nineteenth-Century Contexts*, 38:3 (2016), 183–93.

Fladeland, B. '"Our cause being one and the same": abolitionists and Chartism', in J. Walvin (ed.), *Slavery and British Society, 1776–1846* (London: Palgrave, 1982).

Flanders, J. *The Invention of Murder: How the Victorians Revelled in Death and Detection and Created Modern Crime* (Hammersmith: Harper Press, 2011).

Foucault, M. *The History of Sexuality 1, An Introduction*, trans. R. Hurley (London: Penguin, 1979).

Frijda, N. H. 'The lex talonis: on vengeance', in S. H. M. van Goozen, N. E. Van de Poll, and J. A. Sergeant (eds), *Emotions: Essays on Emotion Theory* (Hillsdale, NJ: Lawrence Erlbaum Associates, 1994).

Frost, T. *Forty Years' Recollections: Literary and Political* (London: Sampson Low, 1880).

Fryckstedt, M. 'Douglas Jerrold's Shilling Magazine', *Victorian Periodicals Review*, 19:1 (1986), 2–27.

Gillingham, L. 'Ainsworth's *Jack Sheppard* and the crimes of history', *Studies in English Literature 1500–1900*, 49:4 (2009), 879–906.

Gillingham, L. 'The Newgate novel and the police casebook', in C. J. Rzepka and L. Horsley (eds), *A Companion to Crime Fiction* (Chichester, West Sussex: Wiley-Blackwell, 2010).

Grossman, J. H. *The Art of the Alibi: English Law Courts and the Novel* (Baltimore, MD and London: Johns Hopkins University Press, 2002).

Hackenberg, S. 'Vampires and resurrection men: the perils and pleasures of the embodied past in 1840s sensational fiction', *Victorian Studies*, 52:1 (2009), 63–75.

Harden, E. F. (ed.) *Selected Letters of William Makepeace Thackeray* (New York: New York University Press, 1996).

Haywood, I. *The Revolution in Popular Literature: Print, Politics, and the People, 1790–1860* (Cambridge: Cambridge University Press, 2004).

Heppenstall, R. *Reflections on the Newgate Calendar* (London: W. H. Allen, 1975).

Himmelfarb, G. *The Idea of Poverty: England in the Early Industrial Age* (New York: Alfred A. Knopf, 1984).

Hollingsworth, K. *The Newgate Novel, 1830–1847: Bulwer, Ainsworth, Dickens, and Thackeray* (Detroit, MI: Wayne State University Press, 1963).

Holyoake, G. J. *Sixty Years of an Agitator's Life* (2 vols, London: T. Fisher Unwin, II, 1893).

Hughes, K. *Victorians Undone: Tales of the Flesh in the Age of Decorum* (London: 4th Estate, 2017).

Hughes, L. K. 'Mary Howitt and the business of poetry', *Victorian Periodicals Review*, 50:2 (2017), 273–94.
Humpherys, A. 'An introduction to G. W. M. Reynolds's "Encyclopedia of Tales"', in A. Humpherys and L. James (eds), *G. W. M. Reynolds: Nineteenth-Century Fiction, Politics, and the Press* (Aldershot: Ashgate, 2008).
Humpherys, A. 'G. W. M. Reynolds: popular literature and popular politics', *Victorian Periodicals Review*, 16 (1983), 79–89.
Humpherys, A. 'Popular narrative and political discourse in *Reynolds's Weekly Newspaper*', in L. Brake, A. Jones, and L. Madden (eds), *Investigating Victorian Journalism* (Houndmills: Macmillan, 1990).
Jackson, W. *The New and Complete Newgate Calendar or Villany Displayed in All its Branches* (6 vols, London: Alexander Hogg, 1795).
Jacobs, E. 'Edward Lloyd's Sunday newspapers and the cultural politics of crime news, *c.* 1840–43', *Victorian Periodicals Review*, 50:3 (2017), 619–49.
Jacobs, E. 'The politicization of everyday life in *Cleave's Weekly Police Gazette* (1834–36)', *Victorian Periodicals Review*, 41:3 (2008), 225–47.
James, L. *Fiction for the Working Man, 1830–1850* (Harmondsworth: Penguin University Books, 1974).
James, L. 'The trouble with Betsy: periodicals and the common reader in mid-nineteenth-century England', in J. Shattock and M. Wolff (eds), *The Victorian Periodical Press: Samplings and Soundings* (Leicester: Leicester University Press, 1982).
James, L. 'Time, politics and the symbolic imagination in Reynolds's social melodrama', in A. Humpherys and L. James (eds), *G. W. M. Reynolds: Nineteenth-Century Fiction, Politics, and the Press* (Aldershot: Ashgate, 2008).
John, J. 'Introduction', *Cult Criminals: The Newgate Novels, 1830–1847* (Abingdon: Routledge, 2000).
John, J. 'Reynolds's *Mysteries* and popular culture', in A. Humpherys and L. James (eds), *G. W. M. Reynolds: Nineteenth-Century Fiction, Politics, and the Press* (Aldershot: Ashgate, 2008).
John, J. 'Twisting the Newgate tale: Dickens, popular culture and the politics of genre', in J. John and A. Jenkins (eds), *Rethinking Victorian Culture* (Houndmills: Macmillan Press, 2000).
Joyce, P. *Democratic Subjects: The Self and the Social in Nineteenth-Century England* (Cambridge: Cambridge University Press, 1994).
Joyce, P. *Visions of the People: Industrial England and the Question of Class, 1848–1914* (Cambridge: Cambridge University Press, 1991).
Joyce, S. *Capital Offenses: Geographies of Crime in Victorian London* (Charlottesville, VA and London: University of Virginia Press, 2003).

Joyce, S. 'Resisting arrest/arresting resistance: crime fiction, cultural studies, and the "turn to history"', *Criticism: A Quarterly for Literature and the Arts*, 37:2 (1995), 309–35.

Knapp, A. and W. Baldwin (eds), *The New Newgate Calendar* (5 vols, London: J. Robins and Co. Albion Press, 1819).

Knapp, A. and W. Baldwin (eds) *The Newgate Calendar* (4 vols, London: J. Robins and Co., 1824–28).

Knight, S. *Crime Fiction since 1800: Detection, Death, Diversity* (Houndmills: Palgrave Macmillan, 2nd edn, 2010).

Knight, S. *Form and Ideology in Crime Fiction* (Bloomington, IN: Indiana University Press, 1980).

Ledger, S. 'Chartist aesthetics in the mid nineteenth century: Ernest Jones, a novelist of the people', *Nineteenth-Century Literature*, 57:1 (2002), 31–63.

Lovett, W. and J. Collins. *Chartism: A New Organization of the People* (New York: Leicester University Press, 1969).

Lucas, A. '*Oliver Twist* and the Newgate novel', *The Dalhousie Review*, 34:1 (1954), 381–7.

Lukács, G. *The Historical Novel*, trans. H. and S. Mitchell (Harmondsworth: Penguin, 1981).

Maidment, B. 'Magazines of popular progress & the artisans', *Victorian Periodicals Review*, 17:3 (1984), 83–94.

Martin, A. M. (ed.) *Martin's Annals of Crime; or, New Newgate Calendar* (2 vols, London: William Mark Clark, 1837 and 1838).

Marx, K. 'Preface to *A Contribution to the Critique of Political Economy*', in R. C. Tucker (ed.), *The Marx-Engels Reader* (New York: Norton, 2nd edn, 1978).

Mather, F. C. *Chartism and Society: An Anthology of Documents* (London: Bell & Hyman, 1980).

Mayhew, H. 'The Literature of Costermongers', *London Labour and the London Poor* (London: Penguin, 1985).

Mays, K. J. 'Slaves in heaven, laborers in hell: Chartist poets' ambivalent identification with the (black) slave', *Victorian Poetry*, 39:2 (2001), 137–63.

Mbembé, A. 'Necropolitics', trans. L. Meintjes, *Public Culture*, 15:1 (2003), 11–40.

McCalman, I. *Radical Underworld: Prophets, Revolutionaries and Pornographers in London, 1795–1840* (Oxford: Clarendon Press, 2002).

McWilliam, R. 'Introduction', *Sweeney Todd: The String of Pearls* (Mineola, NY: Dover, 2015).

McWilliam, R. 'Liberalism lite?', *Victorian Studies*, 48:1 (2005), 103–11.

McWilliam, R. *Popular Politics in Nineteenth-Century England* (London: Routledge, 2012).

McWilliam, R. 'The French connection: G. W. M. Reynolds and the outlaw Robert Macaire', in A. Humpherys and L. James (eds), *G. W. M. Reynolds: Nineteenth-Century Fiction, Politics, and the Press* (Aldershot: Ashgate, 2008).

McWilliam, R. 'The mysteries of G. W. M. Reynolds: radicalism and melodrama in Victorian Britain', in M. Chase and I. Dyck (eds), *Living and Learning: Essays in Honour of J. F. C. Harrison* (Aldershot: Scolar Press, 1996).

Meisel, M. *Realizations: Narrative, Pictorial, and Theatrical Arts in Nineteenth-Century England* (Princeton, NJ: Princeton University Press, 1983).

Mitchell, J. 'Aesthetic problems of the development of the proletarian-revolutionary novel in nineteenth-century Britain', in D. Craig (ed.), *Marxists on Literature, An Anthology* (Harmondsworth: Penguin, 1975).

Mitford, M. R. *The Life of Mary Russell Mitford, Told by Herself in Letters to her Friends* (2 vols, New York: Harper and Brothers Publishers, II, 1870).

Novak, M. '"Appearances of truth": the literature of crime as a narrative system (1660–1841)', *The Yearbook of English Studies*, 11 (1981), 29–48.

Page, N. *A Dickens Companion* (Houndmills: Macmillan, 1984).

Panek, L. L. *Before Sherlock Holmes: How Magazines and Newspapers Invented the Detective Story* (Jefferson, NC and London: McFarland and Company, 2011).

Pearson, G. *Hooligan: A History of Respectable Fears* (New York: Schocken, 1983).

Pelham, C. (ed.) *The Chronicles of Crime; or, The New Newgate Calendar* (2 vols, London: Thomas Tigg, 1841).

Perera, S. *No Country: Working-Class Writing in the Age of Globalization* (New York: Columbia University Press, 2014).

Peterson, T. B. 'T. B. Peterson's lists of books', in *The Birthright: A Novel* by C. G. F. Gore (New York: Harper and Brothers, 1843).

Rancière, J. *The Philosopher and His Poor* (Durham, NC: Duke University Press, 2004).

Reynolds. G. W. M. *The Mysteries of London* (2 vols, Kansas City, MO: Valancourt Books, 2013).

Reynolds. G. W. M. *The Seamstress; or, the White Slave of England* (London: John Dicks, 1853).

Richards, J. 'The "Lancashire novelist" and the Lancashire witches', in R. Poole (ed.), *The Lancashire Witches: Histories and Stories* (Manchester: Manchester University Press, 2002).

Roberts, F. D. 'More early Victorian newspaper editors', *Victorian Periodicals Newsletter*, 16 (1972), 15–28.

Roberts, S. 'The later radical career of Thomas Cooper, c. 1845–1855', *Transactions of the Leicestershire Archaeological and Historical Society*, 64 (1990), 62–72.
Rodrick, A. B. '"Only a newspaper metaphor": crime reports, class conflict, and social criticism in two Victorian newspapers', *Victorian Periodicals Review*, 29:1 (1996), 1–18.
Rose, J. *The Intellectual Life of the British Working Classes* (New Haven, CT and London: Yale University Press, 2002).
Royle, E. *Chartism* (London: Longman, 3rd edn, 1996).
Rudé, G. 'The Gordon Riots: a study of the rioters and their victims', *Paris and London in the 18th Century: Studies in Popular Protest* (London: Collins, 1970).
Rymer, J. M. *Ada, the Betrayed, or, The Murder at the Old Smithy. Lloyd's Penny Weekly Miscellany of Romance and General Interest* (London: Edward Lloyd, 1843).
Rymer, J. M. *Varney, the Vampire; or, the Feast of Blood* (London: Wordsworth, 2010).
Rymer, J. M. or T. P. Prest. *Sweeney Todd: The String of Pearls* (Mineola, NY: Dover, 2015).
Rymer, J. M. or T. P. Prest. *The String of Pearls; or, the Barber of Fleet Street* (London: E. Lloyd, 1850).
Sanders, M. *The Poetry of Chartism: Aesthetics, Politics, History* (Cambridge: Cambridge University Press, 2009).
Schwarzbach, F. B. 'Newgate novel to detective fiction', in P. Brantlinger and W. B. Theising (eds), *A Companion to the Victorian Novel* (Massachusetts: Blackwell Publishing, 2002).
Shirley, M. H. 'G. W. M. Reynolds, *Reynolds's Newspaper* and popular politics', in A. Humpherys and L. James (eds), *G. W. M. Reynolds: Nineteenth-Century Fiction, Politics, and the Press* (Aldershot: Ashgate, 2008).
Slater, M. *Douglas Jerrold: 1803–1857* (London: Duckworth, 2002).
Springhall, J. '"A life story for the people"? Edwin J. Brett and the London "low-life" penny dreadfuls of the 1860s', *Victorian Studies*, 33:2 (1990), 223–46.
Stephens, J. R. *The Censorship of English Drama, 1824–1901* (Cambridge: Cambridge University Press, 1980).
Straub, K. 'Feminine sexuality, class identity, and narrative form in the Newgate calendars', in D. Todd and C. Wall (eds), *Eighteenth-Century Genre and Culture* (Newark: University of Delaware Press, 2001).
Sutherland, J. 'Harrison Ainsworth, 1805–1882', *Lives of the Novelists: A History of Fiction in 294 Lives* (New Haven, CT and London: Yale University Press, 2012).

Taylor, M. *The Decline of British Radicalism 1847–1860* (Oxford: Clarendon Press, 1995).
Thackeray, W. M. *Catherine: A Story*, in *Fraser's Magazine. Vol. XXI. January to June, 1840* (London: James Fraser, 1840).
Thackeray, W. M. 'Going to see a man hanged', in *The Works of William Makepeace Thackeray. Vol. XIV* (London: Smith, Elder and Company, 1884).
Thackeray, W. M. 'Horae catnachiannae', in *Fraser's Magazine. Vol. XIX. January to June, 1839* (London: James Fraser, 1839).
Thompson, E. P. *The Making of the English Working Class* (London: Penguin, 1980).
Turner, E. S. *Boys Will Be Boys: The Story of Sweeney Todd, Deadwood Dick, Sexton Blake, Billy Bunter, Dick Barton et al.* (London: Michael Joseph, 1975).
Ulin, D. 'Reforming Wordsworth: William Howitt and the "great Republican Conservative"', *European Romantic Review*, 20:3 (2009), 309–25.
Vail, A. 'Birmingham's protestant nonconformity in the late nineteenth and early twentieth centuries: the theological context for the "Civic Gospel"', in I. Cawood *et al.* (eds), *Joseph Chamberlain* (London: Palgrave Macmillan, 2016).
Vargo, G. *An Underground History of Early Victorian Fiction: Chartism, Radical Print Culture, and the Social Problem Novel* (Cambridge: Cambridge University Press, 2018).
Vincent, D. *Literacy and Popular Culture: England 1750–1914* (Cambridge: Cambridge University Press, 1993).
Vinthagen, S. *A Theory of Nonviolent Action: How Civil Resistance Works* (London: Zed Books, 2015).
Walton, J. *Chartism* (London and New York: Routledge, 1999).
Weltman, S. A. '1847: Sweeney Todd and abolition', *BRANCH: Britain, Representation and Nineteenth-Century History*, D. F. Felluga (ed.), Web (18 August 2018).
Williams, R. 'Forms of English fiction in 1848', in F. Baker *et al.* (eds), *Literature, Politics and Theory: Papers from the Essex Conference* (London: Methuen, 1986).
Williams, R. *Modern Tragedy* (London: Chatto and Windus, 1969).
Woloch, A. *The One vs. the Many* (Princeton, NJ: Princeton University Press, 2003).
Worth, G. J. *William Harrison Ainsworth* (New York: Twayne Publishers, 1972).
Worthington, H. 'From the Newgate calendar to Sherlock Holmes', in C. J. Rzepka and L. Horsley (eds), *A Companion to Crime Fiction* (Chichester, West Sussex: Wiley-Blackwell, 2010).

Index

(Literary works can be found under authors' names; 'n.' after a page reference indicates the number of a note on that page; page numbers in italic refer to illustrations.)

Ainsworth, William Harrison 21, 48, 49, 53, 57–8, 69, 70, 72, 80n.3
   Jack Sheppard (1839–40) 5, 14, 15, 18n.22, 36, 47–85, 105, 115
   Rookwood (1834) 47, 55, 72
Alexander, Lynn 161
Altick, Richard 10, 90, 99, 100, 156
Anatomy Act (1832) 90, 102–3
Andrews, Kerri 136
'Argus'
   'Republican: a tale of the French Revolution, The' (1840) 44n.50
Ashton, Owen 7, 90, 96

Barton, Ellen
   'Ida Walton; or, a Tale of Trials' (1847) 93
Bender, John 65
Bennett, Tony 8
Bloody Code 26–7, 64
Boone, Troy 115–16, 117, 126n.22, 146

Borrow, George
   Celebrated Trials (1825) 22–3, 24–5, 28–9
Bourdieu, Pierre 141
Browne, Hablot Knight ('Phiz') 35
   Manchester Massacre (1841) 41–2
Buckley, Matthew 56, 66, 80n.2
Bulwer, Edward Bulwer 21, 49, 50, 56, 58–9
   Eugene Aram (1832) 47, 53, 68, 75
   Paul Clifford (1830) 47, 68
Burke, Edmund 24–5

Campion, William 23
Carlyle, Thomas 8, 17n.3, 169
Carver, Stephen James 64, 65, 70, 80n.3, 137, 156
Chambers, William 86
Chartism 2–19 *passim*, 32, 35–40 *passim*, 56–7, 66, 75, 79–80, 86, 88, 89, 90, 95, 100, 111–12, 114, 116, 128n.39, 140, 141, 146, 152, 169, 171n.16, 175–6, 178–9, 180,

183, 189–90, 193, 197–9, 210–11, 213, 214, 215n.1
Chartist fiction 3, 4–5, 6, 9, 10, 12, 13, 16, 18n.21, 40, 52, 62, 71, 73, 75, 79–80, 88–9, 95–8, 108, 121–2, 137, 139, 144–50, 153, 154, 176, 178, 179, 185, 188, 191–2, 195, 196–7, 201, 214
separation into physical and moral forces 4, 5–6, 38, 39–40, 89, 96–7, 116, 128n.40, 141–2, 146, 177–80, 194–5, 196, 198, 214, 215n.4
Chevasco, Berry 140
Cleave, John 18n.22, 86
Cobbett, William 32, 110
Collins, Wilkie 28
'condition-of-England' narratives 5, 185, 193, 217n.59
Cooper, Thomas 128n.39, 180, 191, 194–5, 211, 214, 220n.120, 220n.121
'Kucky Sarson, the barber; or, the disciple of equality' (1845) 104
Costello, Diarmuid 163
Courvoisier, François Benjamin 36, 54, 57
Creechan, Louise 90
Crone, Rosalind 10, 91–2, 94, 101, 125n.1, 125n.6, 126n.20, 143
crowds 37, 45n.68, 63, 66, 76–8, 114–17, 214
Cruikshank, George 47, 63, 78–9

Dawson, George 199–200, 218n.82
Denning, Michael 90
Dickens, Charles 8, 14, 16n.2, 21, 48, 49, 50–3, 89, 140, 166–7
Barnaby Rudge (1841) 47, 69, 77

Oliver Twist (1837–38) 47, 48, 50–1, 53, 55, 59, 60, 62, 64, 67, 71–2, 77, 81n.7, 134

Egan, Pierce
Life in London (1821) 63–4, 136, 204
Engels, Friedrich 171n.16

Falke, Cassandra 56
Flanders, Judith 156
Forster, John 53
Foucault, Michel 65, 77, 83n.49
Fox, Henry 51
Fox, W. J. 191
Frijda, Nico H. 159, 161
Frost, John 38
Frost, Thomas 94, 120, 127n.27, 133n.148, 145
Fryckstedt, Monica 202

Gaskell, Elizabeth, 217n.59
Gillies, Mary
'A labourer's home' (1847) 192
'Associated homes' (1847) 195
Gillingham, Lauren 58, 61, 67, 72–3
Gordon Riots (1780) 22, 35, 69, 70
Grossman, Jonathan 60, 65

Hackenberg, Sara 90, 156, 166–7
Haywood, Ian 10, 11, 90, 142, 146, 158
Heppenstall, Rayner 26, 32
Himmelfarb, Gertrude 142, 147, 157
Hodgson, Mrs
'Have Patience' (1847) 196
Hollingsworth, Keith 42n.1, 52, 59, 64, 65, 67
Holyoake, George 188

Hooton, Charles 80n.1
Horne, R. H.
  'Peter Winch: The man who always had a penny' (1847) 188–9
Howitt, Mary 64, 95, 186, 191
  'Beginning and end of Mrs. Muggeridge's wedding-dinner, The' (1847) 186–7
  'Deserter in London, The' (1847) 196
Howitt, William, 86, 95, 180–1, 187
  Howitt's Journal (1847–48) 16, 175–202, 210, 211
Hughes, Kathryn 104
Hughes, Linda 180, 182–3, 185, 191
Humpherys, Anne 10, 137, 142, 154, 156, 171n.19
Hunt, Henry 40–1
Hurrey, John
  'slave of the oven, The' (1847) 197

Irving, Washington 32

Jackson, William
  New and Complete Newgate Calendar (1795) 21, 24, 30
Jacobitism 11, 69–70
Jacobs, Edward 115
James, Louis 9, 10, 88–9, 91, 94, 98, 110, 117, 118, 127n.33, 132n.123, 139, 146, 152, 157
Jerrold, Douglas 95, 194, 202–4, 212–13
  Douglas Jerrold's Shilling Magazine (1845–48) 16, 17n.3, 175, 176–80, 201–13
  History of St. Giles and St. James, The (1845) 205–9

Jewsbury, Geraldine 209–10
John, Juliet 8, 10, 57, 63, 67, 140, 143
Jones, Ernest 79, 128n.40, 136, 140, 145, 146, 148, 170n.7, 193–5 *passim*, 211, 214
Joyce, Patrick 13, 99, 143
Joyce, Simon 54, 56, 66–7, 69

Knapp, Andrew and William Baldwin 21, 28
  Newgate Calendar (1824–28) 21, 26, 28, 29–30
  New Newgate Calendar (1819) 21, 22, 26–7, 29, 30
Kingsley, Charles 1, 14, 16n.2, 215n.1
  Politics for the People (1848–49) 1–2, 16, 123, 175, 176, 215n.1
  see also Ludlow, John and Maurice, F. D.
Knight, Charles 93–4, 178
Knight, Stephen 21, 25, 26, 42n.1

Ledger, Sally 89
Lever, Charles 89
Lewes, George Henry 204
Lloyd, Edward 6, 11, 15, 86, 88–9, 90, 93, 98, 110, 115, 122–5 *passim*
  Lloyd's Penny Weekly Miscellany of Romance and General Interest (1842–46) 15, 89, 120–5
  People's Periodical and Family Library (1846–47) 15, 93–4, 100–1, 132n.140
Lovett, William 38, 172n.46, 180, 192, 196
Lucas, Alec 61–2
Ludlow, John 1
Lukács, Georg 71

Index

McCalman, Iain 89
McWilliam, Rohan 10, 11–12, 91, 101, 118, 126n.20, 136, 139, 145–6, 147, 149
Maidment, Brian 10, 176, 181, 182, 184, 193
'Manchester Operative'
  'Just instinct and brute reason' (1847) 193
Martin, A. M.
  Martin's Annals of Crime (1837–38) 20, 27, 28, 30–4, 42n.1
martyrdom 32, 36, 44n.50, 66, 77–9, 108, 161, 164
Marxian analysis 106–7, 145
Mather, F. C. 39
Maurice, F. D. 1–2, 16n.2
Mayhew, Henry 50–1
Mbembe, Achille 77
Meadows, Kenny
  Heads of the People (1840) 64
Meisel, Martin 56
Melbourne, Lord 51
Meteyard, Eliza 179–80, 185–6
  'Life's contrasts; or, New-Year's Eve' (1847) 185–6
Mitford, Mary Russell 57

Newgate Calendar; or, Malefactors' Bloody Register (1773) 21
New Poor Law (1834) 45n.55, 67, 89, 90, 187
Nietzsche, Friedrich 167
Novak, Maximillian 21, 30

O'Brien, Bronterre 172n.46, 215n.11
O'Connor, Feargus 39–40, 79, 128n.40, 140, 193–5
'old and new corruption' 5, 6, 71, 137, 143–4, 146, 204

'Optimist' 219n.100
'morbidness of literature, The' (1845) 205

Pearson, Geoffrey 56
Pelham, Camden 35, 40
  Chronicles of Crime (1841) 20, 21, 22, 27, 32, 34–42, 46n.70, 63
penny dreadfuls 14, 87, 89
penny bloods 11, 14, 15, 86–98, 125n.6, 126n.22, 136, 152, 155, 156–7
Perera, Sonali 138
Powell, Sally 101, 106
Prest, Thomas Peckett 100
  Newgate: A Romance (1847) 47
  String of Pearls. A Romance (Sweeney Todd) (1846–47) 2, 5, 14, 15, 87, 90, 91, 92, 95, 96, 98, 99–112, 121
  String of Pearls (1850) 106, 112–115, 131n.100
  see also Rymer, James Malcolm

Rancière, Jacques 174n.104
Reform Bill (1832) 49, 55, 92, 118, 215n.11
Reynolds, G. W. M. 6, 11, 14, 15–16, 86, 90, 104, 123, 136–43 *passim*
  Drunkard's Progress (1840–41) 172n.49
  Mysteries of London, The (1844–45) 16, 134–170
  Seamstress, The (1850) 149–50, 151, 160–1
Richards, Jeffrey 69
Roberts, David F. 203–4, 205
Roberts, Stephen 194–5
Rose, Jonathan 87–8
Royle, Edward 215n.11

Rymer, James Malcolm 100, 110, 117
   Ada, the Betrayed (1843) 91, 115, 118–120
   Varney, the Vampire (1840–42) 91, 114–18, 119, 146

Sanders, Mike 179
Scott, Walter 71
Senex, Junius 148
Shirley, Michael H. 146, 158
Slater, Michael 212–13
Smith, Southwood 185
Springhall, John 87, 118
Stephens, John Russell 81n.5
Stephens, J. R. 20, 32, 38, 40
Sutherland, John 69

Taylor, Miles 39
Tell, William 73–4
Thackeray, William 47–8, 50–3, 205, 207
   Catherine (1839–40) 47, 50, 51, 207
Thompson, E. P. 32, 66, 86

Ulin, Donald 180–81

Vargo, Gregory 10, 144, 148, 152
Victoria, Queen 51, 55, 134–5, 138
Vincent, David 90–1, 98–9
Vinthagen, Stellan 184

Walton, John 5–6, 128n.40
Weekly Dispatch 33, 45n.55, 146–7
Weltman, Sharon Aronofsky 130n.75
Williams, Raymond 8, 71, 140
Woloch, Alex 166–67
Worsley, Henry 55
Worth, George 81n.4
Worthington, Heather 25–6, 29, 46n.70
Wright, Henry C.
   'Dick Crowninshield the assassin, and Zachary Taylor the soldier' (1848) 197

Youl, E. 191
   'Bob Rackett's search for shoes' (1847) 192

EU authorised representative for GPSR:
Easy Access System Europe, Mustamäe tee 50,
10621 Tallinn, Estonia
gpsr.requests@easproject.com

www.ingramcontent.com/pod-product-compliance
Lightning Source LLC
Chambersburg PA
CBHW070346240426
43671CB00013BA/2419